D1571825

The Duty to Vote

The Duty to Vote

JULIA MASKIVKER

OXFORD
UNIVERSITY PRESS

Oxford University Press is a department of the University of Oxford. It furthers
the University's objective of excellence in research, scholarship, and education
by publishing worldwide. Oxford is a registered trade mark of Oxford University
Press in the UK and certain other countries.

Published in the United States of America by Oxford University Press
198 Madison Avenue, New York, NY 10016, United States of America.

Library of Congress Cataloging-in-Publication Data
Names: Maskivker, Julia, author.
Title: The duty to vote / Maskivker, Julia.
Description: New York : Oxford University Press, 2019. |
Includes bibliographical references.
Identifiers: LCCN 2019014951 | ISBN 9780190066062 (hardback) |
ISBN 9780190066093 (online) | ISBN 9780190066079 (updf) |
ISBN 9780190066086 (epub)
Subjects: LCSH: Voting—Moral and ethical aspects. |
Political participation—Moral and ethical aspects. |
Citizenship—Moral and ethical aspects. | Democracy.
Classification: LCC JF1001 .M276 2019 | DDC 172/.1—dc23
LC record available at https://lccn.loc.gov/2019014951

1 3 5 7 9 8 6 4 2

Printed by Sheridan Books, Inc., United States of America

To Steven and our two girls, Elena and Sienna, my whole life.

Contents

Acknowledgments

This book developed out of a paper presentation at the American Political Science Association's annual meeting in 2013. The panel was on the ethics of voting. The question of whether there is a duty to vote had been recently tackled by Jason Brennan's book *The Ethics of Voting*, which is, deservingly, a very influential work in the ethics of voting literature. My motivation to write a book on this subject was born out of a concern with what I thought was an unbalanced conversation. Brennan had done a good job of conveying his arguments against a duty to vote; but the literature did not contain any book-length, self-contained treatment of why the duty may be indeed justified. I took it upon myself to write a book to fill this gap.

Two articles on the duty to vote that I authored precede this book, and I draw from them in sections of this work. They are "Being a Good Samaritan Requires You to Vote," *Political Studies*, 66 (2018): 409–424; and "An Epistemic Justification for the Obligation to Vote," *Critical Review*, 28 (2016): 224–247. Shorter versions of these articles also appeared in the *Washington Post* in 2016.

I am thankful to academic audiences for my work on voting at Davidson College, Columbia University, the University of Michigan, Rollins College, the University of Notre Dame, Oxford University, and others. Special thanks are due to my colleagues at the Rollins College Department of Political Science, who have always been supportive and encouraging of my efforts. I would also like to thank Jason Brennan for his advice regarding publication of my book.

I would like to acknowledge the following people, who offered me helpful feedback through the years and some who reread drafts of my work several times in a row. They are Jon Elster, David Johnston, Anna Stilz, Loren Lomasky, Claudio Lopez-Guerra, Roberto Gargarella, Jeremy Waldron, James Nickel, Joseph Parent, Bill Smith, Robert Goodin, Margaret McLaren, Ryan Pevnick, Frank Lovett, Blain Neufeld, Daniel Layman, Mark Tunick, Jeffrey Friedman, Melissa Schwartzberg, Kevin Elliot, Thomas Pogge, and many others.

I would also like to thank Lucy Randall, my editor at Oxford University Press, and her assistant editor, Hannah Doyle, for their helpful advice.

Lastly, I am grateful to Steven and our two precious daughters for making my life so full. I also want to thank my mother, Adriana, to whom I owe so much.

1

Introduction

Voting and Justice

1.1. Voting as a Duty of Samaritan Justice

Is it a duty to vote, or is voting only a right that citizens are free to ignore?

The popular wisdom is that voting is a freedom that citizens have a right to exercise or not to exercise. It is common to encounter the belief that democracy affords us the freedom to "have our voice heard," but if democracy offers us this freedom—the thinking goes—it also offers us the freedom not to care about being heard. In other words, the flip side of the right to vote is the right not to vote if one does not wish to participate in politics. This logic resembles the rationale undergirding freedom-of-speech rights. One has the freedom to express one's views without fearing punishment; but the freedom to speak our mind surely does not entail that we ought to do so. We may just prefer to remain silent. On this view of rights, a freedom to do something cannot, on pain of inconsistency, imply a duty to do the same thing.[1]

However, it is possible for a freedom to entail a duty without risking a contradiction. For example, if expressing your views will not harm you or your loved ones, don't you have an obligation to speak up against rampant injustice when you see it affect those around you?[2] Nobody should be able to punish you for failing to speak up—much less the government—but don't you have a duty of conscience to use your right for a morally significant purpose when doing so would *not* cost you much?[3]

That is the idea that this book defends: We have a duty of conscience to vote with care in order to help society when doing so would not cost us much. My concern is not with justifying a legally enforceable duty to vote, as in compulsory voting systems. However, my aim is to argue that we are bound by a moral duty to vote so as to help society prevent injustice and ensure decently good governance. The latter can be achieved, partly, if voters manage to elect acceptably fair-minded governments and vote out corrupt or inept ones. Voting governments in and out is not all there is to justice; and this book does not pretend to show otherwise. However, we have to start somewhere. Voting seems to be a basic democratic act because elections install governments— understanding the latter as the cadre of representatives that will occupy positions of political power in the society during a given period of time. Governments, in turn, enact policies that can have an immense impact on people's access to basic goods such as security, economic stability, education, peace, healthcare, and others. In short, governments can foster or impede justice via their actions as well as via their failures to act.

Despite the obvious fact that elections put governments in place, voting has taken on an aura of deep suspicion lately. It is common to hear complaints about the low ability of citizens to make good decisions at the polls, and the world seems to be witnessing a worrisome wave of disenchantment with democracy.[4] This sentiment may respond to the fact that, in the last years, democracies around the world have witnessed the rise of powerful anti-democratic, populist movements, many of which appear to be driving their societies into detrimental predicaments. In the face of this trend, some may think it apposite to question the power of elections to protect cherished liberal, democratic values. After all, don't voters give these anti-democratic movements an opportunity to win and rise to the seat of power?

Among some vocal political scientists and philosophers today, it is common to hear concern about voter incompetence, which allegedly explains why democracy stands on shaky ground in many places. For example, Jason Brennan's 2017 book *Against Democracy* argues that elections give voice to the uninformed and prejudiced, which undermines the values that democracy seeks to uphold, such as justice and freedom. Ilya Somin's 2013 book *Democracy and Political Ignorance* proposes that ballot box voting be de facto replaced with "foot voting"— i.e., citizens' ability to choose in which jurisdiction to live so as to influence government directly and counteract the power of uninformed majorities.[5] Other pessimistic treatments of democratic rule are similar in their conclusions about the future of democracy based on the low civic capacities of the average voter.[6]

Do we do well in thinking of voting as a likely threat to fair governance? My book makes a case for thinking of voting as a vehicle for justice, not a paradoxical menace to it. In it, I explore two questions: Do people have a duty to vote, and if so, do they have a duty to vote with care? The central case in the book is that a natural duty of justice requires citizens to acquire minimal epistemic competence and vote with a sense of the common good in order to support fair governance. It is true that many of the governments that we consider deficient or unjust around the world may be the partial result of incompetent or immoral voting. By the same token, however, many of them are the partial result of citizen indifference, which leads to low participation rates and a lack of concern with what elections are capable of bringing about for society and its members.

The idea that it is solely incompetent, uninformed, and ill-intentioned voters who determine a bad electoral outcome is akin to thinking that it is only the number of car accidents a vehicle has been involved in that determines how fast it deteriorates throughout the years. In reality, the owner's failure to have the car serviced every so often also plays a part in causing the vehicle to malfunction. Failure to act, not only acting recklessly, contributes to things happening the way they do. When not enough citizens vote with information and a sense of justice, the incompetent voters may get to determine the outcome of an election. But one could see this result as partly enabled by the fact that the bad (i.e., uninformed or carelessly cast) votes were not canceled out by the good (i.e., informed or carefully cast) ones, especially if the turnout was not sufficiently high. What I want to suggest is that voting may many times be the problem but can also be the solution.

Discussions on the justifiability of voting in particular are alarmingly absent in the contemporary democratic theory literature. No work on normative theories of democracy that I am aware of offers a *specific* account of why it is justified to vote or how one should go about voting if one is to follow certain accepted standards of justice. This dearth of analysis exists despite the abundance of more general accounts of why democracy is a valuable ideal. This book offers a long-overdue argument about why voting deserves attention in its own right. It claims that we can see voting with care—i.e., with information and a sense of the public interest—in the light of a Samaritan duty of aid toward society.

Samaritan duties of aid require us to help others in need if doing so would not be unduly costly for us, but they do not assume that helping will be utterly costless. For example, a duty of aid does not demand from us that we jump into a dangerous situation (such as a fire) and perform a rescue ourselves, seriously risking our life and health. That would be heroic, therefore supererogatory. However, we may be morally required to call in for help because doing so does not seem to pose a risk that is reasonable for us to fear. This book argues that voting with sufficient information and a sense of the common good is a reasonable, non-heroic cost to expect citizens to undertake in the face of the benefit that elections can bring about for society, namely, fair-minded governments and decently just policies (although they can also bring about the opposite, as we all know). Society needs to be rescued from abusive and unresponsive leaders and public officials; and elections provide us with a mechanism to achieve that goal at no unduly high cost to ourselves as citizens.

The book proposes that failing to vote with minimal information can be compared to failing to provide relatively non-costly assistance to those sufficiently imperiled. This may strike some as an incorrect analogy, but the impression is ultimately mistaken. Let me explain why. The most likely image evoked by the notion of the Good Samaritan is a one-time calamitous situation, such as the child drowning in the pond that could be easily saved by a passerby wearing new shoes.[7] One may wonder in what ways society and democracy are imminently imperiled, and whether viewing the vote as a Samaritan obligation is adequate. I think the analogy is sufficiently valid: we should not judge emergencies as such because they happen one time; rather, we should judge them as such because they are threatening enough. The widely accepted understanding of an emergency is something that needs to be addressed immediately, not that it is non-habitual or unusual.

For example, it makes sense to think of dire poverty as an emergency because it causes people to die from starvation. However, if poverty didn't kill but kept the hungry at a continual point of steep suffering, would we consider it less normatively apt to justify help? We would be hard-pressed to think so.[8] Bad governance is a question of degree, for sure, but the worse it is and the longer it lasts, the more it can produce results that are gravely harmful and permanent. Just as poverty may call for ready action, the results of bad governance may also call for ready action despite not being the worst they could possibly be, all the time. Bad governance may mean that children are denied opportunities for healthy growth and a good-enough education. It can also mean that the elderly will be denied opportunities to end their lives with dignity and in financial security. Bad governance can further translate into citizens losing benefits (such as accessible healthcare, to name just one), which many may find necessary to keep on living or to maintain a minimally decent standard of living. Bad governance can also ensue in wrong-headed and expensive wars that cost human lives and deplete valuable resources. These harms can be quite serious for present and future generations even if in some societies they are less acute than in others. In other words, the results of bad governance can contravene basic interests that all rational individuals can be thought to want to further, such as an interest in good health, in a minimally good quality of life, in income security, and in peace, among others.

I believe that we must not feel regret for devoting most of our time and energy to personal projects and relationships, but we should recognize that, sometimes, a Samaritan duty of assistance will call us to act. There are many pressing social problems that could be alleviated with better, fair-minded, morally responsible governance. Under the assumption that the machinery of elections works transparently, voting to elect minimally decent governments in episodic elections is one reasonably easy way to contribute to relieving society from the evils of injustice and incompetence, although by no means the only one or the most effective under all possible circumstances (i.e., if injustice is so rampant that rebellion is the only alternative, or if elections are a mere facade to disguise a de facto authoritarian regime, for example, voting as a collective act turns futile, dangerous, and possibly non-obligatory, ethically).

In the last decade, there have emerged a number of accounts in democratic theory that seek to highlight political participation and political allegiance as duties of justice owed to fellow citizens. For example, Anna Stilz's 2009 book *Liberal Loyalty* argues that political obligation can rest on universal principles of justice and a consequent natural duty to buttress a state that preserves freedom equally for everybody (from this duty, the obligation to participate in politics follows as a mechanism to preserve the justice of government).[9] According to this account, we owe allegiance to our state, but this obligation derives from universal considerations of justice (i.e., the mandate to avoid violence against those that live close to us) rather than reasons of common nationality or common culture. In a similar vein, Waldron's work on what he calls "The Principle of Proximity" shows that a duty to obey the law is called for by a natural duty of justice to avoid disorder and anarchy—*not* by a sense of shared national identity or culture.[10] In turn, Christopher Kutz's 2000 book *Complicity* originally links a duty to minimize complicity with state wrongdoing with a duty of justice in general, which entails, among other things, the duty to engage with the democratic process with an eye to addressing injustice.[11] Interestingly, as I will mention later in the book, he argues that lack of significant causal influence in bringing about injustice is irrelevant to moral responsibility for complicity. What counts is one's *mere intention to participate* in a larger collective effort that is unjust. In a somewhat similar vein, Eric Beerbohm's 2012 book *In Our Name* presents the claim that certain forms of state support (such as taxation) and multiple benefits that we derive from political and economic institutions make us part-authors of the wrongdoing that our state intentionally or unintentionally commits.[12] Using our political voice to exert change, then, is a duty of citizenship, he claims. I cannot do justice to the complexity of the different arguments in these interesting works (and similar others) but I can say that my approach on voting as a duty of Samaritanism is consistent with the idea that we have duties of justice to others *that political participation can honor.* My book differs from the previously described approaches, however, in that its focus is emphatically on the moral justification of voting *alone.* Democratic theory has consistently underexplored the role of the ballot as an instrument of justice. No systematic attention to voting as a self-standing moral issue exists in the literature with the exception of the critical accounts (already mentioned) that reject the need, rationality, and morality of voting. Moreover, my argument for Samaritanism in elections leaves out duties to offset complicity for state wrongdoing and state injustice. I consider complicity arguments extremely important in democratic theory, but my approach to the ethics of voting highlights a duty to help society via the vote *despite* the fact that we, many times, may bear insignificant moral (and causal) responsibility for state and government wrongdoing. My argument is that the duty to vote is a forward-looking duty to help others as a Good Samaritan would (in this case, by voting and participating in the collective activity of elections) regardless of our part in wrongdoing, when doing so would be easy—although I do not quarrel with the argument that contributing to injustice ourselves is cause for moral blame.

The Samaritan obligation to vote with care is premised on a more general duty of justice, which calls citizens to support and encourage the emergence of just institutions and social arrangements. I take this duty to be an uncontroversial premise in our moral discourse. John Rawls brought it to the forefront of discussion in his 1971 book *A Theory of Justice*. He said:

> From the standpoint of justice as fairness, a fundamental natural duty is the duty of justice. This duty requires us to support and to comply with just institutions that exist and apply to us. It also constrains us to further just arrangements not yet established, at least when this can be done without too much cost to ourselves.[13]

Where does the intuition for the duty to support just institutions come from? Rawls does not deal with this particular question. However, I think it would be reasonable to say that the duty to support just institutions derives from a previous, fundamental moral obligation to treat other individuals as equal bearers of rights. This (admittedly) abstract obligation means that we must support concrete institutions and public norms that protect those rights equally for all if doing so would not be unduly difficult for us. In other words, if we see others as equals, we need to support institutions and arrangements that will further that ideal of equality by concretely treating members of society according to principles of equal rights. Echoing this reasoning, for example, Thomas Christiano argues that each human being has a fundamental and natural duty to treat other human beings as equals and this implies that each person must try to realize the equal advancement of the interests of other human beings. . . . Hence, each has a duty to attempt to bring about, and to conform his actions to, those institutions that publicly advance the equal advancement of interests [i.e., justice].[14]

Voting can heavily influence how certain institutions go about the job of enabling the equal advancement of interests in society because many institutions are stewarded by elected officials or their appointees. Thus, elections and voting do matter for justice. They matter for democracy in that they can give voice to the governed, but they also matter because they can work to further—or affront— the conditions of justice in society by virtue of authorizing (bad or decent) governments to govern.

I think it is uncontroversial that policies, institutions, and laws that give citizens equal chances of seeing their interests furthered by society are those that tend to favor the public good. I will understand this admittedly general term to entail the commonality of needs and claims that citizens have qua members of a larger scheme of cooperation with others and which require access to a host of basic social goods as well as rights. Just and fair governance, then, will be here taken to mean governance predicated on the aim of furthering the common good of society, which, in turn, requires fair access to basic social goods such as individual liberty, a minimally good standard of living, peace, decent opportunities for achieving good health, income security, and other goods that it would be reasonable to think all rational agents will want regardless of anything else they want in life.[15]

My understanding of the common good is informed by a particular moral reasoning that privileges impartiality. Impartiality as an ethical principle, as I will argue in later chapters, should serve as a source of moral motivation for the good voter. A voter that casts a considered ballot will not always have perfect knowledge of facts and causal relationships (although she will try to reach a certain minimal epistemic threshold), but she will try her best to vote for the alternative that she deems most acceptable from the point of view of others, not just herself. Thus, the impartiality logic for voting justly centers on the value of putting oneself in the shoes of others when finding answers to questions such as the following: What types of concerns should governmental policies address? Or, more generally, what type of society should we strive for? When we answer questions like these bearing in mind what others, not just us, would find acceptable, we think impartially, as opposed to thinking selfishly. Although disagreement exists about how one ought to interpret what the public interest really entails, this disagreement does not preclude us from drawing conclusions as to what may be intuitively at odds with the public good because it is motivated by selfish concerns. Citizens may not always agree on what particular ideals and policies ought to be followed for the sake of society, but they may listen at each other and believe, in good faith, that their fellow citizens have the best interests of society at heart. Good voting, as defended in this book, requires an acceptably impartial perspective (which is not to say entirely others-oriented in detriment of personal needs) and a modicum of epistemic competence and information when casting one's ballot at elections.

Even though voting may not make a difference as an individual act because one single vote will get lost in a proverbial ocean of votes, we should *not stand by* the promotion of a collective good (such as good and fair governance) that is morally significant. The Samaritan duty to vote is a duty not to stay in the sidelines when we could act so that our actions, *together with those of many others*, help society at no high cost to ourselves. The book suggests that, even if our individual act has no difference-making power by itself, it can still be what someone ought to do because it is part of a collective activity that is valuable for justice-based reasons. Elections are an example of that type of collective activity. Thus, the duty to vote with care is really a duty of common pursuit. In order to bear fruit, it needs to be carried out *by many individuals together*. We could say that the duty to vote as a Good Samaritan is *a duty to cooperate with others* in bringing about justice. But because considerations of Samaritan justice do not require heroism from us, the book's arguments do not prescribe a self-sacrificial duty to be politically engaged all the time. Episodic voting does not have to require constant or even frequent political participation, although it does require attention to issues of concern as important elections draw closer.

This book revives an idea already expressed a long time ago. In his *Considerations of Representative Government*, John Stuart Mill said that we should view the vote as a trust because it gives the citizen power over others.[16] The concept of a trust implies the (benevolent) goal of protecting the interests and rights of another. Despite the fact that Mill was no fan of democracy as we know it—since he advocated for differential voting power according to the citizen's level of education—he still saw the ballot as a vehicle for furthering the well-being of our fellow-citizens and the justice of our society. He said:

> The voter is under an absolute moral obligation to consider the interest of the public, not his private advantage, and give his vote to the best of his judgment exactly as he would be bound to do if he were the sole voter and the election depended upon him alone.[17]

It seems reasonable to interpret Mill as saying that the franchise gives the electorate *collective* power to affect the fate of society since we know, as did he, that individual voters do not have a perceptible capacity to affect elections because their votes will get lost in a proverbial ocean of votes. However, and consistently with Mill's logic, this book proposes the idea that voting with knowledge and a sense of justice can be a truly effective way to aid society by acting in concert when participating in elections—even if it is not the only way or the best way *at all times*.

Voting, in fact, is a form of power besides being a moral duty—and perhaps *because* it is a form of power we can say that it is morally obligatory. We can think of the vote as a form of power because the right to vote can be very costly to public officials and candidates insofar as it makes their tenure in office depend on what the electorate decides, with the all-too-real possibility that they will be ousted from, or never permitted to access, the seat of political power in society. Because of how influential voting can be as a collective effort, we can say that to exercise the right to vote is akin to exercising a sort of power of attorney.[18] This analogy seems apt because voting is "to perform an action which (if enough others also perform it) alters the assignment of rights and duties in the political community."[19] In other words, we can think of votes as *powers* in a *legal* sense because they "determine the legal right of various politicians to occupy high office. And this is not an incidental aspect: it is the point of voting rules to give ordinary citizens this power."[20] The right to vote gives citizens the opportunity to control government—and *who becomes* government. Thus, the vote is not merely a liberty. It is a power that is, collectively, *judicially effective*, as Waldron points out.[21] Hannah Arendt, who viewed political participation as valuable in itself (not just as an instrument to further desirable results) was surely mistaken when she wrote that "the booth in which we deposit our ballots is unquestionably too small, for this booth has room for only one."[22] Voting is anything but solitary. We must see it as a collective endeavor if it is to mean anything at all for democracy.

1.2. The Libertarian Challenge

A distinctive view in the voting ethics literature has been adding to the pessimistic climate concerning the value of elections and democracy. In particular, a libertarian account against seeing voting as a democratic duty has gained much traction in the last few years. We can call this view "libertarian" in a stipulative sense because it claims that voting is a right or a freedom, not a duty. For example, Jason Brennan contends that we have a pressing moral duty not to vote carelessly but he thinks that considered voting is an action that we are free to take but not morally required to choose.[23] In light of most voters' inability to vote with information and rationally, he claims, we do society a service if we downplay the significance of voting and stress, in turn, a negative duty to refrain from voting incompetently or immorally. Geoffrey Brennan and Loren Lomasky, earlier but similarly, suggest that voting is an exercise in futility since the individual impact of each vote is infinitesimally small.[24] Thus, requiring citizens to make informed choices at the polls goes above and beyond the call of duty, they claim. Jones, more classically, intuitively dismisses a duty to vote on the grounds that choosing not to participate in politics is a legitimate preference for life-plans that are non-political.[25] Voting is, on the prevailing view of voting ethics, *not* a duty that we can expect citizens to discharge without hindering their freedom. Moreover, it is futile in terms of its impact on the world.

This book, in contrast, shows that we do not compromise citizens' freedom when we think of voting as a moral obligation because Samaritan duties of justice are not unacceptably demanding. It also argues that voting has moral force despite the fact that it is not always powerful as an individual act. What matters is that it is part of a larger collective activity that is not powerless at all, and highly significant from the perspective of justice.

As I see it, the libertarian critics of the duty to vote rely on the following three claims to base their case against the duty.[26] First, they appear to think that citizens' political knowledge is almost impossible to improve. Second, they argue that voting is normatively uninteresting because it cannot make a difference by itself to the results of elections. Third, they propose that voting is not morally special as a way of furthering the public good because there are many other ways to do so that can be more effective. The chapters in this book, described later, will take on these arguments in elaborate ways; but the answer that the book offers highlights the following reasoning.

First, citizens' competence is not a fact of nature and it can be modified. Some considerable degree of citizens' ignorance and lack of political interest may spring from structural features of the political and economic systems, not from irreparable individual cognitive failures. Much of the (political science and political psychology) literature on voter ignorance has overtly focused on individual-level attributes (i.e., what the individual voter fails to know and how often) and has neglected to pay attention to the political and economic conditions that influence political knowledge. But there is burgeoning research in the voter behavior literature that examines how institutions and wealth distribution affect incentives to seek out political information. This new scholarship offers three potential explanations for variations in political knowledge.[27] First, electoral rules can obscure or clarify the nature of the political process and, consequently, thwart or enhance incentives to seek information. Second, higher levels of economic equality measured by wealth redistribution provide better conditions for access to education regardless of income level and, therefore, also promote higher degrees of political information for the average citizen. Finally, responsive institutions (i.e., institutions that are perceived to work for citizens, instead of against them and that include their input) provide positive incentives to acquire political knowledge, whereas perceptions of institutional unresponsiveness hamper incentives to become politically informed. Unlike prevalent philosophical accounts that object to the duty to vote, in this book I explore how structural (political and economic) factors may affect voter competence. If structural variables can be altered in a way that individual cognitive flaws cannot, then so can average political knowledge. There is no reason to be as staunchly pessimistic about the abilities of the electorate as the critics of the duty to vote have been so far.

Second, voting as an individual act is not morally uninteresting simply because it is not a difference-making action, nor is it meaningless to the voter. We may have a duty to vote so as to contribute to a larger collective activity that will be impactful in terms of justice and valuable because of that reason. In other words, we may have a duty of "common pursuit" to join forces with others and vote, so that we can *all together* benefit society in the way that a Good Samaritan would. This duty of "common pursuit" is a duty to participate in collective projects whose consequences are desirable for reasons that are morally significant. Fair governance is an example. When many citizens cast a considered vote, electoral results will tend to be more consonant with justice as fair governance than if people abstain or vote without knowledge of the alternatives. Voting with minimal epistemic competence and a sense of the common good is an example of an others-regarding duty of common pursuit. This duty is consistent with a logic of collective rationality, so to speak, whereby what we can accomplish together takes salience over what we can accomplish alone.

Collective rationality, by definition, leaves aside the attractiveness of free riding. Someone motivated to participate in a collective activity that is desirable because of its outcome commits to the common pursuit and, as a matter of moral choice, decides not to take advantage of other people's contributions while not contributing himself. A duty of common pursuit underwrites the duty to vote with care because good governments can only be chosen and trusted with the popular mandate *via the collective activity of elections*. Other forms of political participation help people express their support or rejection for a particular electoral alternative; but none of those forms of participation formally (as a matter of law) places public officials in power or strips them of it (although revolutions and mass protests can and do take rulers down, the assumption is that under healthy democracies, elections are the only authoritative mechanism for citizens to become part of government or to lose that role). Thus, the goal of securing good governance via voting is by definition a collective Samaritan effort. In other words, the Samaritan duty to aid society can only bear fruit when many people contribute to its fulfillment *in concert* during elections. The very collective nature of the duty to vote explains why voting is not irrational and why we do not need to demand that the individual act of voting make a difference on the world (or the election outcome) *by itself.*

The critics of the duty to vote disagree with almost everything I have said so far. They have long emphasized that voting as a sole individual action is ineffectual in that its impact on the election's outcome is negligible. A vote can be analogized to a proverbial drop in an ocean of votes.[28] Because of this fact, they claim, we must not conceive of voting as a morally required, or even morally important, act. On this account, the force of any duty seems to be wholly bound up with how consequential our *individual* actions are in making a difference. But this rationale is mistaken.

For example, do we think that paying taxes is irrational, therefore morally irrelevant, because our single tax contribution is negligible among a vast number of other tax contributions? The single average citizen's share of taxes is not necessary to maintain the coffers of the state in a healthy condition. If one individual (average) person refrained from paying taxes, no financial trouble for the government would ensue at all. Schools would continue to be funded and roads would continue to be built normally. Does it follow from the imperceptible impact of the individual average taxpayer that we don't have a duty to pay our taxes, then? Most of us would say that it doesn't. To reinforce the point, imagine an (unrealistic) situation where taxes are fully voluntary and no sanctions derive from failing to pay your share. Under the assumption that the state in question is acceptably just and free, are we to think that we are under no moral obligation to pay simply because we won't be punished for not paying? It hardly follows.

The mere fact that an individual contribution to the common good of society is imperceptible in its capacity to make a difference does not make it morally optional. For example, classical articulations of utilitarianism, which grants value to actions solely on their capacity to impact the world, do not suggest that individual actions must be able to make a discernible impact *on their own* in order to be morally required. Let me elaborate on this point in order to substantiate the idea that an action is *not* morally trivial simply because it will not have a great impact on the world *by itself.*

Jeremy Bentham refers to the "Principle of Utility" as that "principle which approves or disapproves of every action whatsoever, according to the tendency which it appears to have to augment or diminish the happiness of the party whose interest is in question: or, what is the same thing in other words, to promote or to oppose that happiness."[29] Bentham clarifies that an action will be conformable to the principle of utility "when the tendency it has to augment the happiness of the community is greater than any it has to diminish it."[30]

By focusing on the language that Bentham—the intellectual founder of utilitarianism—employs, we can see that he does not emphasize the idea that an action must invariably be able to have a difference-making, or even large, impact on the world in order to be morally valuable (or required). Bentham nowhere suggests that "utility" must greatly vary as a result of the individual's action. More minimally, rather, Bentham's language suggests that a given act must "tend" toward "increasing" that utility. An increasing effect can be marginal or very small and still be consistent with the logic of utilitarianism insofar as the direction of the action is one of improvement, not regress.

In a similar vein, John Stuart Mill describes the Principle of Utility as "a creed that holds that actions are right in proportion as they tend to promote happiness, wrong as they tend to produce the reverse of happiness."[31] Following this logic, one can think that an action is right if it contributes to a collective activity, however marginally, that will in turn have a discernible beneficial impact on utility (welfare). The small contributing act can have the tendency to increase total utility even if it does not greatly change its level. It will not detract from it, and it can add to it by a small amount. "Tending to increase utility" is not synonymous with "greatly or visibly increasing utility." The consequentialist certainly must think that the more goodness an act produces, the more morally right it is, but she does not have to think that a morally right action is only that which *maximizes* the good.

Utilitarianism's call to improve the world is not a call for the individual to exert change-making influence on any one state of affairs. Neither Mill nor Bentham could have conceived of it in such a way because most contributions to the common good that individuals can make are just drops in the ocean of larger collective activities whose final outcome will have a difference-making effect. Differently put, it seems to me that most of what one person can do for the common good (or society's utility) will not be terribly impactful in isolation from other people's actions.[32]

For example, my single (sustained) act of respecting the law is imperceptibly impactful on the stability of my country. If I decided to disobey the law, my community would still be secure from anarchy. My disobedience alone would not jeopardize order. However, allegiance to the law is the type of action that, added to many others of its very same kind, will make a definitive difference. David Hume understood this when he suggested that the reason behind a moral duty to obey the laws of one's state is utilitarian. He said:

> A small degree of experience and observation suffices to teach us, that society cannot possibly be maintained without the authority of magistrates, and that this authority must soon fall into contempt, where exact obedience is not payed to it. The observation of these general and obvious interests is the source of all allegiance, and of that moral obligation, which we attribute to it.[33]

Without going into a discussion of whether Hume had the right theory of political obligation, my aim here is to briefly explain the nature of his reasoning and why it applies to the case of voting: Single, small acts may very well tend to increase utility (or justice, for that matter) but not in a difference-making or clearly ostensible way. However, the fact that they add to many other similar acts can make them valuable instrumentally because of the result that such accumulation (or collective activity) is capable of producing. And if this is true, doing these acts is not irrational or morally insignificant.[34]

Hume surely knew that individual acts of law-abidingness are not terribly impactful per se in guaranteeing order. Rather, they should be considered in conjunction, as part of a collective activity that will maintain us all safe. Furthermore, it is plausible to think that Hume conceived of the duty to obey the law in rule utilitarian terms, although this conceptual category (i.e., rule utilitarianism) was not clearly delineated in his time.[35] It is not far-fetched to think that he saw the rule "obey the law" as beneficial for society overall when a majority of people followed it. Voting with information and a sense of justice is similar to obeying the laws of one's state in that one can view the act of voting as a contribution to a larger collective activity that will increase society's utility (understood in terms of justice, insofar as fair-minded governments will promote it). We can see voting with care as a general rule that will benefit society when enough people follow it and respect it. In the spirit of the Samaritanism argument that I pursue in this book to defend a duty to vote with care, we can say that considered voting could be viewed as a rule that, when followed by the public, will lead to the type of results that motivate good Samaritans to vote. Although I will not defend a particular rule-utilitarian justification for the duty to vote, the preceding paragraphs only suggested that, just because an individual action does not have the power to alter a state of affairs by itself, does not mean that the action is morally worthless or instrumentally senseless.

Many of us believe that a person ought not to vote unless he or she is well versed on the candidates and issues. In fact, the libertarian critic of the duty to vote argues that we do have a moral duty to refrain from voting without sufficient knowledge and information. We don't have a duty to vote with care but we surely have a duty not to do the wrong thing by voting irresponsibly. Brennan aptly explains that, even though what one single voter does will not alter the outcome of the election, we have a duty to avoid partaking of collectively harmful activities. Voting without information contributes to harm because when many people do it, the outcome can be the election of incompetent or evil leaders.[36]

The foregoing argument echoes a view of morality that emphasizes the value of negative duties not to harm others but does not see positive duties to help others as required. As will become clear in subsequent chapters, in the case of the libertarian argument for the duty to refrain from voting badly, however, we can spot a glaring inconsistency: a single bad vote is unlikely to tip an election to a bad candidate. Further, it will also likely be offset by another uninformed voter's vote for the other candidate. If the individual act of refraining from voting badly will not make a discernible impact, we should not view voting with information as a duty that only makes sense if a single ballot can have an impact by itself. It will not, and that is just fine.

1.3. Voting and Other Ways to Help Society

The third general argument that the libertarian critic makes is that voting is morally innocuous, hence not morally required, because other ways to help society would be more impactful from an individual standpoint. That is to say, faced with the options between voting and doing something else for society, the individual act of voting is always bound to be the least impactful. But, assuming this is true, why must our good act for society be the most impactful of all possible actions available to us?

Imagine life if every time we are faced with the possibility of doing something for others, our action had to be the most effective act of help that we could possibly do. We would lead the lives of saints—not humans. How much should I give to charity? Shouldn't I give all of my income except for what is necessary for my strict survival for my help to be as impactful as I can possibly make it be?[37] How much time should I spend helping the less fortunate than me? Shouldn't I spend all of my time, except for what I need to sleep and make a living? It seems that these ways of helping will be the most impactful of all the ways I could spend my time and money improving the lives of others. In the vein of these examples, and others, it would seem to follow that if I can do something for society that is more effective than voting, I should, since I should always do what is the most effective to help others.

Not necessarily, I say. We already saw that utilitarianism—i.e., the philosophy that bestows moral worth on an act according to how impactful that act can be—does not require that we *always* do the optimal thing. Its logic implies only that the more good one does, the better. Sometimes, the morally right act maybe the one that is good enough, not best.[38] If voting with care is an act that we know benefits society by adding to a larger collection of careful votes, then that effect may be good enough to discharge a duty to help others and, in so doing, increment social well-being and justice. The duty to vote with care, then, is not a duty motivated by a maximizing desideratum. Rather, as the book will argue, it is a duty motivated by the moral nature of the collective activity to which it adds, however modestly. That collective activity, when citizens vote judiciously, is the aim of helping society become more just and well-governed via elections. The moral nature of this collective endeavor is highly valuable because justice and fair-minded governance are valuable goods. Thus, even though the collective act of voting gains its worth from the outcome of furthering justice, the *individual* act of voting does not have to maximize that outcome by itself. Its obligatoriness resides somewhere else, namely, in the fact that it *contributes* to it.

Furthermore, even though voting is not the only way to contribute to the common good of society, the fact that citizens elect and establish governments by way of elections makes it morally special. This is so because governments have tremendous power to affect the life of millions in a way that few other entities can by virtue of their power to enact, or block, far-reaching public policy across a wide geographical territory. So, if governments are so influential on people's life prospects, it is not far-fetched to think that the decision mechanism by which governments come to life as such enjoys a moral significance that other mechanisms or institutions do not. The underlying assumption at work here is that governments are morally distinctive "animals" because they are key for the provision of primary social goods that people would not be able to enjoy by virtue of their own efforts, only. This last idea does not negate the possibility that governments act wrongly by being agents of injustice and evil. The book's arguments operate under the assumption that the duty to vote with care is morally stringent only in a context of decent governmental responsiveness. In contexts of deep corruption, unacceptable abuse, or steep governmental ineptitude, voting as a mechanism for bringing about justice may not enjoy the same moral specialness. Indeed, other forms of (more effective) participation may be morally required, provided the individual costs borne by participants are not unreasonably high.

To argue for the moral significance of voting does not entail downplaying the role of other forms of political participation in a democracy. In this book, I do not quarrel with the obvious fact that we can help others in many ways besides voting. Similarly, I do not pretend to negate that other ways of political participation, besides voting, can influence what type of government society chooses. For example, convincing others to vote judiciously is clearly a positive, potentially impactful form of political engagement if done sufficiently en masse. So is driving voters to the polls. What I want to do, however, is to highlight the ethical singularity of voting, strictly, as the undeniably ultimate cause for the establishment of governments, which are morally important entities because they regulate, like no other entity can, the flow of basic social goods in society. Voting is the one collective activity that no other form of political participation could replace because its distinctive function—that of legally installing governments in power—is not quite replicated by any of them, however influential other forms of political engagement may be in other respects. Voting, in other words, is a sine qua non condition for formally putting representatives of the people in the seat of government. Other forms of political participation cannot do this, although they can surely assist in the task in meaningful ways. Thus, my reasoning suggests that voting and other forms of political participation in democratic societies are not mutually exclusive. This means that we should not consider them as zero-sum modes of engagement, whereby if one form of participation takes place, other forms of participation will or should inevitably decrease proportionate with the increase of the first type. There is room for all the participation we need or feel inclined to bring about, at least at the collective level (not at the individual level since time constraints may limit how free we are to devote ourselves to politics, but this happens with respect to many other activities in life; it is not characteristic of political participation per se).

I want to rescue voting as a basic democratic act from (relative) philosophical oblivion. The tendency to relegate voting to a minor aspect of democratic life in the democratic theory literature can be explained by the fact that voting is admittedly episodic and too "rustic" in its capacity to allow for the expression of a grievance or an opinion, for that matter. It does not entail deliberation with others (at least not in itself, although it generally does as a prelude to the election) and it only allows for blunt choosing of an alternative without allowing us to expand on what we expect from said alternative or why we vote against another. In other words, voting is not a *discursive* instrument. It only allows us to say yes to one candidate and no to others.

However rigid voting is as a form of political expression and, importantly, as a form of grievance communication, the truth is that it is at the base of our menu of political participation possibilities. Voting is the foundation stone for political action.[39] Elections put governments in place by virtue of a process of aggregation that reads people's preferences and responds accordingly. Thus, voting has a tremendous potential to affect people's lives because governments and the policies they enact determine the extent to which the population will enjoy basic social goods that they cannot avail themselves of without help. Even though these goods are affected by variables that governments do not fully control such as the international economic climate and what other leaders around the world decide to do militarily, it would be naive to think that governments and leaders who form part of them have no effect whatsoever on the fate of a country's population.

1.4. Voting and Government Responsiveness

At this juncture, a critical question emerges. Do citizens get what they want from the governments they install by voting? Research in political science shows that government responsiveness has been on the decline in the last three decades, which means that, too frequently, there is no clear correspondence between citizens' preferences and policy outcomes.[40] Differently put, people elect governments and vote them out but representatives tend to betray the mission for which they were chosen, which is to faithfully fend for the interests and needs of the mass public instead of favoring select groups such as the powerful, the business class, or the political elite.[41]

Representatives have a duty to represent the people but there is the well-founded impression that the views of regular voters are unlikely to be influential in government nowadays. In the United States, for example, senators and House members tend to be richer, whiter, and more economically advantaged than their electors. American congresspersons and senators don't resemble the people they are supposed to represent. Some political theorists argue that some degree of descriptive resemblance is important for securing responsiveness of the political elite toward the governed. In other words, representatives of the people should actually look like the people in the sense that they should resemble the people they are representing in important respects such as race, gender, socioeconomic background, and others.[42] Even though some degree of descriptive representation is necessary, a more serious problem is that our political system provides the wrong type of incentives for politicians.

For example, in the United States, the system of primaries gives disproportionate voice to politically radical minorities that may come to hold too much sway on a candidate's winning prospects. In the absence of stricter campaign finance regulations, in turn, candidates will raise contributions from powerful groups with much at stake in the result of elections and will be "indebted" to them once in office, besides being constantly dependent on them for re-election. Among other things, the open and perfectly legal nature of lobbying in Washington means that representatives forge close partnerships with agents of the corporate world, who generously fund their campaigns in exchange for political favors. Finally, those partnerships reach their apex when many of those politicians are invited to work in the corporate sector after retiring from office.[43]

Given this reality, it is not surprising that formal political science research finds a disconnection between political leaders and the people that put them in power (and this trend is not only characteristic of the United States).[44] Some theorists of democracy depart from these findings and circumstances to argue for a more "realistic" normative view of democracy—one according to which power relations and the need to suppress domination should take a more central role in our moral and practical reflections on democratic politics.[45] This more realistic approach to democracy takes power imbalances as a central element of democratic societies and de-emphasizes notions of deliberation and cooperation toward justice. These more realistic views, additionally, may claim to dispense with hopes of impartiality and consensus to rely instead on the strength of institutions such as collective bargaining, judicial channels, and others, that can re-balance power disparities at the center of the political system and keep the interests of the most disadvantaged members of society from being forgotten by the political class.

From the perspective of this "power-centered" approach to democracy, an emphasis on voting may seem laughable. What possible solution to the problem of governmental unresponsiveness can voting offer? I agree with the intuition that democratic justice, which centrally requires political responsiveness, encompasses more than free and open elections. My focus on voting is not meant to deny that basic fact. But however complex the conditions for democratic justice may be, one cannot forget that elections continue to be the only coup de grâce for entire governments that do not live up to the people's expectations. This is a simple but important feature of democracy (if its electoral machinery functions transparently and independently of any one political party). It may not be sufficient to make it perfect, but it is sufficient to achieve the end of evicting governments that do not serve the people and replacing them with ones that may. Because of this capacity, voting deserves to be rescued from philosophical oblivion and put back on the map of contemporary debates on democracy.

Despite the foregoing, issues of government unresponsiveness are still central to the health of democratic societies. In particular, I have in mind two types of institutional mechanisms that can help society restore the corroded connection between the elected and the electors. Although I cannot expand on the nature and justification of these arrangements in this book, I would like to mention them here and cursorily explain why they are so necessary. These two institutional mechanisms, which are umbrella concepts for an array of different devices, each seek to give citizens more control over the direction of policy and legislation. They are, in short, avenues for restoring citizen influence and government responsiveness. However, they differ from each other in one important way, namely, the timing in which they are to be used.

One mechanism seeks to give citizens the power to challenge government decisions ex post facto, that is, after they have been made. Phillip Pettit refers to procedures of this sort as "contestatory."[46] Contestatory democracy enables citizens to call public decisions into question on the basis that they violate justice or important avowable interests, and to trigger a review of those decisions in a forum that society can endorse as an impartial court of appeal. For example, an independent system of justice and a strong and reliable ombudsman office are among the contestatory instruments that give citizens the opportunity to revert governmental decisions and practices that affect society at large, or themselves, unjustly.

The second mechanism for increasing citizen influence and restoring responsiveness seeks to give citizens the power to decide what a policy should be in the first place and have representatives honor that decision in virtue of the fact that it came from the people directly. I call this second avenue of influence "participatory" as opposed to Pettit's "contestatory" because it gives citizens the opportunity to have input into the process that will result in the formulation of official policy. Its aim is not to question a government decision that has already been made but to shape the nature of one that is *in the making* or that *is to be made*. Instances of participatory budgeting as practiced in cities like New York and Porto Allegre, Brazil, are good examples of this form of citizen influence. Participatory procedures are subject to feasibility constraints, as we know that many governmental decisions are too complex and multilayered to be left to the people alone. However, participatory initiatives can be limited to general aspects of the issues at hand—not necessarily all the implementation details, which should surely be left to experts. When regular citizens can have binding opinions on what should be the policy priorities for government officials, they gain control of the political process, or parts thereof, and this entails that they can make policy work for the common good—not the interests of individuals in power.[47]

Turning our normative attention toward a moral duty to vote entails the belief that the health of democracy depends not only on the justice of its institutions but also on the attitudes and dispositions of its citizens. In this book, I will not be concerned with arguing for the need that government may have to inculcate the appropriate virtues of character that undergird an ideal of virtuous citizenship. However, I will assume that the moral duty to vote with care that I defend in the book is possible if the citizen evinces a sense of justice that will motivate her to vote for the public interest. As John Stuart Mill brilliantly expressed it:

> Representative institutions are of little value and may be a mere instrument of tyranny and intrigue, when the generality of electors are not sufficiently interested in their own government to give their vote, or, if they vote at all, do not bestow their suffrages on public grounds, but sell them for money, or vote at the beck of some one who has control over them, or whom for private reasons they desire to propitiate.[48]

In the absence of a public-spirited motivation of the sort that Mill describes, only laws compelling discharge of the duty to vote could get the job done. I am not concerned with justifying or opposing this type of laws (i.e., compulsory voting laws) in this work. I assume, rather, than a moral duty like the duty to vote entails the realization that justice calls us, citizens, to discharge it when doing so is not difficult for us. The virtues of citizenship that lie in the background of my argument for the duty to vote, then, are virtues of responsibility and impartiality. A responsible citizen knows that complete political apathy is wrong when the lives of fellow citizens could be improved thanks to the ousting of evil or indecent governments and the installment of fair-minded ones, which voting as a collective activity makes possible. Responsibility as a virtue of citizenship, then, calls us to contribute to worthy common pursuits, such as elections, when doing so would not be unduly burdensome for us.

An impartial citizen-voter, in turn, knows that she is called to see things from the perspective of others, not just her own, when casting a considered ballot at important elections. As will become clearer in the book, this impartial approach to voting is essentially fair-minded, without being self-effacing, because it asks the individual to assess society's needs from a neutral perspective without that reason ruling out justified self-regarding concerns. As I will explain later, there is abundant evidence from political science research confirming that voters frequently take this broader view at the ballot box.

My views on virtuous citizenship, as I will explain in the book, still permit individuals to follow their own conceptions of the good even if those conceptions of the good give little weight to politics— or none at all. The attitudes that render the duty to vote feasible, as I see it, are not necessarily those associated with a "thick" conception of community, which equates active participation in one's society with the "good life." I am not prepared to defend the idea that a life of political engagement is undoubtedly a life worth living. Nor am I prepared to defend the idea that a life of political engagement makes the individual morally upright or virtuous. But I am certainly prepared to defend the idea that voting is worth doing, and a duty, because of its connection with the ulterior goals of justice and fair governance.

The book unfolds as follows.

Chapter 2, "Being a Good Samaritan Requires You to Vote," offers the central argument for the duty to vote with care. First, it explains why considerations of Samaritanism follow from a more general duty to support justice, and, second, it explains why the analogy between a Samaritan duty of aid and the duty to vote with care in order to elect fair-minded governments makes normative sense. The chapter further argues that the act of voting is no less required as a Samaritan act of justice simply because it is one among many drops in a proverbial ocean of votes. Sometimes, Samaritan justice can bear fruit only when we join forces with others, in a common pursuit, so that the desirable benefit (in this case, good governance) can obtain. Elections are an example of how that duty of common pursuit compels us to vote with care, in order to see our obligation of Samaritan aid toward society discharged. The chapter also tackles the issue of "overdetermination," that is, the fact that the goal of good governance can obtain without the contribution of any one particular citizen since individual votes do not tilt elections. The chapter elaborates a response based on fair-play considerations as well as the morality of not standing by in the promotion of a valuable collective good such as justice. In fulfilling the collective duty of Samaritan justice toward society, each one of us has an associated duty not to make ourselves the exception to that obligation. This entails that we ought not to wash our hands of a joint effort that we have objective reasons to want to see succeed. Finally, the chapter dwells on what distinguishes collective activities that call for Good Samaritan duties of aid from other collective activities that are not to be seen through the lens of Samaritanism.

Chapter 3, "What Does It Take to Vote with Care?," addresses the question of what it means to vote judiciously. It outlines a definition of considered voting that centers on the moral principle of impartiality. I understand said principle as recommending the capacity to put oneself in the shoes of others when making decisions about life in common. The chapter argues that voting with care should entail voting on the basis of principles that nobody could reasonably reject—"reasonably" given the aim of finding principles to organize society that could be the basis of un-coerced general agreement.[49] This understanding of voting with care is not meant to favor any particular conception of justice or political ideology. Legitimate disagreement on this front is welcome and expected in liberal democracies. However, there should be bounds to that disagreement. Mere self-interest and positions advocating for the disadvantage of others cannot pass the test of impartiality understood as the ability to put oneself in the place of another. The chapter also argues that critics of the duty to vote do not give enough credit to a large current of scholarly research on voter behavior that offers a more optimistic view of the citizen's abilities to engage in politics smartly. In this vein, the chapter suggests that we should focus on a vastly underexplored reason why many voters may be uninformed about or uninterested in politics, namely, the structural design of the political system and the redistribution of income and wealth in society. The chapter suggests that citizens' ignorance is not only traceable to individual cognitive failures, and this fact offers hope for improvement of citizens' political knowledge.

Chapter 4, "Why Is Voting Special?," responds to one of the most powerful objections against the duty to vote. The objection holds that if we care about civic duty, there are many ways to be a good citizen other than voting. For example, we can give to charity, heal the sick, make art, teach, and even hold a job.[50] The chapter responds that just because there are many ways to further the common good doesn't mean we can fail basic obligations required of us by our conscience. The quality of government significantly affects every person in society. Elections offer us a relatively easy way to improve society if we vote and end up choosing decent governments. Donating to charity (or any of a number of other acts) may be virtuous, but it does not detract from the urgency of electing capable, civic-minded leaders. This view entails that we may be bound by duties of beneficence as well as by the duty to vote but the former cannot replace the latter. The chapter shows that there is a "principle of moral inescapability" that compels us to vote with care when doing so would not be detrimental to our goals, even if it is true that other actions or pursuits could benefit society. This principle of moral inescapability tells us that when we are particularly well situated to provide needed help, and doing so would not cost us much, we commit a moral mistake if we stay inactive. Elections, the chapter reasons, constitute a mechanism that renders help very easy by providing us with the machinery needed to express and have our choice counted. Elections, that is to say, solve a coordination problem because their existence provides an incentive for individuals to contribute to a collective project that can have a worthy outcome in terms of justice.

Chapter 5, "Self-Standing Arguments against a Duty to Vote and Why They Fail," injects some order into the landscape that lurks in the background of discussions on voting. The chapter lists current objections against the duty to vote that exist in the literature and proceeds to debunk them. These objections are not all part of a systematized account; they exist as a patchwork of diverse criticisms, many of which are also commonplace in non-academic circles. I placed this chapter right before the conclusion because it does not pertain to my original case for Samaritan justice in elections. I make that case in all the chapters that precede this one. Chapter 5 is a response to some of the lingering, most common arguments against voting in general, whether voting is justified on grounds of Samaritan justice or other considerations. In particular, the chapter offers detailed responses to two of the most effective critiques against the duty to vote that spring from the literature and from popular wisdom. These are what I call the "Irrationality Argument" and the "Perfectionist Argument." The Irrationality Argument holds that voting is irrational because it is ineffectual from the perspective of the individual. This line of criticism will have been addressed many times in the chapters that precede chapter 5. However, since the objection is so pervasive in the political science as well as philosophical literatures, chapter 5 devotes more space to debunking it independently of the Samaritan duty thesis that I present in the book. The Perfectionist Argument, in turn, says that a duty to vote violates freedom because it entails a narrow view of what makes life good and this is oppressive. In response to these two objections, the chapter argues that (1) voting is not irrational if we base our idea of rationality on collective rationality, whereby what we can do *together* takes priority over what we can do *alone*; and (2) the duty to vote does not presuppose a moral preference for the political life because it can be justified on considerations of justice—not excellence of character. Furthermore, the chapter argues that the duty to vote enhances choice, not personal virtue, if we think of it as a source of freedom as non-domination for the electorate in general. The duty is freedom-friendly because higher voter turnout improves representativeness, which, the argument is, encourages political elites to cater to the needs of all voters more faithfully, and this fact increases citizens' freedom.

Chapter 6 concludes by reiterating the idea that nobody is morally required to be a saint but that we are surely expected to behave like decent Samaritans toward society if we can easily do so. A minimally careful and informed vote in episodic elections allows us to behave in just that manner by acting in concert with others in a common pursuit.

2

Being a Good Samaritan Requires You to Vote

This chapter offers the gist of my argument for the moral duty to vote with care. As is clear at this (early) point in the book, the dominant view in the voting ethics literature is that we should see voting as a freedom that citizens have a right to exercise or not to exercise. The dominant approach in the democratic theory literature presents a different view. Participatory democrats, for example, have long defended the idea that political participation, of which voting is one form, is essential to democracy.[1] That position emphasizes the high value of participation but explains little about the way in which our alleged participatory responsibilities should be discharged.

For example, does it matter that we *just* vote or that we do it judiciously? Does it matter whom we vote for or that we simply vote for someone? The participatory democracy literature is not readily clear about these questions despite being clear about why political participation is a good thing for equality of status and collective self-rule. Most theorists of democracy today are not concerned with the nature of citizens' choices but only with *the opportunity (and right) to exercise choice.* The following paragraph, by Thomas Christiano, illustrates my point:

> Let us focus more closely on the basic ideals of democracy. First, in a democracy the people rule. *Popular sovereignty* implies that all minimally competent adults come together as one body to

make decisions about the laws and policies that are to regulate their lives together. . . . Second, each citizen has the right to participate as an equal. *Political equality* implies equality among citizens in the process of decision-making. . . . Third, each citizen has the right to an opportunity to express his or her opinions. . . . Each has a right, as well as a duty to participate in open and fair *discussion*. These are the ideals of democracy.[2]

I think I am not mistaken if I say that most theorists of democracy emphasize variants of the conditions Christiano enumerates as cementing pillars of the democratic ideal. I agree with all those views, but I also think that they relegate to the sidelines an important question that matters when discussing the value of democratic rule; and that is the question of what goal citizens should *seek to further through their political participation*. Are there any reasons, besides equality and popular sovereignty, that call us to participate in the political life of our society? In other words, is political participation only valuable, and perhaps a duty, because of what it symbolizes or signifies (i.e., equality of status and self-government), or because of what it can help citizens achieve (i.e., justice as good governance)?[3] I think that political participation can be valued for both reasons, but my arguments for the duty to vote with care as defended in this chapter suggest that political participation can be *especially* valued because of its capacity to *improve the lives* of people. In particular, I will suggest in this chapter that we should see voting with care at episodic, important elections as a democratic duty required by considerations of Samaritan justice.[4]

The question of whether voting should be seen as a duty is rarely asked in the political philosophy/theory literature, although—as mentioned in chapter 1—some late accounts of the value of democracy touch on the obligation to engage politically due to justice reasons as varied as the duty to minimize complicity with evil (Beerbohm, Kutz) and the duty to uphold a fair state (Waldron, Stilz).[5] Treatment of the "ethics of voting" in particular is surprisingly scarce in contemporary democratic theory. Recently, however, new accounts have started to emerge. The prevalent position in voting ethics—which I refer to as the libertarian position—is that voting is a freedom, not an obligation. The libertarian argues that we have a pressing moral duty not to vote carelessly—without information or based on prejudices—but he thinks that careful voting is an action that we are not required to take, although it would be praiseworthy. In other words, voting with care, if possible, is above and beyond the call of duty. Jason Brennan, for example, says:

> On my view, citizens generally have no standing obligation to vote. They can abstain if they prefer. However, they do have strict duties regarding voting: they must vote well or must abstain. Voting well tends to be difficult, but discharging one's duties regarding voting is easy, because one may abstain instead.[6]

This chapter situates itself in opposition to the libertarian account and develops an argument in favor of (1) a moral duty to vote, and (2) a moral duty to vote with care.

As advanced in chapter 1, I understand a careful vote as that which is motivated by a conception of the common good of society, which entails putting oneself in the shoes of others as well as voting with enough factual information. But of course people disagree about the common good, so my arguments imply something less than an "objectively right" conception of justice. People don't have a duty to vote for the "objective" common good; instead, they only have a duty to vote for a conception of the common good that is arrived at by thinking impartially. People thinking from this perspective may still disagree about what the common good turns out to be, but they are still obligated to vote through the lens of an "impartiality test" enabled by an honest effort to take the perspective of others—not just their own—when justifying support for a particular electoral outcome with their ballot.

The detailed discussion of what it means to vote with care, however, I leave for chapter 4. In the present chapter, I focus on the argument that voting with care is required from the individual citizen by reasons of justice. Thus, for the purposes of argumentation, I ask the reader to temporarily suspend thinking about the question of voter competence and whether defining the conditions for a good vote is possible epistemically and morally. Interrupting consideration of this issue for the purposes of this chapter does not undermine the logic of my arguments. The consistency of the latter should be assessed independently of empirical considerations about voter competence (I do think, however, that it is not empirically unfounded to assume that voter competence can exist, and be improved).

Here, I want to explore the idea that citizens are bound by a moral duty of Samaritan justice to aid society via the ballot. In other words, I want to explore the idea that being a Good Samaritan may require us to vote with care, i.e., with sufficient information and a sense of justice, for the good of society. Samaritan duties of aid bind us when an intervention would not be unduly costly—not when it would be totally costless. I argue that voting with care is a cost that society can reasonably expect citizens to assume given what elections have the potential to achieve, namely, the installment of acceptably just governments and the ousting of deficient or unresponsive ones.[7] Failing to vote with minimal information can be compared to failing to provide relatively non-costly assistance to those sufficiently imperiled. As I explained in chapter 1, this may strike some as an incorrect analogy, but the impression is ultimately mistaken. Bad governance can cause harms that are quite serious, both for present and for future generations, even if in some societies they are less acute than in others. In other words, the results of bad governance can contravene basic interests that all rational individuals can be thought to want to further, such as an interest in good health, in a minimally good quality of life, in income security, and in peace, among others.

We must not feel regret for devoting the lion's share of our time and resources to our personal projects and relationships. My defense of a duty to vote with care based on Samaritan considerations of justice is not inconsistent with a set of priorities according to which the personal sphere will take moral precedence over the collective sphere. Samaritanism is *precisely* appealing because it allows for this hierarchy of importance: As I see it, the decent Samaritan does not sacrifice anything of moral significance when she acts to help others.[8] She does not have to subordinate her personal ends to the ends of the community. When it comes to aiding one's fellow citizens, participating in the collective effort that will materialize that help—i.e., elections—is not unduly demanding. In other words, voting to elect minimally decent governments in episodic elections is one reasonably easy way to contribute to relieving society from the evils of injustice and incompetence, although by no means the only one or the most effective under all possible circumstances (say, if elections are not open and fair).

2.1. Voting with Care Is Not Heroic

In the last decade, political theory has witnessed the potent emergence of what I call the "libertarian" argument against the duty to vote. As I clarified in chapter 1, I use the name "libertarian" in a stipulative sense because proponents of this position sustain that there is no duty to vote: Voting is a *freedom* and a *choice,* not an obligation. Defenders of the libertarian view further remark that the only duty regarding the vote is a duty *not* to vote incompetently. In particular, the libertarian offers the idea that voting badly—with no information and based on prejudices—is immoral because it contributes to harming society by leading to bad governance and the emergence of unfair policies.[9]

Behind the libertarian argument against the duty to vote we find a more basic understanding of common-sense morality: This is the idea that, when it comes to our duties to others, we are only required to refrain from hurting other people (a negative duty), but we are not ethically required to help them (a positive duty). This understanding of morality explains why the libertarian defender of the no-duty-to-vote does not think we ought to vote responsibly, he simply begs us not to vote carelessly. Voting without care can ensue in bad governments being chosen, and that is a high price to pay for ignorance. However, nobody should be required to make an effort to vote well. Instead, citizens should only feel morally required to refrain from voting if unable or unwilling to do so carefully.[10]

I do not think that voting with care is beyond the call of moral duty. This is so because positive duties—duties that call for some type of action—do not have to be ipso facto terribly demanding for the individual. For example, coming across a fire on our way to work, we are not expected to jump into the flames and heroically carry people in peril out of the burning building; but we may certainly be expected to immediately call the firefighters. A compelling duty of aid does not demand from us that we jump into a dangerous situation and perform the rescue ourselves, seriously risking our life and health. That would be heroic, therefore supererogatory. However, we may be morally required to call in for help because doing so does not seem to pose a risk that is reasonable for us to fear.

I want to press the point that voting with care—which entails voting with a sense of the common good and with enough information—can be compared to a duty of easy aid. It is reasonable to believe that we are all bound by duties of aid when our intervention would be easy. These duties of "Samaritan assistance" are commonplace in our moral vocabulary. For example, if you are driving by a desolate area and see a pedestrian in distress by the side of the road—say, having an epileptic attack—it makes sense to think that you are obligated to stop and call in for help. Duties of assistance are stringent if they are not unduly costly to the assisting. If you were on your way to the hospital because you think you are having a heart attack, in no way are you expected to help someone else needing assistance. But in normal circumstances, you would be. Why not think of voting as a duty of Samaritan assistance in circumstances that make your intervention expected?

If good governments can be chosen at elections when people vote judiciously, why not think that a duty to promote the common good entails a duty to vote with care, i.e., with information and a sense of responsibility? Societies need to be rescued from unaccountable, corrupt, and indifferent leaders, and one salient way to do that (although not the only way) is to put more of the good ones in power and more of the bad ones out of a job. Elections are the mechanisms that enable this change. Voting with a sense of responsibility for society at presidential elections does not amount to becoming a *homos politicus*. One can have a life away from and still be a virtuous, happy human being. But at certain points we ought to get involved. When? When elections afford us the opportunity to assist society by way of choosing governments that we expect to rule minimally fairly—or more fairly than all the other realistic alternatives at play.

As explained in chapter 1, the duty of Samaritan justice to vote with care is rooted in a general duty to support just institutions and just social arrangements in one's community. This prior duty calls us to act as good Samaritans toward society via the ballot because of a basic moral requirement to further our fellow citizens' equal consideration of interests, when possible. But how is one to further the equal consideration of interests in society? This abstract requisite necessitates that we support institutions and practices that further equality of concern. Unless we are influential personalities in our society that can visibly affect justice by acting alone, the best way to make a contribution to the common good of society is to support, and not obstruct, the functioning of those institutions and practices that favor the equal advancement of interests. Governments chosen electorally can have a significant impact on how basic institutions treat citizens and further their interests fairly. Many times, elected officials and their appointees will steward and administer those institutions and will affect the prospects of the electorate in non-trivial ways, possibly producing undesirable harm and suffering. Thus, one could say that, in the same way as we have a basic duty of humanity to save the drowning infant when doing so would be relatively non-costly to us, all things considered, we also have a basic duty of justice to relieve society of bad governance—or the cadre of officials responsible for it—when doing so would not be unduly difficult to us. We can contribute to this task by participating in elections with a considered vote, arguably, an easy thing to do.

But someone could object that voting is indeed costly. After all, voting with care consumes time and resources that we need to gather information. Information-seeking efforts and the physical act of going to the polls entail time we could be using for other pursuits. In economic jargon, we could say that voting has "opportunity costs." But doesn't everything we do in life have an opportunity cost since we can't be in two places at once? It is true, duties of aid are not costless. Stopping to aid the person in distress may make us late for work. But this is a morally innocuous datum. Duties of aid are binding provided the cost is not *too* high for us—not provided the cost is zero. Voting with information and a sense of responsibility for society could be seen as an acceptable cost to undergo in order to contribute to an important collective good such as good governance.

The conclusion that some actions may be a matter of duty—not mere freedom—evokes a Principle of Minimal Altruism that most theories of ethics find uncontroversial.[11] The principle makes the altruism morally required, as opposed to morally optional, because of its non-burdensome nature under regular circumstances. The Principle of Minimal Altruism derives from a general concern with impartiality as a basis for political morality in society. Impartiality as a political morality asks that I put myself in the shoes of others—while others put themselves in my shoes—to choose basic norms of coexistence we can all live by without disrespecting each other. This unbiased attitude to justifying norms of social organization can help us understand norms of moral behavior. The unbiased point of view seems to entail that people be willing to aid others in need out of a concern with how they would like to be treated when in need themselves. On this reading, the norm of impartiality can naturally justify positive duties to help others—not just negative ones to refrain from hurting them.

The Principle of Minimal Altruism is not a matter of moral choice despite its misleading name. However, it is not unaffected by the division between "morally expected" and "heroic" actions because common-sense morality does not demand burdensome sacrifices on the part of the individual. Like the duty to call for help, the duty to vote with care requires from us that we act—it is a positive duty—but it is not unreasonably burdensome because it is episodic and does not entail an interrupted, overwhelming commitment to politics. Nor is it insurmountable. Other moral considerations (and duties) can override the duty to vote under particular circumstances. For example, our duty to care for a sick relative on election day may be stringent enough to take precedence over our duty to vote. Many other examples of the duty to vote losing to other considerations exist.

It may be thought, on first inspection, that negative duties are by definition more stringent than positive ones because of the (correct) intuition that we all have a duty to go to almost any length to avoid violating the rights of others (for example, we ought to go to almost any length to avoid killing another person) but we don't have a parallel duty to go to almost any length to help others.[12] But this conclusion is not warranted.

One reason why individuals are not obligated to sacrifice excessively in order to maximize harm-prevention is that it would be inequitable to require big sacrifices of those in a fortuitous position to help when others not in that position are spared the burden. One reason why we don't have a duty to go to almost any length, as individuals, to save others is that the duty to help others is more efficiently discharged by a coordinated distribution of special tasks in the hands of specialists (paramedics, firefighters, navy SEALs, etc.).[13] It is important to note, too, that discharging one's negative duties hardly demands any degree of excessive sacrifice. For most of us, keeping from killing others does not demand much effort or courage. By contrast, discharging positive duties to help may not be that easy all the time. This is why we don't require excessive sacrifice from the helper; it is *not* why we conclude that positive duties *altogether* are not really duties in the relevant sense of the word. We may not have a duty to jump into the burning flames to save the imperiled, but we have a duty to call the firefighters; and this duty is as stringent as the duty to refrain from violating the basic rights of others. They are both comparatively easy to discharge, generally. Society collectively "has preempted [the duty to assist] and reassigned it in fair shares to private individuals. *Collectively,* [however] there is hardly any limit to how far we are prepared to go to prevent serious harms to individuals."[14]

Generally, it is indisputably clear why we should *not* act in certain ways. For example, it is uncontroversial that we have a duty to refrain from inflicting harm on other people if not for self-defense reasons. But, if this is so, it should be easy to see why acting in certain ways may also be morally mandated. We can press the skeptic libertarian by calling attention to one principle at the center of most theories of morality: the idea that "morality is fundamentally (though not exclusively) concerned with avoiding states of affairs that are harmful for individuals. Such states of affairs, clearly, can be avoided not simply by refraining from harming but also by preventing harm."[15] As Buchanan aptly expresses it, what matters is their *harmfulness* whether or not those states of affairs were the outcome of someone's act of harming. For this reason, there is *at least* a presumption that there are some moral rights to receiving aid that prevents harm—if we assume that rights-principles express what is central to morality and if, as the libertarian believes, there are rights not to be harmed.[16]

Some positive duties are stringent *because* omitting to act may result in morally condemnable results that are equivalent to those that spring from doing harm directly. This equivalence is not automatic, but it can exist. The philosophical literature is familiar with the argument that a *failure* to *act* can at times be as harmful as an *injurious act* properly speaking. For example, Cicero writes:

> [T]here are two types of injustice. One committed by people who inflict a wrong, another by those who fail to ward it off from those on whom it is being inflicted although it is in their power to do so. For a person who unjustly attacks another under the influence of anger or some other disturbance seems to be laying hands, so to speak, upon a colleague; but the person who does not provide a defense or oppose the injustice, if he can, is just as blameworthy as if he had deserted his parents or his friends or his country.[17]

In a similar vein, John Stuart Mill writes that "a person may cause evil to others not only by his actions but by his inaction, and in either case he is justly accountable to them for the injury."[18]

In matters of voting, we commit wrongdoing when we vote badly—without information and not caring about the nature of our vote. Although this is the most clear and direct sense of wrongdoing when it comes to voting behavior, we also act wrongly if we fail to vote with care even when we don't vote badly either. Failing to vote with care, following Cicero's logic above, amounts to refraining from taking action to "ward off" an injustice of which we are a witness. It amounts to being indifferent when a situation presents itself in which we could intervene to assuage or prevent a wrong—the wrong of bad government—at no unduly high cost to us. Failing to vote with care, thus, could be interpreted as indifference in the face of a relatively easy course of action, and thus, as a nontrivial moral failure. Not acting in this case—i.e., not voting with care—can be equated to a failure to prevent injustice; and, as Cicero thought, we do have a duty to prevent injustice if doing so would not be unduly costly to us. The law may not be morally justified in forcing us to discharge a duty to vote with care, but morality alone can be stringent enough to demand that we behave as *minimally decent* Samaritans by utilizing the ballot as a vehicle of justice without jeopardizing our self-interest. I am invoking only the familiar point that the duties of ordinary people must be less demanding than the performances of saints and heroes. Not all Samaritan acts are heroically demanding. In the case of considered voting, a minimally decent Samaritan takes steps that ameliorate the risk of bad, unfair governance by voting with some reasonable degree of care; but she is not expected to sacrifice anything of value to her—like excessive time or lifestyle—for politics. Thus, it is not unreasonable to think that the duty to vote with care can be premised on a general Samaritan duty of justice to contribute to helping our democracy fight injustice when doing so is not unduly burdensome.

A central assumption in my approach to voting, then, is the idea that by omitting to vote in a considered fashion, individuals are indeed contributing to injustice: They are contributing to the harm that results from bad voting on the part of others as well as to the bad governance that results from those bad votes. This contribution is not causally direct, however, in the same way as pushing someone down the stairs is, for example (or voting badly oneself). Omissions are not direct causal contributors to states of affairs.[19] However, omissions can be causally implicated in the emergence and sustenance of states of affairs because when the individual acts, her actions can modify a given situation even if the individual herself did not cause that situation to come into being. For example, I can prevent someone's death if I throw him a lifesaver when he's drowning in the pool even if I played no part whatsoever in how he fell into the water. In this example, my failure to act when I stumble upon the struggling swimmer is one (sufficient but not necessary) causal factor that explains the swimmer's death.[20]

The concept of "causal factor" can fruitfully be applied to discussions about the morality of voting. Voters may not be directly responsible for the bad policies that governments enact and implement. They may have been deceived or betrayed in their expectations of good governance, so they may not be to blame for the bad performance of governments all the time. Additionally, no individual voter can be said to be causally responsible for good or bad governance since her impact on the result of the election is likely to be negligible. Voters may encounter themselves, in a way, in a similar-enough situation as the bypasser who spots a person drowning. The bypasser hasn't caused the harm himself, but he can assuage or prevent it. By the same token, voters have the *collective power* and the collective means, via elections, to avert the prolongation of injustice by removing the incompetent and corrupt from office and putting someone better in their place. Because of this collective power—and assuming that exercising it with others is not unreasonably costly for the citizen—refusing to stand by should be seen as a duty, not a choice that the citizen will not be blamed for avoiding. In the same way as we are, under general circumstances, morally expected to lend a hand to the troubled swimmer, we are also morally expected to avoid or minimize societal injustice by devoting some limited time to voting for the sake of good governance in society. Our individual contribution to reducing injustice may not be strictly necessary to attain the collective result of good governance. However, our contribution is surely valuable if we conceive of it as part a larger collective activity that we have objective reasons to value highly because of its potential impact on justice. Thus, the duty to vote is a Samaritan duty to contribute to a collective activity that can have a discernible (worthy) effect. It is, ultimately, a duty of *common pursuit*.[21] It calls us to cooperate with others in the attainment of a worthy goal, to wit, just governance (or less unjust governance).

2.2. Individual and Collective Samaritanism

We may say that democratic elections are justified by their capacity to produce good and just governance (although they can certainly produce the opposite). This statement may sound too reductionist, but it is not intended to be so. As advanced in the introduction to this chapter, democracy surely has intrinsic value. It is a valuable form of collective self-rule and it signifies the equal moral and political status of individuals. It gives everyone an equal say, at least formally, and in doing so, it honors the noble ideal of popular sovereignty or collective self-government. In other words, democracy is of worth in itself because it reflects the ideal that citizens are their own masters—who may delegate their power to rule in their representatives—as well as morally and politically equal among each other. However, democracy also has instrumental value in that it is a decision-making procedure that produces governments, which, in turn, enact legislation and policies that will profoundly affect (negatively or positively) the lives of millions. Governments that citizens elect determine if we go to war, the nature of the taxation scheme we all live under, the generosity and duration of the welfare benefits we will receive throughout our lives, and countless other issues of practical importance for people's lives. Thus, despite being valuable as a procedure and on philosophical principle, democracy can be valued for the outcomes that it brings about for people, families, and entire communities.

Elections enable the basic task of registering people's preferences about governments at a massive scale. Thus, voting as a collective effort is in principle instrumentally valuable because—if done carefully—it will result in the promotion of welfare and justice for the general population as a result of citizens choosing governments that care about those things. If people's preferences about what type of government should occupy the center of power are judicious enough, elections will ensue in a result that we have (good) reason to value because of its potential to promote justice and good governance—even though we know that justice requires more than merely fair-minded leaders (it also requires durable and independent institutions that operate justly).

Some may fear that valuing something for its results will lead us to ignore the importance of individual rights and individual needs. For instance, some may value a certain national security policy because it will keep us safe even if said policy entails violating personal rights to privacy and non-discrimination—as in cases of racial profiling at airports or train stations. Instrumentalism as a form of valuation can be morally suspicious at best. But not all forms of instrumentalism are of this kind. Instrumentalism means "valuing something because of what it can help bring about," but the yardstick of measurement may very well be "justice." It is not incongruent to think that a course of action is valuable because it helps promote justice understood as good and fair governance. In other words, justice may be the goal that an instrumentalist approach seeks to further.

We can value a course of action, policy, or decision because it will help promote a state of affairs that we consider just or more just than its alternatives. We do this all the time in the realm of human rights, for example. We consider human rights conventions and laws valuable because, all things equal, we believe that countries adhering to them will show concern for preserving basic liberties for their populations. We do not value human rights conventions regardless of their effects. They may have symbolic worth—and that is a significant aspect of theirs—but the reason international human rights law is a serious endeavor for many people is because human rights conventions can make people's lives better by making their governments more accountable for abuses. Voting as a collective activity can be analyzed in the same way: We can see it as desirable because, if utilized right, it can lead to results that we value in terms of justice.

As advanced in the introductory part of this chapter, valuing the collective act of voting for its potential results is not always how democratic theorists go on about elections. In the democratic theory discourse that enjoys prevalence today, political participation is usually defended and praised because of its tight association with collective self-rule and equality of political status. Collective self-rule is central to democratic life because the citizens' right to govern themselves via their representatives (or directly as in the case of referenda) is one irreplaceable pillar of democracy. Without self-rule, there is no democracy *by definition*. Collective self-rule, in turn, is the flip side of political equality (or equality of status). Only in a system where all have equal opportunity to have their voice heard in the political process can we say that collective self-government is *truly* collective. This is what government *by* the people means.

But we also understand democracy to be government *for* the people—an ideal that the celebrated phrase by President Lincoln also immortalized. What can government *for* the people mean? I think it must mean, at a minimum, governance that is not detrimental to essential interests of the people that the government is supposed to represent. In other words, government *for* the people must entail governance that is attentive to considerations of justice. Thus, we can value political participation, and voting in particular, because of the ideals it represents and honors—such as political equality and self-rule—but we should also value participation, and voting, because of its capacity to further a particular (collective) goal, namely, the goal of improving justice or preventing injustice. In short, we can value elections for (collectively) instrumental reasons.

The individual vote is a different matter, however. Rational choice theory has tirelessly suggested that the impact of a single individual vote is negligible in large elections. Individual votes get lost in a proverbial ocean of votes, making almost zero impact on the quality of governance in society.[22] However, even though our single good vote may not be terribly impactful, it is not unreasonable to believe that we ought not to *stand by* in the promotion of a collective good that is morally important such as good governance and fair policies, if doing so would not be unwarrantedly costly to our interests.

The notion that individual contributions to larger collective activities can very well be the object of moral evaluation (and duties) is not foreign to our most common forms of moral reasoning. Generally, we condemn individuals that participate in morally spurious activities *even* if their particular contributions would not usher in evil consequences by themselves. For example, we would surely think that a person donating a modest amount of money to a government-sponsored genocidal plan acts contrary to duty—i.e., the duty not to inflict harm—even if the money would not suffice to produce any considerable evil by itself because it will not buy the murderous leaders any weapons of mass annihilation. Moral duties to act or refrain from acting are not necessarily justified by the agent's capacity to alter an outcome. However, the moral nature of the collective activity in the backdrop of which the person acts is not irrelevant for assessing the ethical nature of that individual action. If it makes sense to say that acting in certain ways is wrong regardless of how perceptible our individual impact really is, it should also make sense to say that acting in other ways is right regardless of how perceptible our individual contribution may be. Moreover, some actions may not only be morally right, but they may also be required if they are not unduly costly to the individual. In the backdrop of this reasoning, it becomes clear why the moral stringency of the duty to vote with care is not diminished just because the act of voting will have a negligible impact among millions of similar acts during elections. Let me explain further.

The value of our single vote lies in the fact that voting with care is the kind of act that, *together with many similar acts*, will lead to a collective result that we have good (objective) reasons to prefer. Those reasons are the promotion of the common good and societal justice. Individually, then, our single vote is valuable because it is part of a collective process whose final outcome is valuable—as

I assume that there is consensus on the notion that furthering the common good is valuable. The collective enterprise is valuable instrumentally—*because* it promotes justice and the common good—and any action that forms part of that collective enterprise is therefore valuable despite the fact that it would not amount to much *by itself*. The value of our action derives from the value of the larger project of which it forms part—*not* from its power to make a difference. We could say that the larger project's value "trickles down."

I am evoking, then, a two-tiered valuation scheme that applies to small, individual actions that partake of larger collective activities.[23] In our case, the larger collective activity is *the election* and the smaller individual action is our *single act of voting*. The two-tiered structure of valuation dictates that the larger collective activity is valuable because it will help further a worthy good—such as justice in society. Because this is such a praiseworthy collective result, small acts that contribute to it are also valuable even if they cannot produce the outcome by themselves. I believe that there is normative space for two types of (intertwined) valuation here. When we see our tiny actions in the backdrop of our participation in collective endeavors that we have (objective) reasons to value highly, our single contribution acquires a moral salience that is not contingent on the difference-making potential of our single, small act. We could say that the overall value of the collective project mediates the value of the individual act. For example, I can consider that what I may donate to cancer research will not make much of a difference to the plight of the sick. "But when I see my donation as part of a coordinated fundraising effort, its significance changes."[24]

In arguing that our actions matter even when they are not *individually* powerful, I evoke a non-difference-making view of moral assessment.[25] According to that view, we do not assess the moral permissibility of individual actions according to their *difference-making* impact on a collective result. Rather, we assess individual actions according to the nature of the collective activity to which they contribute. To reinforce the argument, think about the

following situation.[26] Imagine a collection of people that work together toward a goal they all endorse. Additionally, suppose that
no single individual contribution will make a difference to the
achievement of that goal because the contribution will be too small.
As Beerbohm points to, if what really matters to assess the worth
of an individual act is whether that act changes things, then all
participants in this enterprise may act fully permissibly even if the
collective goal that they support is not. For example, if the joint goal
is the destruction of some community's clean environment (as part
of an extermination war, let's say), then each individual act of purposely spilling a few drops of poison onto the targeted community's
river can be seen as morally permissible since its impact on the
overall level of pollution will be almost nil. However, the intention to cooperate in the joint goal of environmental destruction
is condemnable and it should therefore play a part in evaluating
the individual's action. In this case, each individual is willingly
participating in the production of a goal that is morally repugnant.
Sharing intentions that are connected to a larger, condemnable goal
bespeaks a type of complicity that can be source of blame for the individual. The blame is a direct consequence of the larger collective
project's moral character. On this view, the individual acts inherit
the moral qualities of the larger enterprise of which they are parts,
and this is independent of how perceptible those individual acts are
on their own.

In the same vein, sharing intentions that are connected to a
larger morally valuable goal—like bringing about just governance
in society—denotes a moral disposition that is an apt candidate for
moral praise. Many acts denote moral praise because they signify
a supererogatory action, that is, individuals who did them went
above and beyond the call of duty. However, many other acts may
also deserve praise because the individual simply did them, and
the individual was expected to do them because the acts were not
too costly or difficult, and they provided needed help to someone.
The non-costly individual act that resonates with a larger goal of

relieving suffering or injustice can very well be morally obligatory under circumstances we can imagine. In the case of an individual good vote, the potential to determine an election's result is virtually zero. However, in the same way as contributing to a morally suspicious project is ethically troubling for the individual *even* if his contribution to the final outcome is negligible, taking part of a larger collective effort oriented toward improving justice in society should be seen as valuable *even* if the single individual's capacity to determine a result is also negligible.

The logic should be the same for both cases. If it is morally problematic to form part of a collective effort that seeks to harm others, by parity of reasoning, it should be morally praiseworthy to form part of a collective effort that seeks to reduce injustice affecting others. But there is more. If it is morally obligatory to refrain from participating in activities that purposely harm others—it is not *just* recommended—then, we should see that it is morally required to participate in activities that relieve injustice and suffering affecting others *provided that* doing so does not burden us unduly (in other words, the positive duty must fall within the purview of the Principle of Minimal Altruism). We ensure that other people's dignity is preserved *not only* when we refrain from violating it ourselves but also when we can, easily and non-expensively, do something to secure a general respect for that dignity, especially if is being patently jeopardized by others or by a particular situation (as when governmental injustices undermine people's well-being and rights). This is what impartiality as a principle of social morality mandates. It does not require us to act like heroes, seriously sacrificing ourselves for other people. But there is a long way inbetween Samaritanism and sainthood.[27]

There are many examples of acts that we see as morally obligatory even though we know that our single contribution will not determine a result. For example, we tend to believe that we ought to lend a hand in certain compelling situations, even though we know that many other people will be doing the exact same thing, rendering our single contribution not terribly noticeable, strictly speaking. Imagine that the government asks everyone to contribute one bucket of water to help alleviate the plight of residents living in a badly draught-stricken area of the country. Your singular contribution, or lack thereof, will not make the cooperative enterprise succeed or fail. However, common-sense morality suggests that it is wrong to stand by and do nothing in this sort if situation—if you could easily lend a tiny hand—even though we know that doing something would not change anyone's predicament ostensibly. Similarly, imagine that a homeless child lies sitting against a street wall on a chilly winter night asking for a small donation to buy a coat. The child is not asking anyone for the whole monetary amount that is necessary to purchase the piece of clothing. Aware of the overbearing nature of that demand, he is responsibly requesting individual donations of four dollars each. Do you act wrongly if you fail to disburse four dollars (which, we assume, you don't particularly need?) We may think so. Does the child have a claim to your help that he can enforce against you? No. You have an overriding legal right to do the wrong thing.[28] However, doing nothing in all these situations speaks to the type of person that we are, not to the perceptible effect that our actions have. It would not be unreasonable to say that you have failed to discharge a moral (albeit not legal) duty to contribute to assisting others in all these cases.

In elections, although a single vote will not have a discernible impact *by itself*, an accumulation of many certainly will. Our reason for action can be a duty of Samaritan justice even if we know that we would not achieve much *by acting alone*. The duty to aid calls us to join forces with others, in a common pursuit, by participating in elections when we would not incur high costs by doing so. It is not far-fetched to think that we ought to commit to participating in a collective endeavor that is instrumentally valuable for reasons related to the promotion and protection of justice. This is a duty *not to stay in the sidelines* when we could act so that our actions, *together with those of others*, help society at no unreasonable cost to ourselves.

At this point, someone could object that a duty of aid that needs to be carried out in conjunction with others to be impactful cannot be binding on the individual. How can one be bound to do something that will have no effect on the world? Despite intuitive, the foregoing reasoning is mistaken. Duties of aid do not lose moral stringency when they need to be carried out by many, collectively, in order to have a discernible effect. To see why, think of the following hypothetical situation, which I borrow from Virginia Held.[29]

In a subway car, an individual attacks a passenger. A number of subway riders, unrelated to each other but sitting in the same car where the attack is taking place, witness the aggression. No individual rider by himself is assured to be able to stop the attack (and it may be too dangerous, therefore costly, to do so). However, all together will be able to subjugate the aggressor easily. If this is so, all the riders witnessing the attack have a duty to act in concert in order to protect the victim from further harm, by stopping the attacker from moving. Similarly, we have a duty to vote with care—acting in concert with other members of the electorate at elections—in order to prevent the harm of bad governance on society, regardless of the insufficient effect of our vote alone.

Despite the preceding rationale, one could fear that the smallness of one single vote may at last weaken the moral stringency of the duty to vote. Because one individual vote is so minuscule in its effects—unlike the act of helping restrain an attacker—it can be superfluous because the threshold needed to win the election will be met without it. Am I still required to vote if I know that a given result will easily unfold without the need for my contribution? Differently put, am I still required to vote with care (or vote at all) if I know that my vote is not necessary to secure the result I favor?

The fact that each single vote in isolation will most likely be superfluous in the final count is hard to deny, but such mathematical truth does not detract from the moral force of a duty of aid via the vote. Everybody's vote is unnecessary in a mathematical sense since it is almost sure that the threshold of votes needed to win an election will be met regardless of any one citizen's participation. Thus, everybody would seem to have an equal claim to not fulfilling the duty to vote with care. However, this conclusion makes little sense from a neutral, broader viewpoint. It may be empirically true that my actions are superfluous in enabling a given result, but if this is true, so are everybody else's. Does it follow, then, that nobody has a duty to act? Imagine for a second the subway attack-scenario already described: if only five people were necessary to stop the attacker, but there are six riders witnessing the attack, does it follow that none of them has a duty to intervene? It would hardly follow. It makes more sense to think that everybody has an equal duty to act regardless of over-causation because it is difficult to see anyone's claim to be relieved from the duty as more weighty than another's.[30]

Furthermore, as I have already suggested here, an individual action that is not impactful by itself may still be morally required because it is the type of act that derives its value from a worthy, larger effort. In other words, an individual contribution that is negligible in its effects may still be morally valuable (and required) because it is the type of action that, together with many other actions of its kind, produces a valuable result.

Derek Parfit echoes this reasoning when he explains that "Even if an act harms no one [because it is negligible] this act may be wrong because it is one of a set of acts that *together* harm other people. Similarly, even if some act benefits no one [because it is negligible] it can be what someone ought to do, because it is one of a set of acts that *together* benefit other people."[31]

Parfit's logic above can support a duty of common pursuit— that is, a duty to cooperate with others in a collective activity— whose stringency will spring from the moral value (or disvalue) of a certain collective outcome. Some examples may help to clarify this point: even though I would not do any noticeable harm by dumping my trash into the river nearby my house, when the whole neighborhood follows my lead, the harm will be noticeable; thus, it is morally wrong to dump my trash. The collective result of everybody dumping trash is morally reproachable; thus, contributing to it, however marginally, should also be.[32] Likewise, even though I cannot modify pollution levels as a result of my individual act of recycling, when the entire city takes to recycling, pollution will decrease; therefore, I ought to recycle. This conclusion stands regardless of whether other individuals will actually recycle—or refrain from dumping trash onto the river. They may or they may not; but the point I want to make (and reiterate) is that an individual contribution derives its value from the value (or disvalue) of the larger outcome of which it forms part. Because of this fact, we cannot say that we are morally permitted to pollute simply because others are polluting, for example. However, we should not be morally required to make up for other people's failure to contribute (say, by recycling their trash ourselves). We are only required to do our fair share of Samaritanism.[33]

The point I have made before stands: wrong or right tiny actions are so because of their *association* with certain noticeable results that we have good reason to value or disvalue. We know that *if* many people recycle, pollution levels will decrease, thus, it is right to recycle. The rightness or wrongness of an individual small action hinges on its derivative worth. Voting with care, I want to suggest, is a case in point because the cumulative impact of small contributions (i.e., good, informed votes) helps bring about good governance, which we have good reasons to value highly. This is so even if one sole vote will not make a difference on the result of the election. A careful vote is still the type of action of which the morally desirable result (i.e., the electoral outcome that is preferable in terms of justice) that we value "is made of" so to speak. And thus, our commitment to it is *not* morally trivial and, under circumstances we can imagine, it may well be required.

The idea elaborated in the previous paragraph does not evoke a (Kantian) generalization argument. In other words, saying that voting with care is a moral duty because of its effects when many other individuals also vote with care is not the same as saying that, if nobody voted at all, disaster would ensue, and, therefore, we all ought to vote.[34]

Kantian generalization arguments center around the following question: What would happen *if* everybody did X (or nobody did Y)? The Kantian-minded person asks this question in order to assess the moral permissibility of an action or whether it is a duty to do, or not do, a certain act. The reason why the question centers on this hypothetical situation is the all-too-familiar Kantian universalization requirement for moral action (as entailed by Kant's categorical imperative). An action that cannot be willed to be permissible by everybody cannot be morally right, let alone a duty, according to Kant.

In the case of voting, the Kantian-minded individual could ask herself: What would happen if *nobody* voted? The answer to that question would be "nothing good" because a society in which nobody whatsoever took to the polls to cast their ballots would be a society without government! (or a society where there is no effective well-established method to choose one, which would gravely impair good governance). Because this situation would be unwanted (nobody can will it to be universal without incurring in a contradiction), the Kantian-minded voter would conclude that the decision not to vote cannot be universalized, therefore, there is a duty to vote.

Despite the simplification of the Kantian generalization argument for the purposes of this discussion, we can say that the logic has met with stark criticism when it comes to justifying duties, and in particular, the alleged duty to vote.[35] One can challenge the Kantian generalization argument by objecting to the hypothetical scenario experiment. Imagine for a second that I'm persuaded that it is my duty to become a medical doctor. My reasoning is that, if nobody studied medicine to become a doctor, society would be in deep trouble because the sick would die (and it is a contradiction for the individual to will this). But the fact of the matter is that a lot of people *do* study medicine regardless of how I feel about the importance of medicine. The hypothetical scenario experiment is unrealistic. In reality, there are many doctors and there will be many of them despite the hypothetical catastrophic theoretical suppositions. But most importantly, the fact that if nobody became a doctor, society would meet disaster does not mean that *any one particular* individual is morally required to become a doctor. It simply does not follow.

In the case of voting, even though a society where absolutely nobody voted would be catastrophic because no government could be elected, the *fact of the matter* is that many people do vote. But most importantly, the critic could say that, in the same way as the individual is not obligated to go to medical school despite the disaster that would ensue if nobody on earth wanted to become a doctor, she is not obligated to vote despite the catastrophe that would ensue if nobody voted and no government was established.[36]

I am not going to defend the Kantian generalization argument because I think it is flawed in its application to the issue of whether we have a duty to vote, or to become doctors for that matter. However, my defense of the duty to vote as espoused so far escapes the Kantian generalization logic. To understand why, we need to rehearse the gist of my argument for the duty as defended up to this point. This logic is nicely encapsulated in the earlier examples involving pollution and trash collection: We know that if many people recycle, pollution levels will decrease, which is why we are morally required to contribute to that desirable result, however marginally, if doing so is not costly to us. In the same vein, if many people dump their toxic trash onto the river, pollution levels will rise, which gives us a reason to know that we are obligated not to dump our trash, however marginal our act may be in its overall impact. Thus, unlike proponents of the Kantian generalization argument, I am *not* saying that individual action X is wrong because if everybody did X (i.e., something usually unlikely in reality), disastrous consequence Y would ensue. Instead, I am only saying that individual action E is right because when many or enough people do E, beneficial consequence Z *usually* follows. I am also saying that individual action R is wrong because, if many or enough people do R, undesirable consequence M *usually* follows. This is not the logic of Kantian generalization; it is the logic of cumulative altruism, or collective rationality, whereby we don't focus on the difference-making potential of our single act but, rather, on the value of the larger endeavor to which our contribution is *actually* adding, however modestly.

2.3. Voting as a Duty of Common Pursuit

In many circumstances of social cooperation, it is generally the case that free riding is a realistic option for the individual absent a legal sanction for his failure to contribute. Generally, economists have explained that free riding is difficult to avoid for non-excludable goods (such as clean air or good governance, for that matter) because those goods are hard to keep away from citizens not willing to contribute their fair share to their maintenance or creation. In the case of voting, absent a compulsory voting system, there is no clear penalty that the free-rider will fear. The free-rider acts rationally, from a strictly selfish perspective, because he doesn't bother to go to the polls or obtain the information necessary to vote carefully but he still benefits from the work of others, whose votes will result in the installment of a government.

But even if it's individually rational to free-ride on others during elections, we have a duty of "common pursuit" that counsels against that behavior. This duty entails nothing more than the duty to be well disposed toward cooperating with others in the framework of a larger collective enterprise that we have reason to value highly because of its overall effects, such as the furthering of justice, good governance, or the protection of rights. It's a prima facie duty because it is not absolute (it cannot require us to cooperate if doing so is unduly costly to us or if doing so collides with another duty or moral consideration that should have priority in particular cases). The duty of common pursuit is really a duty to see the merits of collective rationality over the merits of individual rationality narrowly understood as the pursuit of personal utility. Cooperatively disposed people understand the stringency of this duty, which is not supreme to all other duties, and act accordingly when doing so is not unduly burdensome. Cooperatively disposed citizens reason that, when one's contribution is added to many similar contributions by others, the outcome will be more beneficial for all than the individual cost that each bore by cooperating. Multiple social duties can be seen through the lens of this logic.

For example, most Americans think that paying their fair share of taxes is a moral duty and they do so duly, regardless of the fact that their sole tax payment is unlikely to make a tangible difference to the financial solvency of the state.[37] Likewise, many people contribute to large charity causes and organizations as a matter of moral duty to help the less fortunate even though it is undeniable that, for the most part, each individual contribution is immaterial to the larger pool or resources collected to help the needy. These forms of cooperation illustrate two things about human rationality: First, they indicate that the individual may possess a notion of instrumental action that emphasizes incremental additions to a large pool of contributions instead of a single act's potential to make a perceptible difference to a given state of affairs. Second, they suggest that the individual can be ethically motivated to act by a sense of commitment and a linked obligation not to stand by while others contribute to a worthy project that is likely to bring about desirable consequences for all (i.e., enhanced public services, decrease in poverty, increased well-being, a more just society, etc.).

The distinctive aspect of the form of collective rationality that undergirds the duty to vote with care is that it does not require the individual to make sure that other individuals are acting similarly so that he avoids being "the sucker." The collective rationality mindset does not evoke an assurance game—i.e., a game where the agent's willingness to cooperate hinges on whether the other agents participating in the venture also cooperate. Rather, the collective rationality mindset that undergirds the duty to vote with care reflects a different form of morality; one characterized by commitment.[38] The gist of the commitment morality that calls us to vote with care is the principle that everybody *ought to* act as if others were acting similarly. Parfit, in his seminal book *Reasons and Persons*, for example, supports this rationale. When explaining what makes co-operation morally required, he explains that (*a*) if we assume that the best outcome is that in which people are benefited the most, (*b*) each person in a given group *could* act in a certain way, and (*c*) they would benefit other people if *enough* of them acted in this way, then (*d*) each of them *ought to* act in this way.[39]

Note that Parfit's reasoning does not assume that the individual's contribution can make a discernible impact by itself on the predicament of another person. It is only when a sufficient number of individuals contribute that the group can make a difference *collectively*. If this is the case, one can hypothesize that the motivation driving the individual to cooperate will not be the goal of effecting change through her single act. What can it be, then? The same reason that animates the voter to cast a considered ballot among millions of votes: a sense of commitment to a collective enterprise that she has good reasons to see bear fruits when others contribute as well.

In the case of elections, and according to the morality of commitment just explained, the voter asks: "What should *we each* do so that all of us as a group achieve a particular result?" In contrast to the classical, rational choice individualistic mindset, she does not ask: "What will *I* do given what others are actually doing?" The individualistic rational choice mindset treats other people's degree of compliance as a standard for determining our own degree of compliance with a duty to do something. The rational choice mindset also suggests free riding on others if one can get away with it and still receive the benefits of other people's contributions. In the case of voting, if enough others are making the effort to vote, I may as well save myself the trouble. Similarly, if nobody is voting at all, I may as well think that I should not be the only one bothering.[40] But this is in no way the only type of rational thinking of which human beings are capable. People also evince a capacity for *collective* rationality, that is, they are capable of seeing beyond the mere individual utility of free riding, and can concentrate on the gains of full collective cooperation.[41] People normally do things for others in disregard of what others similarly situated are doing themselves. Charity rallies, blood donation, organ donation, food drives, foster parenting, abandoned pet adoption, and the hiding of Jews from German authorities in Nazi Europe are just a few examples. Some of these instances of non-selfish behavior are quite personally costly—so what unchangeable law of human nature says that much less costly communal behavior is not actually possible?

The argument of commitment is analytically different from an argument based on reciprocity, which sustains that it is unfair that some cooperate in the promotion of a good while others, who will benefit from that good, do not. The reciprocity argument is concerned with the allocation of distributive burdens and, by extension, with the free-rider problem that arises when someone shirks his fair share of the cooperative burden. Reciprocity-based duties are duties of cooperation among members of a particular community, or collective enterprise, that distributes a common benefit to its members, which is generally a public good, although not always. My argument of commitment, which derives from the value and humanity of a natural duty of justice, is instead concerned with what I call—in an admittedly morally charged way—rectitude of character. This quality of moral rectitude, when it comes to our role in a group, is a common human characteristic, and it should not be taken to be an unattainable trait. Indeed, critics of the rational choice approach to human behavior have time and again highlighted it as a commonly found aspect of human cooperation. There is nothing extraordinary in acting with the common good in mind in situations in which self-interest is not gravely jeopardized for doing so. In fact, people do this all the time, perhaps moved by what Amartya Sen calls "a concern for decency of behavior," or a perfectly human sense of commitment to a larger cause, without that commitment overtaking their lives and other goals.[42]

I posit that we are doing two immoral things at a time when we fail to vote responsibly. We are free riding on the cooperation of others in the community by allowing them to vote while we save ourselves the effort; *and* we are choosing to *stand by* instead of being part of a consequentially valuable enterprise, collectively speaking. These are two related, but analytically different, phenomena. Free-riding concerns speak to considerations of fairness as reciprocity in the distribution of the burdens of social cooperation. Voting, on this reading, is a cooperative burden because it is necessary to sustain democracy by installing a ruling coalition in power. Thus, when someone shirks from the responsibility, he is taking advantage of those that diligently don't and reaping the benefits of their efforts. Democratic governance is a public good in the sense that we all benefit from it even if we have not, as individuals, contributed to its emergence and survival by voting or participating politically in other ways.

Arguments about a duty not to stand by, in turn, speak to considerations of moral commitment *regardless of allocative concerns*. They revolve around duties that we have toward others when they need us and when we are able to lend a hand because doing so would not be detrimental to our personal goals. Our positive duties of justice, among which we find duties of aid, can be owed to society as well as particular individuals in need of assistance. That said, we can still value voting as an individual act and fully acknowledge that it is not tremendously effectual as a single helping action. But that is not a reason not to engage in it. Indifference would be immoral because it is immoral to stay in the sidelines when a valuable collective good such as good governance is being forged or maintained via elections, and when acting would not detract from our self-interest in any meaningful way. Either when we act as part of a larger group of people to effect aid (as in elections) or when we act individually to aid a particular person, standing by speaks badly of who we are even if we have a legal right to be mindless.

The logic of commitment and the coupled duty of common pursuit explain why some actions are morally required even if they will not alter an outcome (such as an electoral outcome) by themselves. Earlier in this chapter, we established that some actions are morally prohibited because they are wrong in themselves even if the doer of those actions will not affect or alter a larger outcome discernibly. The genocide supporter who donates a small amount of money to the state-sponsored genocidal plan is one case in point. I bring this example back to consideration because I want to make note that, interestingly, the libertarian advocate of the no-duty-to-vote agrees with the idea that some actions are morally wrong even if they are negligible in their impact. The no-duty-to-vote defender claims that it is morally wrong to engage in collective activities that harm others *even* if our specific role in the activity is ineffectual. In particular, it is immoral to "pollute the polls" with a bad vote. Brennan, for example, states:

> I will argue that one has the duty not to vote badly because this violates a more general duty not to engage in collectively harmful activities. A collectively harmful activity is an activity that is harmful when many people engage in it, though it might not be harmful (or is negligibly harmful) when only a few individuals engage in it. . . . But voting is collectively, not individually, harmful. The harm is not caused by individual voters, but by voters together (in this respect, voting is unlike [bad] surgery or [bad] driving). When I refrain from voting badly, this does not fix the problem. Still, it is plausible that I am obligated to refrain

from collectively harmful activities, even when my contribution has negligible expected cost, provided I do not incur significant personal costs from my restraint. I will argue that this is the reason I ought not to vote badly.[43]

Following Brennan's reasoning, I want to suggest that, if voting badly as an *individual* act is immoral *regardless* of the fact that our single act of voting badly won't have harmful consequences by itself, failing to vote judiciously as an *individual* act can also be immoral *regardless* of the fact that our single ballot will not produce any discernible benefit by itself. The foregoing logic explains why my defense of a duty to vote with care can counteract what I call the "threshold criticism."

The threshold criticism evokes the objection of overdetermination dealt with earlier in this chapter. It sustains that the benefits of good voting can emerge when a sufficient number of people vote with care—i.e., when a threshold of good voters is met—but that it is not necessary that all citizens vote with care for democracy to function adequately and fairly. Votes can be redundant: we don't need all possible voters to vote for an election to be defined and a good government to be elected. The threshold criticism is technically correct, but so is the fact that it is not necessary that every person that could vote badly refrain from doing so for a bad electoral outcome to be avoided.[44] It matters only that *enough voters refrain from voting badly*. This is explained by the logic of the threshold argument but in reverse. If voters need to reach a certain threshold to tilt an election, that means that we do not need *all* possible good voters to vote for a good electoral result to come about, we just need those that will constitute the threshold amount. This entails, logically, that we don't need all possible bad voters to refrain from voting badly for a bad electoral result to be avoided, only enough of them. Thus, libertarian detractors of a duty to vote cannot say—on pain of inconsistency—that there is a moral duty to refrain from voting badly *but* that there is no moral duty to vote with care because it is not necessary that everybody vote with care for good governance to obtain. They can't use that logic because it is not necessary that everybody refrain from voting badly for bad governance to be avoided, either.

Jason Brenan thinks, rightly, that it is wrong to participate in collective activities that, as a whole, result in harm. Voting badly (i.e., when many people do so) is such a collective activity. But if it is wrong to contribute to morally suspicious larger goals, it should be clear that it is morally right to contribute to morally good ones. However, ought we to do so or are we merely free to engage in morally good behavior? My argument so far has been that we ought to contribute to a praiseworthy collective effort as a matter of Samaritanism when we are in a position to do so at no high cost to ourselves. Elections offer us the structure that enables us to reach that helping position *in conjunction with others*. The fact that our single vote cannot achieve much by itself is irrelevant in the same way that refraining from casting one single bad vote is ineffectual in the collective effort of avoiding unfair governance. If we have within our reach a structure that can materialize the help that the Samaritan duty calls for—such as elections—we ought to do something to participate of that structure.[45] Our tiny action is of value, as I said, not because of the difference it can make—it will not make any difference in most cases—but because of its derivative worth, which springs from the larger enterprise of which it forms part (i.e., elections). In other words, our tiny action is of worth because it contributes, however marginally, to a larger valuable project. That larger project is valuable, generally, because it supposedly furthers a worthy human good such as justice, freedom, or fair governance. Elections, in this vein, are valuable because they can bring about a version (however imperfect) of those goods.

At this point, one may rightfully wonder whether making a small contribution to a collective project with a large (valuable) impact invariably counts as an instance of the Samaritan duty of justice to aid others. In other words, are all cases of easy altruism also cases involving Samaritan justice? It stands to reason that not all instances of cooperation in a collective project can be required by Samaritanism. Even though I use the term "Samaritanism" in a slightly non-traditional way, since aiding society does not equal aiding someone at (physical) risk of dying, strong conceptual parallels exist given the urgency of what is at stake when societies are governed unfairly and indecently. What is at stake when societies are governed immorally or inaptly is access to primary social goods and the fulfillment of basic interests in having access to those goods. Situations in which access to these goods is imperiled or diminished, I argued, could be compared to situations where ready aid is called for because of how indecent it would be to leave individuals without attention. Governments have the capacity to affect the flow of primary social goods; thus, failing to act toward ensuring that fair-minded leaders gain access to the seats of power in the first place seems to violate considerations of Samaritanism. It would seem to follow from this reasoning that instances of cooperation not geared toward restoring or gaining access to primary social goods are not motivated by considerations of Samaritanism, however important and necessary those joint efforts may be. I think it is uncontroversial that there is minimal consensus about the idea that most rational human beings will have an interest in having ready access to things like income security, decent healthcare, peace as absence of violence and war, and freedom from oppression, among others. Considered voting as a collective endeavor can enable access to these goods; therefore, it is not far-fetched to think of it as required by considerations of Samaritan justice.

In the next section, I will dwell on the (possible) moral equivalence between harming and failing to prevent harm, and on how it applies to the duty to vote with care. By focusing on the possibility of this equivalency when it comes to voting, I will show that the individual duty to vote with care is grounded in moral considerations that we should normally see as *binding, not merely as morally optional.*

2.4. Benefiting, Non-harming, and Failures to Prevent Harm

As the libertarian position on voting suggests, one reason why many may oppose the duty to vote with care springs from the widespread belief that negative duties always take priority over positive duties. In particular, the central belief is that the duty not to harm is always more morally stringent than the duty to provide aid—or to prevent harm from happening *when one is not the agent inflicting the harm.* Following this line of thought, some may say that voting with care confers a mere benefit on society. Since common-sense morality only requires us to refrain from harming others, the reasoning goes, we are not morally obligated to benefit anyone by voting. The logic that justifies this conclusion revolves around the central idea that "one who harms another makes that person worse off than she would have been had the agent not done what he did [but] one who fails to aid does not make someone worse off in this way."[46] In light of this difference, the familiar belief that we should be held morally responsible for making the world worse via our actions but not for failing to make the world better takes salience.[47]

In particular, the opponent of the duty to vote can avail herself of two related but different claims. She can say that voting with care is a form of aiding (benefiting) society but that we are *not morally* obligated to aid anyone. We are *only* morally required to refrain from harming them. She can also say that even under the assumption that voting with care prevents a harm (the harm of bad governance), we are not morally obligated to prevent a harm, we are only obligated not to do harm ourselves. Let me address these two claims separately.

Is the non-voter failing to bestow a mere benefit on society by not doing his share to increase the quality of governance when he stays home instead of taking the time to vote with care? This interpretation is highly intuitive. A non-benefit does not necessarily amount to a harm. For example, if I fail to regale you with a million dollars,

I certainly fail to benefit you, but I certainly don't harm you—and I'm not obligated to give you my money (short of any contractual duty or promise to do so). This conclusion rightly rests on the belief that a negative duty *not to harm* others is much more stringent than a positive duty to help others by bestowing *benefits* on them. But the objection, in order to bite, must understand "benefit" as a windfall benefit, that is, a benefit that will elevate our well-being and bring it above a baseline of normalcy, so to speak.[48] A windfall benefit positively affects a human interest by improving it in a way that is not strictly necessary to meet universal minimal requirements of human well-being. Preventing a harm, by contrast, is usually understood as an act that will prevent an interest from being adversely affected and/or from worsening below that baseline of normalcy. It can also be understood as an act that will stop or slow down the deterioration of an interest that is already being adversely affected.[49] If you give me champagne to appease my thirst, you are putting me above a recognizable minimal standard of human welfare because you are giving me more than I need to feel well; water would quench my thirst just fine. If you fail to give me water when I'm thirsty, in turn, you are not failing to regale me with a benefit in the sense that we are using that term here. We could say you are hurting me. Thus, making water available to me when I need it equals the prevention of a harm. Unlike champagne, there is little doubt that water is necessary for a decent existence.

The objection that voting with care *only* confers a benefit, and is therefore non-morally obligatory, is too simplistic. In general, taking action is not always equivalent to providing an unnecessary, windfall benefit; it can amount to restoring a situation that was worsening to its "normal" state. *Doing* something can also amount to slowing down the rate of worsening even if we are not restoring the situation to its "normal," previous, state. For example, when a doctor treats a sick patient by actively doing something such as medication prescription and medical procedures, the doctor is not bestowing a benefit understood in the sense of a non-needed, superfluous gain in welfare. Rather, the doctor is restoring the patient's well-being to a "normal" (prior to disease) level. She is bringing the patient back to a universally accepted-as-needed state of comfort. More dramatically, if the patient is a terminal patient, the doctor's actions may be intended to slow down the rate of the patient's physical deterioration and to alleviate her pain. In this vein, voting with care is not equivalent to regaling democracy with a gift or a welcome-yet-not-needed benefit. It is not equivalent to lifting society to a level of well-being that is *not* morally required based on universal standards of basic justice and human dignity. Rather, voting with care is conducive to securing society's basic fairness and protecting it from the erosion of good governance without demanding from the voter that she face an unreasonable cost. Electing fair-minded governments, our ousting indecent ones, is the main goal of elections as a mechanism of collective choice. It is hard to see how this basic purpose could be thought of as an un-necessary, yet welcome, benefit on society. Rather, it is more com-pelling to see voting as a mechanism that can contribute to securing the conditions necessary for just governance. Just governance, in turn, is to be understood as governance that enables and enhances access to primary social goods such as income security, peace, min-imal opportunity for advancement, decent healthcare, and so forth. These goods are not luxuries; they are social necessities because their absence would make a person's life grim. In other words, lack of access to these goods would *harm* people.

The second possible claim against the duty to vote with care as presented here maintains that one does not have duties to prevent harm, only duties *not to inflict* harm on others. Thus, the oppo-nent of the duty to vote may concede that voting with care is in-deed a form of preventing the harm of bad governance, but she may nevertheless refuse to recognize that there is an obligation to do something to prevent the evil in question short of not contributing directly to it by voting badly. This reasoning means that the indi-vidual sees himself as morally permitted to be *indifferent* during elections. He believes he is morally permitted to be indifferent because of the alleged fact that positive duties to act for others make unduly heavy demands on the agent, even if it's harm—not superfluous benefits—that we are talking about.

This chapter has challenged the idea that common-sense morality excludes positive duties from its repertoire, however. The opponent of the duty to vote is right in claiming that considerations of cost should affect the obligatoriness of individual actions. However, he takes an extreme view about the type of costs that supposedly impose an unduly high burden on the individual. The libertarian position against the duty to vote—and the position that rejects duties of Samaritan aid in general—assumes that *anything* beyond the cost of refraining from inflicting harm via our own acts is too high, therefore, not morally obligatory. But there is much room for disagreement over this issue. Philosophers share no consensus over the idea that there is no binding duty to make the suffering of others less pressing, if doing so would not place oneself in an unacceptable predicament.

It is, after all, a matter of dispute that all actions done for the sake of minimizing suffering or preventing harm are unduly costly for the individual. Helping others may perfectly be as costly as not harming them. For example, donating $100 to charity may be less costly than refraining from buying clothing made in sweatshops abroad. The latter way of not contributing to harming others (by refraining from participating in the global dynamics that exploit cheap labor in poor countries) may be too burdensome for the agent on two counts: first, it is cheap to dress in clothes that come from sweatshops and, second, it is incredibly easy to find them in the marketplace. Avoiding them systematically may impose financial and time-related costs on the individual that surpass the monetary cost of the charity donation. One can think of other examples to illustrate the real possibility that not contributing to harm is equally or less costly than helping others or preventing harm. The idea that negative duties are *invariably* more stringent than positive duties because they are less demanding on the agent cannot be sustained without a doubt. It is not empirically accurate all the time.

Even if it was true that negative duties not to harm invariably impose lower costs than do positive duties to aid or to prevent harm, one could question the idea that positive duties are always unduly burdensome. An often-used example may help clarify this point. Is calling for help using a mobile phone at the scene of an accident too high a cost for the agent that happens to pass by? One may think that stopping to make a call may conceivably make the passerby late for an important appointment, or it may impose an inconvenience that it would be rational to want to avoid. It is true, helping others is not totally costless—but is it always *unacceptably* costly? The passerby may not suffer grave consequences for being late once his boss knows he was helping save a life. Or he may, in particular cases, but not as a matter of definition.

It seems to me that a useful way of thinking about how considerations of cost affect the obligatoriness of actions addressed at preventing harm to others consists in understanding what the relationship is between costs borne by the helper and the benefit received by the person being helped. If the good furthered by helping is comparably more weighty (morally) than the sacrifice undertaken to get it, it may be true that there is a strong moral reason to do the sacrifice, all else equal. For example, if the cost of jumping into the water to help a drowning child is ruining our shoes, and the good promoted by said cost is saving a life, it becomes quite reasonable to think that the cost should be outweighed by the benefit, making the rescue morally obligatory.

This reasoning may give room to not so palatable possibilities, however. For example, if the cost of jumping into the water is catching pneumonia, does the good of saving a life still render the rescue obligatory? What if the cost of jumping into the water was losing a leg? From an impersonal standpoint, the good of saving a life will seem to justify the cost of losing a leg because nothing is worse than death (allegedly). However, this is not the perspective that we might want to take.

A cost-benefit analysis in its most crude form may not be fully appropriate to think about what makes harm prevention morally obligatory. Besides it, we need to adopt a threshold logic. A threshold logic indicates that no matter how great the good promoted by an act of harm prevention may be, the agent is not morally obligated to do such act if the cost of doing so is above a *reasonable standard of sacrifice*. I understand that this terminology invites questions about what that standard would precisely be, and how one is to arrive at it. I do not have available the most specific answer to those questions, but I do not think that the idea is difficult to pin down in its general form. This standard of sacrifice may perfectly include costs that are not as high as considerations of life and death yet are weighty enough to render certain acts only morally optional (not required). In the case of elections, it is not far-fetched to think that, under circumstances one can imagine, voting with care is not a cost that surpasses the reasonable standard of sacrifice in question.[50] Furthermore, the harm prevention that is possible when voting with care is prevalent is of such high value, that contributing to it seems to be justified by the cost of a considered vote. This is the idea that this chapter defended in previous sections.

As we know, the libertarian opponent of the duty to vote with care places the act of considered voting into the category of supererogatory action, that is, action that is morally praiseworthy but not morally obligatory. This assumption not only is a conceptual error, but it also is a normative mistake because the duty to vote with care is a specific application of a broader duty of justice that is not optional (although it may be overridden under specific circumstances that make other moral considerations more urgent—this being the case with practically all duties). The duty to support justice in society requires more than forbearance. It requires active steps to make sure that injustice does not take control of our institutions. Cicero's reflections on justice, among others, echoed this idea when he said that failing to prevent an injustice done to a neighbor when it would be easy to do so is as grave as doing the injustice oneself.

At a societal level, even basic rights to physical integrity, security, property, and equality before the law that are paradigmatically associated with negative duties not to intrude and not to harm require positive actions to be effective. These positive actions include the levying of taxes to fund the police and the judicial system, among others. Negative duties to refrain from interfering with the rights of others are ultimately enforced by a state that punishes and prevents those violations. And that costs money and requires much more than non-interference. It requires resources and positive measures necessary to maintain a system of justice and law enforcement working. Justice, in summary, does not survive only on negative duties of forbearance. If forbearance is not all there is to justice, it becomes easier to understand why positive action is not inconsistent with justice. In particular, voting with care is an act that, under circumstances we can imagine, not only is consistent with justice, but also is required by it given the utter importance of the good that it helps promote, namely, decently fair governance.

A society where citizens make an effort to vote with care for the sake of good and fair governance is guided by the moral rule of easy altruism, which we mentioned earlier in this chapter. The principle of Mininal Altruism, despite its name, does not *just* recommend charitable, altruistic behavior. Rather, it tells us that helping by preventing harm or suffering, under circumstances of low cost to the helper, is not optional because it is the just thing to do. The principle of easy altruism is nothing else than a principle of impartiality. Generally, impartiality encapsulates the basic notion that we are all entitled to equal consideration regardless of separating factors such as race, gender, sex, etc., so that we can stand an equal chance of having our basic, shared interests fulfilled. Basic shared interests are interests that we can reasonably attribute to most rational human beings; they include the yearning for things such as security, a decent livelihood, good healthcare, and peace, among others.

When the citizen casts a considered vote with the intention of promoting fair governance in her society, she is seeing her fellow citizens as deserving of consideration equal to her consideration of herself. She is discharging a duty of justice via the vote and expecting others to do the same so that the government elected can be trusted with protecting and furthering the basic interests of all, not just a few, or not just the elite's. This approach is valuable because it highlights the importance of equality of status in the eyes of government. But the considered vote, collectively, is also valuable because it has the capacity to relieve our fellow citizens from injustice, even if it does not always achieve perfect justice.

This chapter has attempted to show why voting with care is an obligation given its connection with justice and its allegedly low cost. In the next chapter, I focus on one of the most powerful criticisms against a moral duty to vote, namely, the idea that voting is not morally special because it is not the only way to help society and the common good. In the following pages, I will argue that voting with care is morally special *enough* to be thought of as a duty even if there are many other ways to further the common good of society.

3

What Does It Take to Vote with Care?

3.1. Two Conditions for Considered Voting

The duty that this book defends is not merely a duty to vote; it is a duty to vote with care. If the main goal of voting is to help society fight injustice, in the spirit of Good Samaritanism, then voters' choices must reflect this sense of instrumentality. Not all types of votes will do this successfully, only those judicious enough to be capable of collectively bringing about an electoral result that is recommended by justice. But a careful or considered vote must meet certain minimal conditions to qualify as such. What are those conditions? In this chapter, I will give an answer to this fundamental question.

But first, I want to reiterate a concern that I expressed in the introduction to the book. This concern is important to address so as to be prepared against a challenge that critics of the duty to vote forcefully offer, namely, the idea that voters are predominantly unable to vote smartly and, therefore, that elections play no significant role in influencing justice (if anything, they are all the more likely to cause *injustice* because ignorant voters will choose inadequate governments).

In this book (and chapter) I suggest that we are morally bound to vote as Good Samaritans, i.e., with a sense of the common good of society and with necessary information for the sake of good governance. This requirement is predicated on the argument that, when it is not unduly costly to help, we should try our best to do so. Empirically, it may be the case that many people are unable or unwilling to honor and discharge this duty. This fact does not automatically render the duty morally invalid, however. Rather, it points to the possibility that individuals are not well-equipped or willing to act on it. As I claimed in chapter 2, the world is full of people that are derelict in their duties. People lie, kill, and steal for no justifiable moral reason, most of the time. Does that mean that the duties to not lie, steal, or kill are morally toothless? It would hardly follow.

But one could still wonder whether the duty to act as a Good Samaritan through the ballot asks too much of human beings. In other words, is the duty to vote with care consistent with a realistic understanding of human psychology? If it is not, we could question its moral stringency altogether since it is not far-fetched to think that moral duties should be as consistent with human nature as possible. They should not ask individuals to do impossible things or to undertake heroic missions as a matter of routine ethical demands.

However, I do not think that considered voting is an example of an impossible ethical demand. An alleged duty to donate most of one's income is such a demand, or to die for others, or to completely forgo personal self-realization for the sake of society. But voting every so often at important elections is not that burdensome. It is true that it is not *totally* costless since voting minimally competently requires acquiring knowledge, which takes some time and effort to internalize—but this cost is not morally *unacceptable*. The fact that some may shy away from it does not make it so, in the same way as the fact that some shy away from paying taxes does not make taxes morally unjustified, for example. One can imagine individuals spending some time learning about the policy positions of the different candidates without this hindering in any morally relevant way their life-plans or personal goals. It is strange to say that voting takes away from other things in life in a way that makes any moral sense unless your preferred way of life is one of utter isolation from society, in which case we can discuss whether there may be exceptions to the duty to vote with care based on objections of conscience or similar reasons.

Importantly, I reiterate, the duty to vote with care is not *too* demanding just because we know that many individuals are unable or unwilling to discharge it. There may be reasons that explain this inability or unwillingness that are *not* related to limits germane to the human condition. In other words, the reasons that explain why many people cannot vote smartly or won't bother to attempt to do so may not be reasons based on psychological limitations that affect humankind as a matter of definition. Instead, they may be reasons pertaining to the structure of the political and economic systems under which many individuals live; a structure that may be setting the wrong incentives when it comes to voting and acquiring information. For example, certain electoral rules may be making it harder for citizens to understand what is at stake in an election if voters get fatigued due to the many different levels of public office that they are supposed to decide on at once. Furthermore, political elites may conveniently manipulate or pass information to the public that is not completely factually accurate, and some media outlets may acquiesce in this shady practice, contributing to mass misinformation on certain key issues. Additionally, relatively skewed distributions of wealth and income in a country may cause steep educational disparities, which may explain why a more educated minority tends to possess political knowledge but the vast majority of less well-to-do citizens are not equally competent politically. More structural reasons can be given. This chapter will pursue this line of argumentation because critics of the duty to vote have too often ignored it. My aim is not to suggest that structural reasons are all there is to account for voter ignorance and political disinterest. There are also individual-level reasons of cognitive incompetence. However, as I will explain below, the latter have gotten disproportionate attention in the ethics-of-voting literature compared to other plausible explanations for voter ignorance and voter disinterest. I believe that voter ignorance can be explained by various different reasons; and I do not see those different reasons as mutually exclusive. However, I do think that the literature has laid too much emphasis on one type of reasons (i.e., individual-level cognitive failures) to the detriment of others (i.e., structural and contextual factors). I will clarify what all this means in the following sections. Next, I lay out the general goal of this chapter, namely, defining the notion of a considered vote.

My rationale for what is to count as a considered vote consists of two general parts. One is normative and the other is epistemic. The normative part tells us that voting with care must entail voting with a particular mindset. A careful, judicious voter casts a ballot consistent with her most conscientious opinion of the common good; she is fair-minded in her decision-making at the ballot box. I call this the "fair-mindedness condition" for careful voting. The epistemic aspect of good voting, in turn, tells us that voting with care requires sufficient information about facts necessary to assess the superiority of one electoral option over others (or the equal lack of appeal thereof). I call this the "minimal epistemic competence condition."

With respect to the first condition (fair-mindedness), we are wise to accept a rather thin conception of what it means to cast a good-enough ballot. Based on the reality of pluralism—which means that individuals in society will reasonably disagree about issues of morality—I do not think that we can tie, nor should we want to, a particular conception of justice to the notion of a considered vote. However, we can suggest that the good voter is the person that takes a broader view than his self-interest justifies when thinking about his electoral choices. This requisite entails, also, that immoral prejudices and biases disguised as concerns for the common good cannot pass the test of considered voting, however sincere those may be due to self-rationalization. The reason why self-rationalized bias and self-rationalized personal advantage must remain out of a person's true motivations for voting is that the reasoning evinced by the voter who falls prey to self-rationalization would not reflect impartiality (the voter may think it does, but in reality, it would not). Thus, the fair-mindedness condition for considered voting entails something else besides a pro-social attitude on the part of the citizen. It entails striving for an impartial thinking process. What does it take to think impartially?

I submit that fair-mindedness in voting should entail voting on the basis of principles that nobody could reasonably reject—"reasonably" given the aim of finding principles that could be the basis of un-coerced general agreement. Even though some results are unacceptable under this understanding of the common good, there can be many non-identical sets of rules and notions of justice that pass this test of non-rejectability.[1] This understanding of the common good is not merely "epistemic" because it requires a bit more than the use of correct information and rational thought-processing. It requires a basic commitment to thinking in impartial terms.[2] A commitment to impartiality is akin to a process of "democratic deliberation within."[3] This internal deliberation requires that, in matters of political decision-making, people imagine themselves in the position of other people and ask, "What would they say about this candidate and her proposals?" This deliberation does not necessarily require an actual dialogic process with other interlocutors, but it does require taking into account other people's perspectives and concerns when assessing the merits of a political decision. I suggest that we ask for this disposition from voters in a democracy besides the modicum of knowledge and rationality that must accompany any voting choice. This disposition does not require academic familiarity with philosophical theories of justice. It only requires a disposition to see things from the viewpoint of others, not just oneself, and to make an effort to suppress biases that may lead one to prefer an alternative that others may have a *justified* reason to reject. Abundant political science research confirms the fact that many voters vote with the common good in mind.[4] Although this tendency doesn't say much about *how* they conceive of the common good, it tells us that others-regarding reasons for voting are not an implausible thing to ask from citizens.

With respect to the second condition for considered voting (the minimal epistemic competence condition) one must bear in mind that there are at least two diametrically opposed positions on the subject of voter capacities. One position views the average voter as unable to reach a modicum of competence. The other position sustains that many voters can reach that minimum—which is not unacceptably burdensome—and more will be able to do so under enhanced conditions (i.e., better education, better access to impartial and balanced discussion in the media, and higher income equality, which distributes more evenly the resources needed to acquire information and time for participating in politics). The "pessimistic" approach that mistrusts voter competence is exemplified by theorists such as Bryan Caplan, Ilya Somin, and Jason Brennan, among others.[5] They claim that voters tend to vote irrationally, ignoring experts' knowledge, and erratically. The "optimistic" approach to voter competence is epitomized by theorists such as Arthur Lupia, Samuel Popkin, and Phillip Tetlock, among others.[6] They propose that voters can be rational choosers despite their lack of expert knowledge since they can take epistemic shortcuts to know what selection would be superior. The cognitive shortcuts literature shows that despite lacking perfect knowledge, citizens can learn what they need to know to make a satisfactory choice at the polls. This literature is complemented by studies showing that public opinion has been consistent and coherent across time, even if not all voters can be said to be epistemically competent individually.[7]

These two blocs of literature are both empirically strong since authors rely on survey studies and statistics, which means that it wouldn't be scientifically correct to discard either of them at the expense of the other. I believe, however, that the voting ethics literature has been co-opted by the pessimistic camp. My arguments in this chapter do not pretend to ignore the empirical and philosophical issues around the capacities of average citizens. However, it aims to add more balance to what I think is an imbalanced conversation. In particular, this chapter will emphasize the idea that it is plausible to believe that public knowledge can improve with the right public policies and institutional reforms, which include, but are not limited to, more civic education, less influence for special interests in politics, less party polarization, which leads to disaffection, and the simplification of electoral laws.[8] If we can affect citizen knowledge, we can know that political ignorance is not a fixed, unalterable datum of reality. Even though much political ignorance can be attributed to individual cognitive failures, much of it can also be attributed to structural political variables such as distance between citizens and public officials, low sense of political efficacy among would-be voters that leads to disinterest in politics, and outright manipulation of media messages by interest groups with vested interests in particular policy outcomes. Individual cognitive failures are difficult to undo, but it makes sense to think that we can improve failures of information due to structural factors in the political system by reforming the political system itself.

In relation to the issue of voter competence, Jason Brennan argues that we can effectively classify citizens into three basic categories.[9] These conceptual archetypes each reflect the citizen's attitude toward politics as well as her level of political knowledge. According to Brennan, we can divide citizens into *hooligans, vulcans,* and *hobbits*.[10] Hooligans are citizens that have strong political opinions and are highly motivated to participate in politics, but they consume political information in a biased way, confirming their already existing views, and they show contempt toward those that disagree with them. Hobbits are citizens that show high degrees of apathy and disinterest in politics. They are largely ignorant of facts and evidence relevant to understanding important societal issues and have no strongly felt beliefs of a political nature. Brennan thinks that the hobbit is the typical non-voter in the United States, at least. Lastly, vulcans are the most rational and knowledgeable of all three types of citizens. They have solid knowledge of social science and other matters that permit them to understand the evidence for and against political arguments. They are obviously interested in politics but they are not biased and, because of that, they can engage in rational dialogue with others. They can also argue against opposite points of view dispassionately; they don't care about "winning"—they care about the truth. They show no contempt toward those that disagree with them.

Brennan never tells us that he bases his taxonomy of citizens on extensive survey work on the American, or other, electorate. He seems to justify his categorization on purely observational or anecdotal information, collected by him. In what follows, then, I will rely on the same methodological approach. I think that Brennan's classification of citizen-types is incomplete. In my view, we need (at least) a fourth category to understand citizens' attitude toward politics. For lack of a better term, I call this additional category the Moderately Interested Voter (MIV). MIVs are largely well-predisposed to acquiring new information about political matters and they process it with an open mind because they do not have strong preexisting biases. They are generally aware of their knowledge deficiencies in key areas but they seek to educate themselves on some of the basic issues that seem to be at stake in the election—given the time constraints that they have (which may be significant). Their command of social science is not solid but they do a good job of isolating the basic causal links that are central in some of the most pressing issues under exploration. Their sense of identity is not tied to their political views so they do not care about winning arguments for the sake of winning them. They are genuinely concerned with *not* making a vastly uninformed choice at the ballot box. They may not be overtly concerned about politics outside of the election period but, when the voting approaches, they take pains to fulfill what they believe is a civic duty of due diligence, so to speak.

I know many people like this. They don't read the *New York Times* or the *Wall Street Journal* every day, and they do not have high terminal degrees, but they are conscious enough about the seriousness of elections, even if politics take the back seat to other aspects of their lives most of the time. Brennan ignores them completely, but he should not because they may be an important reason why not all is lost for democracy. In his work, Brennan argues that most citizens eligible to vote are hobbits or hooligans. Of course, he is right in thinking that vulcans are destined to be a minority. However, I am not sure he is right about hobbits and hooligans taking the first place *together*. In the absence of a formal survey of the electorate, the claim that MIVs may be as numerous as hooligans or as hobbits is prima facie equally reasonable. At least, from a common-sense perspective, it is not clear to me that hooligans are more numerous than MIVs. Hooligans are very invested in politics and generally very knowledgeable, although unduly biased in their favor. They spend inordinate amounts of time participating politically in various ways and consuming political information. They consider politics an essential part of their lives. I would say that, in tune with the observation that most people are too busy to care that much about politics—which Brennan seemingly shares with me—it would be reasonable to think that MIVs are more common in society than hooligans. The latter may be more visible and vociferous—and that is exactly why Brennan thinks they are so numerous but he may be mistaken.

In what follows, I explain in more detail what my idea of careful voting requires from citizens and the possible criticisms that it may receive. I address those critiques as well in the rest of the chapter.

3.2. Fair-Mindedness in Voting

I want to suggest that the fair-mindedness needed at the ballot box could be partly understood in the backdrop of John Rawls's notion of "perfect procedural justice."[11] As mentioned, the impartiality requirement for good voting is not merely epistemic because it asks us for more than rational and informed reasoning. However, it is procedural—not substantive—because it does not predict a particular ideal of justice. Rawls argues that a lottery is an example of perfect procedural justice. Insofar as the lottery is not weighted, the outcomes that spring from it will be considered just because everyone had an equal chance of being selected. This means that we do not hold a criterion of justice that is *independent* of the procedure itself. If the procedure in place is applied correctly, that procedure renders the result, whatever that is, just.

Voting with a sense of impartiality (or fair-mindedness) resembles the logic of perfect procedural justice. If people vote predisposed to assessing the merits of the electoral alternatives through a lens of impartiality, they will think about what others would find acceptable, not just themselves, and the results of the election should pass the test of justice—for the purposes of this discussion, at least.[12] This fair-mindedness should be accompanied by epistemic conditions that include information and rationality. But in the same way as lotteries will yield different results when played many times, the same election could, *in theory*, yield different electoral outcomes *even* if voters vote following the fair-mindedness requirement and rationally every time. This is so because voters may hold different views of justice and still be acting within the bounds of the logic of impartiality as here defined.

What I want to ague, thus, is that my understanding of what it means to vote with care is not meant to favor any particular conception of justice. Legitimate disagreement on this front is welcome and expected in reasonably liberal democratic societies. However, there should be bounds to that disagreement. Personal-advantage-based positions (however disguised they may appear) cannot pass the test of impartiality understood as the ability to put oneself in the shoes of others. This is why the principle of impartiality is not merely epistemic. The principle of impartiality does not merely require us to be free from logical error and misinformation. However, it is procedural, not substantive, because it stresses the exercise of a particular method, i.e., the "deliberative" or "reflective" method.[13] This method of decision-making entails making choices about what we think is just from a viewpoint that nobody *could* reasonable reject, but there is not a sure set of principles of justice that are invariably and conclusively to be preferred as a result of doing this (although there are, admittedly, a set of outcomes that we would reject because they would not follow from impartial deliberation. Following the lottery analogy, we could say that certain results could only derive from a weighted, therefore unfair, lottery).

The fair-mindedness approach to morality is motivated by a particular conception of how we should relate to other human beings when thinking about some of the most important and impactful decisions that concern life in common. This approach is characterized by our ability to justify our behavior to each other in a way that others will find difficult to reject because it would not be reasonable to do so, save on self-interested reasons that fall astray of mutual consideration. For a moral principle predicated on impartiality, an action is wrong (unjust) if it would be forbidden by a system of rules governing social interaction that no one could reasonably reject.[14]

This mutual concern position is appealing as a philosophical theory of morality and as an account of moral motivation. As already mentioned, there is plenty of empirical evidence in the voting behavior literature that shows that socio-tropic voting— i.e., voting that is not primarily motivated by narrow self-interest but by a concern with the common good—is common in large elections.[15] In this vein, my normative account of voting with care is not detached from reality. In order to follow the spirit of the fair-mindedness standard of good voting, voters do not need to be expert philosophers, adept at analyzing the intricacies of different theories of ethics and justice. Instead, they have to be psychologically attuned to others and make decisions that are not exclusively driven by narrow self-interest but that are good for society overall—especially those that need help the most.

This attention to society's well-being does not necessarily negate one's own individual needs as a voter. The fair-mindedness approach to voting, as I will explain in what follows, is not blind to self-regarding considerations; it just tries to combine self-interest with the common interest understood as those results that nobody will have objectively valid reasons to reject. In this account, "each person has a veto on all proposed principles for regulating social life."[16] Thus, fair-mindedness does not equal self-effacing behavior. By contrast, it reconciles a neutral concern for others with a justified concern for ourselves.[17] Scanlon puts it this way:

> Part of what it is to be reasonable in this context is to have a care for one's own well-being. Another part is to have a care for what others, given their outlooks, could consider to be acceptable terms of interaction. The guiding thought is that one is looking explicitly for terms of cooperation that no one will reject, were they each seeking to identify terms of cooperation that avoid imposing undue sacrifices on any party to the agreement.[18]

In a more classical tone, J.-J. Rousseau also highlighted the coexistence of two considerations, i.e., self-interest and the common good, when thinking about voting. He remarked, throughout his work on the social contract, that each member of the community created by the consent of the people must vote from a public perspective qua citizen, expressing not simply her private beliefs but her judgments about what is verified from the perspective of all.[19]

The intuition that self-regarding reasons can be reconciled with a concern for the common good to motivate the individual to vote is not far-fetched. This account of voting, one could say, highlights the idea that "nobody should accept a rule that would require a unilateral sacrifice of their interests."[20] In this vein, Brian Barry says: "It is true that it is not unreasonable to be generous. But it is one thing to be praised for behaving generously against a background norm which leaves the act optional and quite another to be led by generosity to accept a rule that would expose one to moral condemnation unless one were to sacrifice oneself unilaterally. It would not be reasonable to accept the latter."[21]

So a good voter that follows the moral standard of fair-mindedness to cast her ballot *will not* be expected to be utterly altruistic in detriment of her class-based or individual interests. She, if wealthy, for example, would not be expected to lend her support for a social rule that prejudices her capacity to keep her wealth (via the legalization of expropriation measures, for instance). However, she will be expected to withdraw her support from rules that help her keep her wealth at the expense of interests that the non-wealthy may have valid reasons to see respected such as the establishing of a taxing system that burdens everyone proportionally to their income. These are just punctual examples. Many more can be given. The point I want to make is that altruistic and self-regarding considerations can peacefully coexist in the voter's heart and mind. The fair-mindedness approach to voting values both; and it does not expect one to totally overshadow the other. The moral notion of impartiality does not eschew individual reasons. In other words, fair-mindedness, as I understand it here, does not impose on the individual a burdensome requisite of benevolence toward others.

The idea that both self-interest and the common good can, and do, figure in voters' mindsets underscores a philosophically important question: How are we to understand what the common good is? This question of definition is too big to be tackled in its entirety here, but I want to briefly address it because it is related to our discussion of voters' concern for the fate of society.

3.3. Interpreting the "Common Good"

A long and respected tradition in political thought—which has spilled over into theoretical political science—conceives of the common good—or public interest—as an unintended, natural consequence of a free market in which everybody cares about and works toward the satisfaction of their selfish preferences. This account of the common good sprang from a particular view of economics centered on the metaphor of the "invisible hand." In this story, "the behavior of consumers in an open market ensures the satisfaction of the wish on the part of each to be able to buy goods and services at the lowest feasible price. Consumers are each disposed to buy something of a given quality as cheaply as possible. . . . Producers of the commodity or service are disposed to undercut one another's prices in order to maximize revenue; if they are not then others will have an incentive to enter the market and challenge them. And the effect of the interaction between the dispositions of the two groups is to push producers to sell at the competitive price."[22]

None of the actors involved in this story act with anything different from pure self-interest, "and the effects of each acting on those wishes is that, as by an invisible hand, the wishes are satisfied."[23] After Smith made waves in economic theory with this image of the invisible hand as an explanation of how public benefit derives from private interest, the image was adopted in political theory. As Pettit aptly summarizes, James Mill—a compatriot of Smith—made the invisible hand mechanism the center of his theory of government in his *Essay on Government*, written in 1819. In that essay, Mill argued that by designing an effective (i.e., appropriately proportionate and representative) electoral system, it would be possible to rely on an invisible hand to promote the public interest in Parliament. Mill departed from the then common assumption that people were first and foremost motivated to satisfy their selfish preferences in politics and in every other realm of life. James Mill's great adaptation of the invisible hand mechanism to politics consisted of the idea that the community—or government—had the duty to check self-interest before it got out of control. Mill thought that an effective solution to the threat of selfishness invading and ruining public life was a representative system.[24]

In particular, to work as an effective invisible hand toward the common good, the representative system would have to be inclusive enough to be reflective of a wide range of interests, and elections would have to be as frequent as possible. In this way, the system would force representatives to reflect and further the interests of constituents in their voting, and "the decisions reached [would] reflect a compromise that is going to promote the greatest aggregate satisfaction of essentially self-interested agents. This satisfaction is what he [Mill] takes to constitute the public interest."[25]

James Mill was a utilitarian, so he understood the public interest as the greatest aggregate amount of well-being or happiness in society. However, the invisible hand mechanism can still make (theoretical) sense if one holds a non-utilitarian view of the public good that is still centered on the satisfaction of self-interest. J.-J. Rousseau provides us with an example of this possibility, despite the much more common interpretation that his political thinking negates self-interest completely.

At some point in the *Social Contract*, Rousseau defines the general will like this: "[the general will] considers only the general interest, whereas [the will of all] considers private interest and is merely the sum of private wills. But remove from these same wills the pluses and minuses that cancel each other out, and what remains as the sum of the differences is the general will."[26] In this logic, it appears to be the case that the public interest is given by the commonalities that exist among all the private interests *combined* in society. In contrast to the more common interpretation of Rousseau's political theory, this account does not presuppose mutual adaptation to the concerns of others—in search for fairness. Instead, it only presupposes a mathematical operation according to which concerns that are not shared as a private interest by all will not pass the test of public acceptability. Robert Goodin refers to the foregoing rationale as the logic of the "least common denominator" because it highlights the preexisting shared interests and leaves out the differences.[27]

In a much more contemporary tone than Rousseau, pluralist theories of power in political science and political theory also put private interests at the helm of a theory of the public good. In the pluralist picture, groups of individuals try to maximize their interests and make government work to their advantage by channeling and furthering those interests. Bargaining and the use of influence, rather than reason and mutual concern, are key elements in how politics operate and function, according to the pluralist approach. Under conditions of relative distributive and social equality, this model of politics guarantees that competition and self-interest derive what is best for all because no political actors will be extremely more effective than anybody else in getting what they need from government. Additionally, the fragmented nature of government (division of powers, checks and balances, federalism in some cases) prevents political power from concentrating and being abused by a few.[28] This view of the common good highlights the formation of a democratic equilibrium among competing groups and private interests.[29] Although it does not exclude moral reasoning and deliberation, it is primarily centered on the notion of a *strategic compromise* in the backdrop of fair democratic procedures and relative equality of political influence.

The theoretical accounts of the public good that rely on some invisible hand mechanism that will "magically" result in the public interest being served naturally rest on a view of human nature that many would call rightly individualistic. In tune with classical social contract theories of government, they seem to take self-preservation and political survival as the key aim of politics. The invisible hand logic explains why, in the framework of appropriate rules, when everyone is self-interested, everyone ends up benefiting. J. S. Mill, who did not share his father's dogmatically utilitarian view, explains the power of self-interest clearly when he says that "the rights and interests of every or any person are only secured from being disregarded, when the person interested is himself able, and habitually disposed, to stand up for them."[30]

John Dewey, much later, evoked a similar view of self-interest in government when stating the pedestrian, but powerful, idea that each citizen knows best, after all, "where the shoe pinches."[31] Neither Dewey nor J. S. Mill was an advocate of selfishness in politics, but they did see political participation as a self-protective activity. Understanding politics as a self-protective activity entails the assumption that rights have to be safeguarded from infringement by others, who may use politics and government to attempt to weaken those rights. Centrally, understanding politics as a self-protective activity entails the previous implicit assumption that, if not you (or your delegate), who will protect and fight for *your* concerns?[32] However, J. S. Mill also offered a magisterial defense of politics as an *impartial* endeavor. Political participation permits us to put ourselves in the shoes of others and, particularly, of society as a whole. He said:

> Still, more salutary is the moral part of the instruction afforded by the participation of the private citizen, if even rarely, in public functions. He is called upon, while so engaged, to weigh interests not his own; to be guided, in case of conflicting claims, by another rule than his private partialities; to apply, at every turn, principles and maxims which have for their reason of existence the common good.[33]

The fair-mindedness approach to voting that I am proposing in this book does not take the invisible hand mechanism as a cause for the common good. It does not conceive of self-interest *alone* as a sufficient motivation to further the public interest. The impartiality approach to voting takes self-interest as one ingredient to the common good, but it is not as cynic as to ignore the power of a human concern for others. In fact, J. S. Mill recognized the dual nature of political participation, and especially voting, quite well when he said:

But it is not the fact that the possession of a vote would enable you only to protect yourself. Every citizen possessed of a vote is possessed of a means of protecting those who cannot vote, such as infants, the sick, idiots, etc. as well as a means of helping others who can vote to do good in every conceivable way in which just and provident legislation can affect human happiness.[34]

From now on, when I refer to the "common good," I will be alluding to the possible set of (acceptably) just outcomes that may result from elections. It is an admittedly abstract term. Because impartiality derives from a fair-thinking process on the part of many balanced-minded voters and public officials, there is no one common good consensus that all voters must arrive at, although there are some outcomes that would be flatly inconsistent (and disallowed) by the rules of reasoning implied by my standard of considered voting.

People disagree with each other, however. How can they all vote with a view to justice *if they will not see eye to eye on what justice requires*? How can we be so confident in proposing any given standard of fair minded-voting that is not equipped to produce consensus (or even large agreement) on the policies and ideals that would honor justice? It is undeniably true that we live in pluralistic societies where people have different views on justice, religion, and what makes life good overall. The fact of pluralism is an ineradicable characteristic of liberal democratic communities—and this diversity makes these societies not only vibrant but also tolerant and fair.

The (welcome) fact of pluralism and the difficulties that it creates regarding the possibility of citizen agreement brings to the fore an enormous literature that is useful to reflect on the validity of the fair-mindedness standard that I present in this chapter. This literature is known to those familiar with the debates as the "public reason" literature. The term "public reason" is associated with John Rawls's notion of "justice as fairness" and, later on, with his (modified) defense of "political liberalism." Over the decades, however, the literature has given room to an immense gamut of views and counterviews on what it means to find reasons that others can endorse as acceptably fair—or that they cannot reject as unfair.[35]

I do not, in particular, endorse a Rawlsian view of public reason in its full form—but it is undeniable that the spirit of my argument goes back to Rawls—and its Kantian and Rousseauian intellectual roots. I cannot do justice to the full complexity of the debates in the public reason literature here, but I will explain their fundamental form because criticisms to the main arguments in that literature parallel a serious objection against my conception of careful voting. In particular, the objection is that fair-mindedness will not do the trick in elections. It won't allow us to reach useful solutions to problems of justice because people will disagree with each other on those fundamental issues, and their votes will not reflect any plausible view of fair-mindedness, in consequence.

The public reason doctrine is nothing more than a form of political justification that makes decisions and deliberations legitimate in the eyes of citizens. This doctrine demands that the fundamental political and ethical rules that structure life in society be justifiable to all those persons over which the rules are to apply and have authority (coercive authority, in most cases). Undergirding the public reason ideal is the notion that persons should be assumed to be equal and free, in the sense of not being naturally subject to the authority of others without a valid, agreed-upon reason for that subjection. Thus, acting on the basis of the public reason doctrine entails supporting rules, norms, and political decisions that we have reason to believe, sincerely, that others could conceivably endorse, or not unreasonably reject as biased or self-interested. In order to do this, the doctrine, in its traditional formulation, asks us to *only* appeal to publicly shared reasons—that is, widely shared political values about justice in society's organization—and refrain from supporting rules based on more controversial beliefs of a religious or philosophical kind, which are supposedly less likely to enjoy the support of all those affected by the putative rules in question. The assumption, clearly, is that it is easier to agree on questions of *political justice* than it is to agree on questions about *conceptions of the good life and religion*. It is important to note, thus, that the (traditional) idea of public reason "derives its content from liberal political conceptions of justice that are supposed to be autonomous or independent of any particular comprehensive doctrine."[36]

In fact, according to the public reason doctrine's main formulation, citizens may endorse decisions and rules that are justified by their comprehensive doctrines such as their religion or a particular view of what makes life worthwhile, but they can only do so provided that they can support their decision with political considerations, ultimately,[37] and so long as they sincerely believe that these public reasons will be acceptable to others affected by the rules in question.[38] As we will see shortly, it is not clear that questions of justice are easier to settle than questions related to more "comprehensive doctrines."[39] But we have to wait a little bit to deal with my elaboration of that point.

In Rawls's (prevalent) view of public reason, citizens will be conscious of the need to appeal to political reasons ultimately because it is widely accepted that "the burdens of judgment" give rise to reasonable disagreement over moral or philosophical issues. The burdens of judgment include a number of (normally expected) obstacles to human cognition under conditions of freedom. They comprise the fact that (1) scientific evidence may be complex to analyze or conflicting, (2) people may disagree about the weight that different considerations should carry in a decision, (3) concepts may be inherently vague and abstract, (4) life experience may shape our assessment of political values, and (5) social and political institutions are limited in the number of values they can incorporate.[40]

The public reason doctrine (as formulated initially by Rawls) tells us that reasonable citizens will accept these typically human obstacles to judgment and expect diversity of ideas on justice and the good life *because* of them. But this acceptance will lead them to commit to neutrality on comprehensive philosophical and/or religious doctrines and only focus on political issues so as to avoid paralysis and disagreement. The idea is that the (well-meaning) motivation to find a reasonable justification for common norms and rules in society will render it necessary for citizens in the public sphere and in their voting decisions to *restrict the use of reasons that are likely not to be appealing to a majority of other citizens because they are not broadly shared.* The traditional view of public reason, then, upholds a rather idealized conception of what makes a constituency of "reasonable" citizens. It takes for granted that (1) there will be a set of *shared* political or justice-based considerations that citizens will willingly and gladly support, and (2) citizens will all be reasonable enough to limit themselves in the use of broader philosophical or moral and religious ideas when attempting to justify their point of view to other citizens.[41]

Do we do well in assuming that citizens will be sufficiently reasonable to be able to reach wide agreements on political issues of justice? Is it realistic to expect them to leave behind their comprehensive views about the good life and God, for example? On first inspection, a look at contemporary liberal democracies suggests that the main assumptions in the public reason literature as described so far are both unrealistic and normatively worrisome. They are unrealistic because most societies are witness to fierce disagreements on the most basic questions of justice—ranging from how generous the welfare state should be to whether the law should grant rights such as the right to abortion or to assisted suicide. Moreover, we do see that many religious or comprehensive doctrines are used in public debate and do figure in people's voting decisions at the polls.[42] The basic assumptions of the public reason literature may also be normatively problematic—most centrally—because it may be ethically wrong to demand from citizens that they leave their most dear comprehensive ideals out when appealing to others in justifying public norms. After all, don't freedom and equality—distinctively liberal values—encompass a right to the practice of religion or to adhere to a larger than political view of the good life as long as no relevant harm to others is done?[43]

Without going into more depth in a debate that is too big to fully address here, one could summarize the possible objections to the public reason doctrine (therefore to my standard of fair-minded voting) in the following way.[44] The lingering fact of deep disagreement among citizens in liberal democracies means that the outcome of public reason (that is, the outcome of citizens' thinking processes when justifying their vote to others) may lead to (1) inconclusive policy results—the problem of inconclusiveness—or to (2) indeterminate policy results—the problem of indeterminacy.[45] The problems of inconclusiveness and indeterminacy concern the *actual* capacity of public reason to offer *any* solutions to the most important moral and political questions that society faces.

Concretely, the problem of inconclusiveness means that, with regard to a particular controversial question, a multiplicity of answers may be plausible within the boundaries of public reason, and appealing to our shared (justice-based) beliefs and values cannot clearly tell us which one of those answers is the most reasonable. The problem of indeterminacy—which will turn out to prove more serious—means that public reason may be incapable of providing *any* solutions whatsoever to a particular controversial issue under discussion in society. Resorting to shared values and beliefs may prove insufficient to find a solution because the set of sharable reasons will be too thin. People disagree on the fundamental philosophical and moral values they uphold—and many issues may not be amenable to assessment if these doctrines are not allowed to be used in the process of justification.[46]

Inconclusiveness may unfold in a case like the following. Some citizens may oppose abortion rights because they may deem that a fetal right to life, as required by justice, should rank higher than a woman's right to be treated equally in terms of her right to bodily autonomy—in the first trimester of pregnancy. Others may defend abortion rights because they think that women's right to bodily autonomy should rank higher instead.[47] Similarly, some may believe that the Catholic Church has a right to not hire women as priests if it so chooses because it is a private association—and liberal democracies afford freedom to these. Religious freedom is an important justice value. Others, instead, may believe that private associations such as churches should not be exempt from anti-discrimination laws—also required by justice.[48] All these conclusions, at least on first inspection, appear acceptably reasonable based on the justice values that they purport to evoke. Citizens involved in these controversies all seem to accept the basic justice values under scrutiny. What separates them is the weight and ranking that they give to the different considerations (i.e., rights) at play.[49]

Indeterminacy in the results of public reason, in turn, may exist in cases like the following. Someone deeply devoted to a life of religious asceticism and service to God may reject the right to recreational drug use because the latter involves seeking pleasure for pleasure's sake—which follows from a hedonistic view of what makes human life worthwhile. Others may believe that recreational drug use for individual purposes should be perfectly legal because they do not think that religious considerations should have authority to dictate how people should live, or because they do not believe in God altogether—even if they are not hedonists.[50] In the same vein, some people may reject the right to gay marriage based on their religious views, while others may accept it also based on their religious views if, say, their particular religious affiliation required of them to be tolerant toward others. In cases like these, there is no set of shared values that can provide a set of reasonable alternatives to choose from, and we have a stand-off.

Is my standard of fair-minded voting vulnerable to the difficulties so far mentioned? Is citizen disagreement liable to always—or most frequently—produce inconclusiveness and indeterminacy when it comes to what we see as a just society? I say no. In what follows, I will defend the fair-mindedness standard against these criticisms.

First, the problem of inconclusiveness may not be a real problem, after all. The standard of good voting that I propose, and the public reason literature on which it relies, do not demand that there *always* be perfect consensus among citizens. My notion of fair-minded voting is perfectly consistent with lack of (collective) precision on what justice requires—so long as voters are thinking about their electoral choices within the orbit of the impartiality logic. In other words, people may disagree on the weight and/or ranking of rights and moral values, but "their shared normative framework of reasonableness ensures that the reasons grounding their conflicting arguments are at least mutually acceptable."[51] Furthermore, voting and other aggregative means of decision-making exist to settle disputes that fair-mindedness may be unable to solve. There is nothing wrong in admitting this and using those means in a healthy liberal democracy to further public officials' capacity to enact public policy. Moreover, my arguments for fair-minded voting do not entail the idea that citizens must have concrete answers to all questions of policy and fine-grained legislation. It is only the job of their representatives to have those answers readily available, although it is the job of regular citizens to have a sound idea of what the abstract goals of policymaking should be.[52] If they disagree on those goals to a degree that is reasonable and expected, I consider the work of the fair-mindedness standard in voting satisfactorily done, nevertheless.

At this juncture, someone could raise the point that citizens may not disagree to a reasonable extent but may disagree unreasonably. For instance, in the abortion and priesthood examples respectively, some citizens may completely deny the normative value—not just the weight or specific ranking—of a right to equality for women. In circumstances of this sort, I would say, the citizen denying this value is being unacceptably unreasonable and, therefore, unfit to satisfy the fair-mindedness test when voting. The same conclusion would hold if the denial was rooted in a religious or comprehensive secular doctrine that the citizen sincerely embraces—not just a political conception of justice. The fact that fair-mindedness allows for ideological diversity does not mean that such diversity can be completely limitless, if we want to be fair-minded at all. Certain ideas involving hatred toward others cannot be said to be just or reasonable—however sincerely held by the citizen—since they violate the minimum requirement of seeing others citizens as free and equal members of society. But this is not a normative problem for the validity of the fair-mindedness test, in the same way that the existence of murderers does not pose a normative threat to the idea that unjustified killing is morally wrong. Furthermore, and on a more practical sense, just because some kill does not mean that all do. Similarly, just because some vote unjustly does not mean that all will.

A second answer to the problem of citizen disagreement lies in the "convergent" justifications account of public reason.[53] In this view of political justification, each person may have her own, unique reasons that lead her to endorse public principles and policies.[54] People do not necessarily have to leave out parts of their comprehensive beliefs when deliberating on the nature of social and political rules, but they should attempt to discover how their particular reasons can justify a point of agreement with others. In voting matters, this requisite may entail that voters must try hard to put themselves in the shoes of other citizens without, for that reason, "forgetting" their philosophies of life or religious views. This line of argument seems more adequate to address the indeterminacy objection in public reasoning (and careful voting). According to this model of justification, there can be convergence (consensus) on a law or decision *without* agreement on the reasons for that law or decision. For example, think about a situation in which a universal healthcare bill is put up for a popular vote. A devout Catholic voter may, arguably, conclude that providing affordable and widespread insurance is consistent with (and maybe required by) basic scriptural principles, and lend his support to the bill. An atheist voter may also support the measure for very different reasons, having to do with economic considerations (i.e., the need to count with a healthy workforce so that productivity increases and so does economic growth). Thus, in this case, citizens decide what interests should be shared by the community *rather* than try to find preexisting commonalities among individuals. In other words, the common good consists of interests that people want to have in common—*not* in interests that they already necessarily have in common.[55] The particular reasons why they arrive at those communal interests may differ (i.e., faith, economic reasoning, public spiritedness, etc.) but what characterizes individuals in this position is their evaluative stance.[56]

This second perspective on how citizens arrive at publicly acceptable views of the common good is more consistent with my ideal of fair-mindedness in voting than the first perspective, which emphasizes preexisting, overlapping agreements among people with different philosophies of life or ideals of the good. The reason why this is the case is that the view of fair-mindedness that I propose in this chapter (and book) does not presuppose any type of "blindness" to factors that may be an important part of the individual's sense of self. In my view of how citizens arrive at an ethically acceptable conception of fair voting, nobody is asked to "forget" her broad moral commitments. Instead, citizens are asked to reflect on whether their own comprehensive ideals of the good would ensue in outcomes that others would find unacceptable for the right reasons and, if they might, to try to adjust those views so that they can coexist with the views of others in the public sphere.

During elections, this conclusion means that the voter is not obligated to leave aside her comprehensive ethical commitments for the sake of others. However, if certain aspects of her views will collide with important rights and interests that others have justified reasons to see protected, then careful voting calls the voter to put herself in the place of others and adjust her views accordingly.

Accepting the convergence model of public reasoning means that people can choose either to support their reasons with political considerations, strictly, or with other type of (broader) considerations, as well. Convergence does not rule out shared reasons; it only allows diverse reasoning.[57] Theories that permit convergence *also* permit consensus.[58] Logically speaking, then, the expansion of usable reasons in the public justification of norms will give us a higher number of opportunities to achieve agreement among citizens because people will be allowed to use more and varied arguments to appeal to others.[59] The availability of more reasons, however, does not mean that anything goes. The idea of "reasonableness" is not abandoned, just reframed. There are still cognitive and moral requirements that citizens may not violate on pain of stepping out of the orbit of fair-mindedness altogether. Differently put, convergence theorists also adhere to the original (Rawlsian) requisite that public justification must take place in the backdrop of the ideal of free and equal persons. They just do not think that this requirement is always and invariably affronted when citizens appeal to reasons grounded in comprehensive moral doctrines and broad philosophies of life.

There is one strong criticism to the convergent model of public justification that could affect my standard of fair-voting. Someone may object that when citizens are allowed to give and hear reasons grounded in comprehensive doctrines that are not widely shared in society, we cannot expect them to be sincere in the formulation of those reasons to others.[60] If I believe that your views are incorrect because you worship the wrong God, how can I ever put myself in your shoes when deciding/voting on basic social and moral rules? The objection is that if there are no shared values among voters, there will be no sincere effort to truly understand each other's different perspectives. This will make citizens into hypocrites that will never attempt to put themselves in the shoes of others when discussing or deciding on common norms for their society. Because of this, one may also object that convergent justifications in public reasoning (and fair voting) undermine the existence of shared commitments to justice because they separate, rather than unite, citizens. In short, they create instability and friction.

I think, however, that convergent justifications may actually encourage putting oneself in the shoes of others. This is so because citizens will remember that certain reasons may or may not be acceptable to others given *their* particular system of beliefs, which may be structurally different from the system of beliefs that we associate with an idealized audience.[61] In the convergence model, citizens are called to realize that what may strike them as unreasonable or irrational may be perfectly reasonable and rational in the framework of a particular belief system that they don't fully know. For example, Patricia may think that Joshua's reluctance to eat pork is unreasonable and irrational—she doesn't go by the mandates of the Jewish Bible as Josh does. However, once she is willing to reassess Josh's behavior in the backdrop of *his* particular belief system (i.e., the Torah), she may *sincerely* find Josh's behavior acceptable and even endorsable.[62] She may be able to relate to Josh even though *she does not share with him* an important (religious) value to him.

Moreover, the fact the citizens may be alluding to unshared principles when justifying their public views also encourages mutual understanding by forcing them to familiarize themselves with the reasons of others in order to deliberate with them effectively. For example, Sarah may believe that David's refusal to support higher taxes for the wealthy is utterly inconsistent with his Catholic faith (which he takes to be central to his identity) because—Sarah argues—Catholic principles mandate deep compassion for the poor, which should translate into a generous welfare state logically funded by high taxes. Sarah is not Catholic, so, she's talking to David from a perspective that is not her own—but her narrative directly appeals to David's particular belief system. In these examples, Patricia and Sarah can eventually find Josh's and David's reasons intelligible—even if they don't share them personally.[63] This alone should be enough for the possibility of sincerity as required by the public reason doctrine.[64] *The sincerity requirement does not mean that one has to adopt another person's belief as one's own.* It means, rather, that one has to have a reason for understanding why that belief is *consistent* with that person's larger system of belief—besides knowing that the belief must not violate the fundamental premise of free and equal persons. Furthermore, convergent justifications may empower historically marginalized groups by giving them the opportunity to use their languages and experiences more freely, instead of having to adapt them to a more idealized, historically prevalent, form of discourse and deliberation.[65]

The literature on public reason in its different variants is too extensive for me to fully explore in this chapter. But, for the sake of finalizing this section, I need to say that the convergence model of public justification is not always a panacea. Just because people are encouraged to expand the type and number of considerations that they can use to justify their position to others in public does not mean that others will *always* find those reasons acceptable—although I believe that the odds of bitter disagreement will be lower. In other words, my intention here is not to deny the realistic possibility of disagreement in democratic societies. But I do not think that I have to deny that possibility in order to propose a standard of careful voting like the one I propose in this chapter (and book). As I stated before, the main purpose of broadly defining what fair-minded voting requires from citizens is to rule out predominantly self-centered and overtly sectarian reasoning from the mindset and attitudes of voters. I cannot expect, nor would I want to, absolute consensus on all issues of morality and justice among them. The public reason literature, in its two main variants here described—Rawlsian and convergent—does *not* presuppose that perfect agreement is possible. My standard of judicious voting does not need to do that either.

3.4. Competent Voting

Much of the literature rejecting the notion of a duty to vote assumes that voting judiciously is difficult. It is not for everyone: some people are prepared to do so, while others are not, and it is a bad idea to ignore this fact. The assumption is that good political participation requires *skill, expertise*, and *training*.

That good political participation requires skill is undeniable. But how burdensome it is to acquire that skill is something that defenders of the no-duty-to-vote position simply take for granted. However, the notion that average citizens can acquire specific skills for public service, for example, is evidenced by the (generally effective) functioning of the jury system, which requires that jurors pay attention to rules of evidence, to standards of fair treatment, and that they have a minimal understanding of the laws in question in a particular case. In this regard, it is worth quoting J. S. Mill (again), who, despite his preference for giving the educated more leverage in elections, said about jury duty and political participation more generally that they tended to promote desirable impartiality and the good use of human faculties. As he put it:

> If circumstances allow the amount of public duty assigned him [the citizen] to be considerable, it makes him an educated man. . . . A benefit of the same kind . . . is produced on Englishmen of the lower middle class by their liability to be placed on juries and to serve parish offices, which . . . must make them nevertheless very different beings, in range of ideas and development of faculties, from those who have done nothing in their lives but drive a quill or sell goods over a counter. [The citizen] is called upon, while so engaged, to weigh interests not his own; to be guided in case of conflicting claims by another rule than his private partialities, to apply, at every turn, principles and maxims which have for their reason of existence the common good.[66]

Whichever stance we take on the effects of participation on the individual strictly, Mill's description of the standards of behavior and reasoning required by basic public functions such as jury duty is illustrative of the tasks that regular citizens in actual democracies must engage in today. There is no reason to believe that these tasks—of which episodic voting forms part—will always be fulfilled unsuccessfully by a majority of citizens. One doesn't have to be a professional expert in economics, public affairs, or foreign policy in order to cast an acceptably good ballot.[67] However, one must put some thought into the decision and take the necessary steps to acquire pertinent information. Also, one must be unprejudiced.

The distinction between expert knowledge and good voting is evoked by John Dewey, who, ironically, is often identified with a "thick" view of democracy according to which democracy should pervade every aspect of one's life. But we don't need to adhere to Dewey's demanding ideal of democracy to share his opinion that "it is not necessary that the many should have the knowledge and skill to carry on the needed investigations; what is required is that they have the ability to judge of the bearing of the knowledge supplied by others upon common concerns. It is easy to exaggerate the amount of intelligence and ability demanded to render such judgments fitted for their purposes."[68]

Aristotle advanced a similar argument in defense of the competence of the layperson when he suggested that politics is one of those "arts" whose products are properly judged by the "consumer," not just the "skilled artist." He said that "there are some arts whose products are not judged of solely, or best, by the artists themselves, namely those arts whose products are recognized even by those who do not possess the art; for example, the knowledge of the house is not limited to the builder only; the user, or, in other words, the master of the house will actually be a better judge than the builder, just as the pilot will judge better of a rudder than the carpenter, and the guest will judge better of a feast than the cook."[69]

Aristotle had no knowledge of the complex conceptual tools that voting behavior researchers have access to today, but I think that his statement on the role of expertise in politics can be applied to voting discussions in current times: many non-expert citizens can still know enough to judge the appropriateness of competing electoral choices. Even if we assume topical incompetence on specific issues of a more technical nature, it is not far-fetched to believe that voters' competence is, or may be, sufficient for a number of "big questions."[70] Topical incompetence does not logically entail global incompetence or the incompetence to realize how incompetent one is, and the need to defer to experts, whom we can identify as such.[71]

Furthermore, there is something to be said about the possibility that expert knowledge is not vastly superior to the knowledge of the average voter when it comes to the power to predict the outcome of various policy alternatives. Philip Tetlock's seminal research on this area suggests that it is reasonable to doubt that experts have far superior predictive skills that non-experts in their fields of expertise.[72] For example, he notes that Bryan Caplan focuses on economists' relative predictive superiority to undergraduates "but [that] it is experts' poor absolute levels of prediction that is really striking and it is striking too that dilettantes do just about as well as experts, and that having a Ph.D. or years of experience in one's field is not a significant predictor of the level of one's predictive capacity."[73] Tetlock defines dilettantes as those individuals that read *The Economist* and the *New York Times* assiduously but lack any technical training or formal education in the field. Additionally, he mainly focuses on economists', political scientists', and historians' ability to predict economic and political outcomes. He notices that they do better than undergraduates but not significantly better than older laypeople. Experts are definitely superior than mostly everybody in what Tetlock calls "determination"—that is, the capacity to determine whether an event *will take place*. However, he explains, they are only marginally better than dilettantes at what he calls "calibration"—that is, the capacity to accurately provide a *level of probability for that event.* Anyone having paid any amount of money to a financial counselor may easily confirm this: Most of them do not do better than the investors themselves in predicting what investment will pay the most and which one would be better to avoid. There is a reason why companies like E-trade and similar do-it-yourself investment sites are so popular and profitable.

Tetlock's research on the differences between expert and non-expert knowledge could be conceptually framed within a Hayekian understanding of how human knowledge is formed and transferred in (market and free) societies. Hayek, an unmistakable proponent of free economic enterprise, argued that many economic outcomes are difficult to predict in real life, away from the technical economic models that make sense in the classroom.[74] Hayek asserted that we rarely know all the real-world variables that intervene in causing or not causing events, and economic models are notorious for not catching them either.[75]

For example, many labor economists seem to agree that increases in the minimum wage will increase unemployment, yet many studies have shown that this effect is not necessarily certain.[76] At best, the empirical data on the impact of minimum wage laws in specific circumstances and places is murky and inconclusive—and in some notorious cases it shows that the predicted unemployment rise does not happen.[77]

Jason Brennan, in his two books on democracy and voting, makes a big deal of the alleged superiority of experts in knowing what is best for voters and society overall. On this superiority he bases his whole normative point about epistocracy being justified *in lieu* of universal voting rights and democracy. But the fact that experts are not significantly superior in giving us information that matters should give him pause. This is not to say that voter ignorance is not a problem; but it is one thing is to say that something is a problem, and another thing is to say that something else is a clear solution to that first problem. In the case of democracy, I don't think that we can see things as simplistically as Brennan does.

Experts do not have vastly superior predictive policy knowledge. If the problem of voter ignorance is pressing because voters may/will choose flawed and incompetent governments themselves, which will harm the interests of the population by enacting unjust policies and laws, then the fact that experts are not significantly superior in predicting the outcomes of policies should alert us to the fact that, perhaps, epistocracy is not all that is cracked up to be.

This conclusion becomes more clear if we consider the fact that experts usually disagree starkly about what it is that should be done. Just one example: Joseph Stiglitz is a distinguished professor of economics at Columbia University and (co)winner of a Nobel Prize in Economics for his work on laying out a theory of how markets function with asymmetric information. Stiglitz is also a fierce critic of the way in which globalization and trade liberalization have been conducted in the last few decades (unregulated and non-gradual) and its (negative) effects for people in the Global South. In this very respect, Stiglitz appeared at first to be an oddity among many mainstream economists who were non-hesitant to defend free trade as a panacea for poverty reduction worldwide. However, increasingly, many acclaimed economists and academics in general disagree among themselves on the roots and causes of inequality globally, and on the remedies to fix it, if that is a goal worth attaining at all. This simple example is just an example of how academics disagree among themselves, but it points to something much deeper, which Brennan and his skeptic friends never care to admit: expert knowledge is disputed many times.

Many times, it is our political and/or economic ideology that will explain why we see certain social goals as worthy of attainment while we see others as calamitous or morally wrong. Many of these goals will be seen by some as required by fairness, while others will think the opposite is true. Regarding goal setting for policy, I don't think we can say that there are "moral experts." Regular citizens are, prima facie, qualified to deliberate on the moral acceptability of different general policy goals, even if they do not possess technical expertise. For example, citizens can have perfectly consistent opinions on the morality of moderate distribution to alleviate poverty, even if they don't have knowledge of taxation systems. They may also have perfectly consistent opinions on the immorality of bloody, prolonged wars, even if they have no knowledge of geopolitics. They may have consistent opinions on the immorality of preventable wage stagnation even if they have no expertise in labor economics; and they may have consistent opinions on the wrongfulness of corruption, even if they don't have much knowledge of how government operates. Other examples could be given. The point I want to press is that, despite the fact of voter incompetence, one should not fall prey to the belief that voters are completely unable to make minimally informed electoral choices because they may lack knowledge of causal effects in economics and institutional design. Thoughtful reflection on the general morality of some of the proposals at issue in the election may be all they need to make a sufficiently careful decision at the ballot box. The rest should be the job of the people they elect.

One may rightly wonder, however, what the cutoff line is, so to speak, at which ignorance of political and economic matters gets in the way of the ability to make good enough choices at the ballot box. This is a valid concern that I do not intend to dismiss. No democratic theorist worried about the justice and quality of democracy should. But there is a world of difference between arguing that no smart or healthy electoral choice is possible when political knowledge is lacking and saying that when *any type* of political knowledge is lacking, that very fact signals an obvious inability to make a sufficiently informed choice at the ballot box. Skeptics of the duty to vote find *any and all* absences of political knowledge discouraging, but they are wrong to be so pessimistic. Not all type of political knowledge is equally necessary for voting smartly or responsibly. Knowing how many representatives your state or jurisdiction has, for example, may not be essential to comparing the current electoral options before you. By contrast, not understanding the most basic ideological differences among the parties that are running candidates in the election may be detrimental to your ability to choose responsibly (as in non-randomly). Opponents of the duty to vote that focus on all types of political knowledge deficiencies equally rarely draw distinctions of this sort.

Because one cannot dismiss the problem of voter ignorance, however, one cannot ignore the following question: Do ignorant voters have a duty to vote too? I tackled this question in the last chapter. Now it will suffice to say that nobody can have a duty to do something that is harmful in all conceivable respects. In this case, voting without relevant knowledge can harm democracy when many people do it because it can install bad, dishonest, or incompetent governments in power, as Jason Brennan rightly points out. But that doesn't mean that all ignorant voters are off the hook morally if they responsibly refrain from voting because they know that they will do more harm than good if they cast an uninformed ballot. This is where my views sharply differ from Brennan's. The duty to vote judiciously must entail a duty to become sufficiently informed to discharge it. If my political ignorance is in some relevant sense my own fault, and could have been avoided at no great cost to me, then, it is not clear at all that abstaining from voting makes me into a dutiful and responsible member of the community any more than driving drunk but deciding to slow down in order to avoid an accident makes me into a responsible driver. Actions taken to minimize collateral damage from previous actions or omissions that were in some sense ethically (and prudentially) questionable do not have the same value as not engaging in unethical (and dangerous) behavior in the first place. But of course, not all cases of political ignorance are the same. In other words, many citizens may be to blame to a lesser degree, or not at all, for failing to know relevant information at the time of voting in elections (if, for example, ignorance is due to uncontrollable factors such as structural poverty instead of controllable ones such as a disposition to waste time). But the fact that there are, conceivably, many degrees of moral blame for being politically uninformed does not negate that there is a moral duty to vote that entails, as a matter of logical necessity, an accompanying duty to become sufficiently informed. For, how can one vote judiciously if one votes in ignorance? It is undeniable that the duty to seek out information is built into the duty to vote with care. It is impossible to do anything carefully but thoughtlessly (one may do so fortuitously but randomness is not to be trusted as a consistent friend).

3.5. The Roots of Voter Ignorance

Despite the foregoing arguments, political scientists doing survey research in the 1950s found that citizens were largely uninformed and had little understanding of some of the most basic facts of politics and institutional design. In this tradition, for example, Phillip Converse finds little ideological content in voters' choices and much incoherence when answering to open-ended survey questions.[78] He concludes that there is no underlying belief structure for most people, although his findings have been challenged.[79]

In the voter behavior literature within political science, psychology, and economics much has been written in reply to the skeptics of voter competence—but not much systematization has been achieved in the responses. Here I propose the following line of reply to the argument that voters are overwhelmingly incapable, therefore, that democracy as a minimally intelligent mechanism of decision-making is bound to fail. Voter ignorance is not an unchangeable law of nature. As a matter of fact, the United States ranks almost last internationally when it comes to voters' knowledge of political issues.[80] This may seem at first to hurt my case rather than help it, but the deeper point I want to make is that, if other voters elsewhere know more than Americans, voter competence is not in principle a rigid human trait bound to persist no matter what. There may be some social and political factors that worsen or improve it.

Relatedly, there is an extensive "revisionist" literature on voter behavior that attempts to debunk the claim that voters are too poorly equipped to vote minimally smartly. As indicated already, this literature analyses the use of "cognitive heuristics" in political decision-making.[81] For example, Lupia and McCubbins distinguish information, which they define as facts, from knowledge, which they define as the ability to make accurate predictions.[82] More information is not necessarily better in order to make a better prediction, and, given budget constraints, usually would cost more than it's worth. For voters to make a reasoned choice requires sufficient knowledge, not vast amounts of facts related to politics. Although these cognitive "savings" require minimal knowledge of the options being evaluated, they serve to keep the information-processing demands of the task within bounds. Some of the most common cognitive shortcuts employed by voters are a candidate's party affiliation, a candidate's endorsements, and a candidate's ideology, among others.[83] Low-information rationality, also called "bounded rationality,"[84] is not necessarily akin to bad voting. Studies show that voters are capable of considering a limited amount of information about candidates, and they consider just enough information to reach a rational decision, minding their preferences.[85]

Further, when measuring voter competence, not all political knowledge is equal. Some of the factual knowledge measured in surveys used to assess voter competence (such as whether the citizen knows who her senator or representative is, or whether she knows which party controls the Senate or Parliament) has been argued to not faithfully reflect voters' capacities to identify general ideological trends that are indeed more helpful to make informed decisions at the voting booth. Some of the factual information required by surveys of political competence has been said to reflect the elitism of their designers, usually academics, and it has been argued to be unnecessary in the use of cognitive shortcuts that may produce satisfactory-enough political choices.[86]

Skeptics of the power of heuristics in politics will say that it is precisely the information needed to engage in these cognitive shortcuts that many citizens lack.[87] The reason for this lack of knowledge may be multifarious, but one of them is the phenomenon of informational free-riding (or rational ignorance). This idea suggests that rational voters will not bother to seek information to vote because their vote is unlikely to be decisive in the final electoral outcome. But, I say, (informational) free riding is not a fact of nature. People vote for instrumental reasons other than decisiveness, such as to increase a candidates' margin of victory or to diminish her margin of loss, and to enhance democratic legitimacy and stability more generally.[88] Negligibility is not the same as futility, and people may still have an incentive to act however small their individual contribution to a larger outcome may be.[89]

Many people contribute to collective activities out of a sense of commitment with a result that they have good reasons to value, even if their individual contribution is not noticeable by itself. The thesis of informational free-riding ignores this plausible aspect of human psychology. It also ignores the fact that, when high personal costs are not involved, many people may place collective rationality (understood as group-regarding reasoning and a consequent propensity to cooperate with others) above individual rationality (understood as purely self-regarding thinking and a consequent tendency to freeride on others if possible).[90]

Another reason that explains voter ignorance, according to the skeptics, is the phenomenon of rational irrationality.[91] According to this thesis, voters in large elections allow themselves the luxury of adopting (epistemically) irrational beliefs because they know that their single vote will not matter to the outcome. Thus, they can afford to indulge in irrationality without any relevant risks because the marginal cost to an individual of holding an erroneous belief is low. This logic assumes that the individual will prefer to have a certain type of belief (i.e., irrational or factually wanting) and that he will derive some type of gratification from it. Rational irrationality, then, describes a situation where it makes sense to be *epistemically* irrational.

The rational irrationality theory may be internally coherent, but it is not empirically conclusive. For a start, it *only* works under the already mentioned assumption that the voter gets a psychological reward from holding irrational biases *regardless* of her capacity to influence the election. Caplan tells us that the voter knows that she won't be impactful, although she may not be conscious of her irrationality. The fact that she won't influence the electoral outcome explains why she unconsciously (or consciously) relaxes her standards of evidence-based reasoning. This seems, on its face, a rather implausible picture of human motivation, for if I know that my act will have no impact whatsoever, why would I even bother to form a belief concerning the election? I am not saying that people are not prone to forming and adopting irrational beliefs, but it seems to me that the assumption that they are aware of how little their vote matters cannot easily be reconciled with a preference for irrationality. It is more tempting to speculate that many people have the false (epistemic) belief that their vote *does* matter, and that is why they support (irrational) beliefs about politics.[92] This seems to me to be a more plausible incentive. The reward structure in the case of someone who knows that his beliefs will not ensue in any noticeable or discernible result may not be effective enough to explain why someone will actively adopt a belief—except for the assumption that it will make him feel good. But if voters are instrumentally rational, they will seek also to be influential—not just contented.

Importantly, Caplan's theory of rational irrationality cannot explain why individuals would acquire a belief that they know to be irrational. In this vein, Stephen Bennett and Jeffrey Friedman criticize Caplan's theory as logically contradictory.[93] They argue that Caplan's theory must assume that the agent is wittingly adopting a factually false belief. After all, the trade-off is between individual gratification and epistemic correctness, implying that one is aware that one is sacrificing truth. But if the person knows that her belief is untrue, then why would she derive satisfaction from supporting it with her vote? This logic doesn't make sense.

As mentioned previously, however, Caplan perfunctorily suggests that the trade-off can be made subconsciously. The individual adopts irrational beliefs in a non-deliberate fashion simply because, under circumstances of negligible individual impact, it is easier for her to relax her intellectual standards and rules of evidence, the result of this being that she becomes more vulnerable to emotional appeals and fallacious reasoning. The whole empirical validity of the rational irrationality theory seems to rest on this one assumption of unknowing irrationality. However, Caplan does not satisfactorily explain the dynamics and psychological probability of this scenario. In the absence of this explanation, we can surely think that knowing that one's vote does not decisively matter in elections does not fly as an explanation for voter irrationality. For the latter to make sense, we would also have to assume that the voter gets some type of psychological reward from holding irrational biases *regardless* of her capacity to influence the election. This seems, on its face, a generalization that warrants more empirical investigation than Caplan offers. He offers none.

Skeptics, overall, seem to place too much emphasis on the role of individual cognitive failures to explain why voters don't know as much as they should know. As mentioned, against the suggestion that many voters may use cognitive shortcuts, they charge that most voters are incapable of identifying the right type of information needed to decide which heuristics to use. Against this backdrop, I want to offer an underplayed response to the objection of voter ignorance. If voter ignorance is not a fixed law of the human constitution (given that it varies cross-country), then, there must be variables that affect it positively as well as negatively. If this is so, one can in principle think that democratic societies may endeavor to improve voter competence instead of retreating toward a deterministic position that sees the electorate as ipso facto incapable of producing smart results. The literature on voter behavior has provided us with suggestions of what the variables that affect political knowledge and political interest may be. I submit that we can group them into three categories: (1) structural variables, (2) contextual variables and (3) cognitive ability variables.

Structural variables are variables that refer to the nature and functioning of the political and party systems in a given country. They have been, in my opinion, vastly underexplored as intervening causes of political ignorance (critics like Somin and Caplan, for instance, make little or no mention of them and instead focus primarily on the third category).

One structural variable that affects the general availability of accurate political information is a political party's incentive to profit from income inequality (which is correlated with less access to information for those with lower incomes). For example, Alan Abramovitz and Steven Webster argue that Republicans in the United States have an incentive to convince voters of the non-problematic nature of inequality because inequality moves voters to the right, which is the party's preferred ideological orientation.[94] This argument can be coupled with the already widespread thesis in political science that political elites play an important role in influencing public opinion.[95] The public opinion literature shows that people do not form political views that politicians will *later* attempt to satisfy and match. The picture is not that simple because the causal arrows moves in both directions.[96] Members of the public tend to follow the elites that share their general ideological or partisan views.[97] Sometimes, the process of public opinion formation is tilted in favor of the political elites, who have interests that not always further the common good, especially if candidates are entangled with corporate groups that donate resources to political campaigns, enabling candidates to win expensive elections. For example, James Druckman et al. show that presidents often use polls to identify the interests of organized groups and lobbies that support the presidents' broad agendas. They then respond to these groups while simultaneously using polls to devise methods to distract other Americans—leading them to focus on personality and image rather than controversial policy.[98]

Climate change is another good example of the influence of elites on the quality of information made available to the electorate. Environmental issues have historically been bipartisan and non-controversial—think, for example, Richard Nixon's role in creating the Environmental Protection Agency.[99] This reality began to change markedly in the mid-1990s when opinions, both in Congress and in the public, began to polarize along party lines. Historical accounts suggest that economic interests organized in the early 1990s with the intention of sowing doubt over the issue of man-caused global warming given the ties between the oil industry lobby and the Republican leadership.[100] Due to these efforts, the discourse of Republican politicians generally became rife with climate change denialism.[101] These efforts appear to have influenced mass Republican opinion to a point where many Republican voters take climate change denialism as a hallmark of their Republican identity. Elite manipulation has also been argued to be greatly responsible for policy results, such as the Bush tax cuts, that were made possible, in part, by the misinterpretation of economic facts by interested politicians.[102]

To add another depressing fact to the description of how many democracies function, especially the American one, it bears reminding critics of the duty to vote that many policy outcomes that we consider largely detrimental from the perspective of the average voter are not necessarily the direct choice of the average voter. The deregulation of campaign finance and the consequent influence of wealth in the higher spheres of government can leave, as a result, a gap between politicians and the common voter's concerns. This gap may be made worse by the latter's ignorance, but that ignorance cannot explain by itself why policy that is bad for the bulk of society is ultimately enacted *all the time* that bad policy is enacted. Or it would be simplistic to assume so.

It is intriguing that, to my knowledge, none of the critical accounts of democratic participation that have emerged in the last decade or so mentions the power of lobbying groups in getting their way *despite* the needs and preferences of the electorate. The gun-control issue in the United States is one study case that exemplifies how this power plays out despite the people's wishes, among many other examples. In the United States, a majority of the population, including a majority of citizens self-identified as belonging to the Republican Party, support regulating the sale and use of weapons. However, the massive influence of the National Rifle Association (NRA), which is only possible because of its monetary donations to political campaigns, impedes any type of reform because the public officials and candidates that receive these donations obey the policy agenda of the NRA in return. If the NRA was precluded from donating such big amounts of money to single candidates and politicians, politicians' incentives would certainly change. Of course, we know that voters may get fed up with this dynamic and vote out the immoral politicians that ignore their will. Be it as it may, it is a structural issue pertaining to how the American political system works—allowing unmatched mass donations to political campaigns—that explains the existence of bad policy—not the people's "idiotic" preferences for dying in mass shootings.

There are many other examples of policy outcomes that are largely a response to the influence of interest groups, rather than being a faithful reflection of the preferences of voters.[103] Trade is one of them. For example, Jeffrey Drope and Wendy Hansen's study on anti-dumping decisions by the International Trade Commission concluded that "industries that are located in more oversight committee members' districts or states enjoy a greater probability of favorable treatment from these regulatory agencies. Even when controlling for economic hardship, the more money that firms and associations that favor protection spend, and the more favorable the pattern of congressional representation, the more likely it is that they will enjoy an affirmative decision."[104] Lobbying may be rampant because it is legal in the United States, but it is not an unusual mechanism of influence in Europe.[105] Lobbying is such an effective mechanism to achieve desired policy outcomes—in the absence of successful regulation against it—because of the asymmetry between concentrated benefits and diffused costs. For many of the interest groups invested in influencing politicians, the benefits derived from getting their way are spread out among a relatively small number of citizens—compared to the larger population—while the costs may be borne by a majority of citizens—but these costs may not be as undesirable to the latter as the benefits are desirable to the former. Or they may be, but lack of coordination capacity (to raise money or to voice complaints collectively) makes it more difficult to protest against the (generally harmful) measures put in place by representatives that respond primarily to the agenda of special interest groups.[106]

Besides elite influence and money in politics, other structural variables that affect the quality of information that flows to the electorate include party polarization,[107] media framing effects (which are connected to the argument that elites influence public opinion),[108] the complexity of electoral laws, and the responsiveness and transparency of political institutions. For example, studies have shown that complex electoral laws that make multiple elections happen in one ballot do not contribute to clear information for the electorate. They have also shown that too repetitive elections cause voter fatigue and that proportional representation, as opposed to winner-takes-all representation, enhances voter knowledge after controlling for education and income.[109] Also, local and primary elections that do not require party brands for candidates—something quite common in the United States—make it difficult for voters to identify issues and are more prone to cause misinformation.[110]

Research shows that responsive institutions also offer good incentives for citizens to become more politically knowledgeable. For example, Nick Clark defines institutional responsiveness as the system's openness to allowing citizens to influence policy. His work shows that where there are electoral or deliberative mechanisms that allow citizens to influence policy, and the extent to which these institutions respond to public input is nontrivial, citizens will have more incentives to become informed.[111] These mechanisms can include direct-democracy-like devices such as ballot initiatives, recalls, or various deliberative fora. His findings echo the seminal research by Michael Carpini and Scott Keeter, who show that there is a strong link between a sense of political efficacy and political knowledge in the population.[112] Other work by scholars researching the relationship between voter attitudes and institutional responsiveness shows that where institutions perform poorly in terms of their capacity to respond to people's input, individuals tend to develop a negative impression of the political process and tend to form a detached attitude, which drives many of them to not seek information that will improve their knowledge of policy issues.[113]

Another structural variable that may influence why some voters know little about politics is economic inequality. For example, Kimmo Gronlund and Henry Milner find that political knowledge appears to be strongly affected by education level in countries where income and wealth are more unequally distributed.[114] They place "Anglo-Saxon" systems in this category such as the United States, the United Kingdom, Australia, and Canada. They also find that in "welfare-state countries" with high levels of economic equality, political knowledge tends to be less tied to education (they primarily focus on Nordic European countries, the Netherlands, and Germany).[115] Paul Howe offers similar findings in his research comparing Canada and the Netherlands: overall levels of political information are similar by educational group except for one difference: fewer Dutch respondents than Canadians know nothing or next to nothing.[116]

It makes sense to think that, in countries where the gap between the rich and the poor is larger, educational quality will be affected by income level since the wealthier will be able to afford better education, whereas the poorer will not necessarily have access to high-quality schools because public services in general will be deficient. In turn, good schooling is important in instilling in the citizen the incentive to get politically informed. The above-mentioned research seems to confirm this hypothesis. As indicated, there is evidence that in countries where inequality of income and wealth is not high, voters appear to show relatively higher levels of political engagement and political interest than in countries where economic inequality is higher.

The second type of variable that affects political knowledge is contextual, and it refers to socioeconomic characteristics of the *individual*. It is not news that education level, income, and wealth affect political knowledge. What I want to highlight in defense of the duty to vote with care is that these variables are modifiable by public policy. For example, improving civic education and working toward ameliorating economic inequality should result, at least in the medium to long term, in some appreciable increases in political knowledge and political interest. In this vein, William Galston shows that civic education has decreased or completely disappeared in US schools curricula and argues that, contrary to findings from 30 years ago, recent research suggests that traditional classroom-based civic education can significantly raise political knowledge.[117] Galston claims that if we compare generations rather than cohorts—that is, if we compare today's young adults not with today's older adults but with the young adults of the past—we find evidence of diminished civic attachment, which goes together with diminished knowledge. He says: "In the early 1970s, about half of the 18 to 29-year-olds in the United States voted in presidential elections. By 1996, fewer than one third did. The same pattern holds for congressional elections—about one third voted in the 1970's compared with fewer than one fifth in 1998."[118] If it is true that young adults' faith in politics and their willingness to participate has decreased because, among other things, schools do not teach the importance of democracy any more, it is not far-fetched to think that the situation could be partly reversed if schools started doing that again.

The third type of variable that affects political knowledge is strictly individual, and it refers to the ability to use cognition logically. I believe that critics of the duty to vote overemphasize this category, which is not to be dismissed. Yet, by doing so, they lose sight of the big picture. For example, Benjamin Page criticizes this individual-level focus when reviewing Ilya Somin's 2013 book on democracy and voter incompetence.[119] For Page, "the chief deficiency of Somin's book may be its focus on low *levels* of political knowledge among citizens, rather than on the more important issue of the nature, extent, and sources (including elite sources) of systematic *biases* in that knowledge."[120]

I suggest that we follow Robert Talisse and distinguish between "agent ignorance" and "belief ignorance" when reflecting on issues of voter competence and voter interest.[121] Agent ignorance is given by cognitive failures that result from faulty thinking processes strictly independent from the existence of full and accurate information. It points to deficiencies in the individual. Belief ignorance, by contrast, is attributable to misinformation despite the presence of cognitive competence. It points to background conditions that affect the flow of information. Thus, belief ignorance is, in theory, more easily alterable. We need to focus on the quality and flow of information in society to change it. To be as strong as its proponents want it to be, the objection against a duty to vote must conclusively show that public ignorance is due to agent ignorance—not belief ignorance. Belief ignorance may be currently accentuated by a host of structural and conditional factors, and so, it may be eased or eliminated, conceivably. Placing the blame for bad political results on the "ignorant voter" squarely is not only unfair but it also signals a narrow social-science view of how democratic politics work. Blaming the individual for his lack of sufficient or elaborate political knowledge entails neglecting the distorting roles of such elite-level, political party and economic system-factors that have a nontrivial effect on people's incentives to know and to care about politics. Thus, focusing only on individual-level deficiencies in cognitive reasoning neglects some promising approaches to improving voter competence and political knowledge.

The focus on individual-level attributes for explaining voter incompetence also reflects a view of human motivation wholly informed by the rational choice perspective on voting. This approach views political information as similar to consumer information, and the "political market" as analogous to the market for products. The rational choice framework says that if the costs of acquiring information are higher than the benefits, the voter will remain uninformed or abstain. But the relationship between voter knowledge and costs is more complex than that. Political knowledge constitutes a multifaceted link between the people and the political elite. While voters need information to hold elites accountable for their actions, the elites can alter, filter, or even block relevant political information and in that way influence popular opinion.[122]

In this chapter, my aim was *not* to dismiss considerations of voter incompetence that we should find troubling. My goal was simply to point to the possibility that the pessimistic tone that undergirds accounts against the duty to vote may not be completely justified. The reason for this doubt is twofold: First, it's not ostensibly clear that a majority of citizens make uninformed decisions. Cognitive shortcuts can make for efficient remedies for imperfect information in politics. Even if we were to concede that many citizens do not know enough to use these cognitive shortcuts effectively, we can think that the information necessary to revert this situation is much less daunting than commonly assumed. For example, it is in principle easier to see how a citizen can learn which newspapers correspond to which ideological positions (broadly understood) and consequently read their editorial views as a possible guide to voting than it is to see the average citizen learning economic theory and congressional history before voting.

The second reason why the pessimistic approach to voter competence may not be completely justified is that it relies too heavily on an individual-failure view of voter ignorance, and, in so doing, it is uninformed by the possibility that contextual and structural factors related to the political and economic systems explain, to a higher degree than admitted, why many citizens don't know or don't care to know about politics. But if this is so, it stands to reason that striving to modify some of the structural and contextual factors that contribute to causing ignorance may have positive results in terms of the quality of electoral choices.

Cognitive aptitude to process information is not the only ingredient to a judicious vote. As this chapter argued, fair-minded reasoning is another. Fair-mindedness is not to be understood as requiring philosophical expertise. It simply requires the would-be voter to adopt a perspective that is broader than her mere self-interest without taking self-interest out of the equation completely. As explained, this broader view entails asking oneself whether our electoral preferences could be rejected by anyone for the right reasons (such as the violation of an avowed basic interest or right).

Prevalent accounts that reject the duty to vote and other accounts that emphasize more generally the ineptitude of the electorate stress the role of voter ignorance in explaining why less-than-appealing leaders are chosen. The culprit is always the dumb voter. These accounts call attention to a real problem, but they are too partial in their examination of what harms democracy. It is not only ignorance that drives voters to fail to vote responsibly—it is also indifference fueled by unresponsive politicians. For example, in the French presidential election of 2017, the runoff between liberal-centrist Macron and far-right-wing Marine Le Pen defied expectations. Would Le Pen be the next president of France? Well, judging from how many people were indifferent to this prospect, she may as well have been. According to polls, the abstention rate in the French election was between 25 percent and 27 percent. A similar trend can be identified in the 2016 US presidential election, where abstention was higher than in the previous one.

Thus, my views in this book seem to entail a contradiction: I defend the duty to vote with care but I also admit that many times citizens may have reason to think of the ballot as a waste of their time because governments elected will still not care to work for the common good. I acknowledged this possibility earlier when elaborating on the morality of lesser-evil voting. I admitted that, in the case that all we face are equally unappealing (electoral) evils, the duty to vote loses moral stringency. However, I also said that, even when candidates are much less than perfect, we have a duty to vote for the one who offers the view that's most consistent with justice. The idea is that voting the unresponsive governments out is still a very effective way to prevent the cycle of unresponsiveness from getting worse. The skeptic may reply, however, that it is precisely people voting in elections that put bad governments in place. But democracy works just like that: elections, and only elections, install governments in the seat of power. This fact means that they are *also* the only mechanism to reverse previous, bad choices at the polls. In other words, elections, by virtue of their capacity to legally make government change hands, are the only way of officially breaking the cycle of unresponsiveness that bad governance brings with it—short of rebellion (but rebellion is not a legal mechanism to officially change governments under a democracy, however ethically permissible it may be under certain circumstances. Furthermore, one could argue that before resorting to the rather extreme option of rebelling, one has a duty to vote to attempt to end the injustice in question via peaceful means *first*).[123] Elections are the only choice method that lends *judicial*, therefore *final*, validity to the preferences of the people when it comes to whom they want to as their representatives. This simple fact makes elections the first step toward eliminating political unresponsiveness.

A rather simple, but not perfect, analogy may shed further light on the foregoing point. A person may use a drug—initially created for medical use—for recreational purposes and (accidentally) die from an overdose of the drug. This unfortunate possibility does not detract from the fact that the drug possesses the curative features that animated its creation in the first place. The drug can be used to do good despite its potential to be used to cause harm. Similarly, elections can be used to elect bad, unjust governments, but such fact does not mean that they are intrinsically useless for choosing good ones. They can do harm but they can do good as well, which is what they were, arguably, designed for. One must take into consideration institutional reforms that will make unresponsiveness costly for politicians, but, in the meantime, voting the bad governments out is only viable thanks to elections. The duty to vote with care is consistent with recognizing the problem of unresponsive governments. Emphasizing this duty may help us in waking people up from indifference. Ignorance is not the only reason why unfit leaders and unfair-minded governments gain access to power. Indifference (understandably) fueled by an unresponsive political class is another. Does the citizen have a moral duty to vote *even* if public officials and representatives are generally unresponsive? The answer to this question should already be clear. Insofar as elections remain functional as the only mechanism to oust unresponsive governments, we should view voting with care as a moral duty. If voting is a duty of justice, what could be more just than the action of contributing to the ousting and replacement of an unresponsive government?

The question of which reforms are necessary to fight the problem of political unresponsiveness is essential to a discussion of justice in democracy, however. Acknowledging that certain reforms will make democracy more just by re-energizing citizens and incentivizing them to vote with care is not utopic. Many political scientists know exactly which reforms are likely to achieve this change. For the purposes of argumentative clarity, we can classify them into three groups: (1) campaign finance reforms, (2) electoral law reforms, and (3) preventing of deadlock reforms.[124] What these three types of reform have in common is that they would am-plify the influence of common voters on policy and government—reducing unresponsiveness on the part of the political elite as a result. Decreasing unresponsiveness would, in turn, encourage people to become more excited, and consequentially more in-formed, about politics.[125] Political scientists have furnished us with evidence that when people have a larger say in politics, they tend to become more politically informed than when they do not.[126] All this is not to deny the problem of ignorant voters as a menace to the quality and justice of democracy. After all, nobody can ignore how much harm uneducated choices in elections can cause. But it is one thing to think that we are doomed because most people are incompetent citizens, and quite another thing to wonder why many of them are, what we need to change so that they no longer are, and why many other citizens are indifferent but not necessarily ignorant.

4

Why Is Voting Special?

In this chapter, I will address a fundamental objection against my views on voting and justice. This is the objection that, if voting with care is not the only way to further the common good, why should we see it as a (moral) duty instead of a simple choice? We can also fulfill a duty of Samaritan justice by helping the common good in many other ways. We can donate to charity, work toward finding the cure for cancer, or do community work, among millions of alternatives. Why is voting so special?[1]

I want to suggest that, despite the fact that voting with care is *one* way among others by which we can help further the common good of society, we don't need to show that voting is superior to other common-good-enabling activities in order to show that voting with care is a moral duty. We do have to explain, however, why voting with care is unique *even* if it is not the only activity that advances justice, or the most effective at all times and under all circumstances (i.e., voting may not be efficacious if elections are fraudulent or if rebellion is the only alternative feasible in the face of a relentlessly abusive government).

4.1. Elections and Governments as Providers of Primary Goods

What's special about voting with care that renders it a duty? To answer this question, it is necessary that we understand what the distinctive function of elections in a democracy is, together with the role that governments play in ensuring access to primary social goods and fair governance for all.

The term "government" can be understood in two different ways, which are frequently confused. The word "government" can refer to formal institutions such as the executive branch or the legislature and to the accompanying norms of procedure that regulate how these bodies operate. But we also use the term "government" to refer to the current administration, that is, the cadre of public officials currently in power. Established government institutions and norms are essential for democracy, but the administrations that steward and run those institutions have the potential to affect justice significantly by virtue of the practical capabilities that taking the reins of power confer. Even though power is not all concentrated in one place in liberal democratic systems, the concerted act of governing results in policies, or absences thereof, that will have a noticeable effect on people's lives. The nature of the government in control, thus, matters to justice. And if this is so, the mechanism that enables a given coalition to install itself in the seat of governmental power has a moral significance that seems unparalleled among other mechanisms of political influence.

The reason why voting is—*collectively*—the most direct mechanism to influence the quality of governance is that elections are the "still agreed procedure for legitimizing governments, and putting into power those who decide whether or not we will go to war, what levels of taxation we will have to pay, whether we are eligible for welfare benefits, and whether it is legal for us to march in a political demonstration."[2] In other words, elections are the standard mechanism by which governments and ruling coalitions are installed, maintained (if they are re-elected), as well as removed by the electorate. Street demonstrations, letters to public officials, and other non-strictly electoral ways of influence may surely have greater impact than elections at specific times (i.e., the civil rights movement in the United States or the fight against apartheid in South Africa), but they do not inevitably and systematically *authorize* governments to act. Elections put governments in place, and by virtue of this fact they always authorize them to put into effect policies and programs that (should) further the common good.

Elections fulfill, we could say, at least three essential functions: (1) they *enable* the *choosing* of a government and its installment in power; (2) they *legally authorize* the chosen government to govern and enact policies consistent with the common good; and (3) they enable citizens to *sanction* bad governments and *remove* them from power; but they also enable citizens to *renew* their trust in good governments and extend their tenure. In the words of political scientists Jose Antonio Chebub and Adam Przeworksi: "Democracy is a political regime distinguished by the accountability of rulers to the ruled, [and] elections are the mechanism through which this accountability is enforced."[3] Even if non-electoral mechanisms such as marches and other citizen-led activities affect the actions of governments, and serve as punishing tools that dissatisfied citizens may resort to, they do not *legitimize* and *install* ruling coalitions in power. They may contribute to the exit of some, and to their fall from grace, but they cannot *officially* enable the establishment of new ones. Only elections can establish governments and *legally* legitimize their actions and initiatives.

Voting governments in and out is not the only task citizens should be responsible for in a democracy. I am in no way advocating for a minimalist role for the citizen, nor do I claim to profess Schumpeterian values of market-inspired electoral participation. From a moral standpoint, however, it follows that if a duty of justice to help society carries any weight, and elections can directly affect the quality of governance by enabling citizens to choose a government and authorize it to implement policies that will affect the lives of millions, then citizens ought to vote with care if doing so would not be detrimental to their individual goals.

Generally, it is safe to say that governments are distinct for enabling us to obtain goods that would be unavailable to us in their absence. For example, a government's decision to massively defund education or healthcare programs can have irreversible effects for segments of the population that cannot afford private provision of these goods. A government's decision to embark on an unnecessary war may have drastic effects on the health of the state's coffers as well as on the psychological and physical welfare of the people. Many other examples of what government can do for people, or against them, are surely available. In sum, "The influence of government on the wellbeing of society can be considered or estimated in reference to nothing less than the whole of the interests of humanity."[4] The test of good or bad government, as J. S. Mill suggested, is inevitably linked to the interests of society (however we define those, although I believe that basic ones are not so difficult to imagine without much controversy). Mill's language may be flamboyant and imprecise, but it encapsulates an important idea. Political representatives and officials appointed by the latter have an immense power to affect people's lives.

Thus, the effect that governments have on the common good—as opposed to the effect that private individuals or organizations may have—cannot be dismissed as morally trivial. I call this the *Governmental Salience Fact* (GSF). It means that governments are massively powerful giants whose policies can influence the economy, the geopolitics, and the general welfare of society in a way that few other entities can. The GSF is an empirical datum that tells us that good and bad government profoundly affects the quality of people's lives. Because of this great impact, it is not far-fetched to think that governments are morally distinctive entities. I call the latter proposition the *Governmental Salience Principle*. The principle builds on the GSF. It tells us that *because* governments are so influential, their justice *should* be seen as a central justification for voting. This is not an empirical datum like the GSF. It is a moral prescription based on the gravity of the effects of governmental policies on society.

Governments are distinguished from other entities and institutions because, it is reasonable to assume, they have more power to affect people's life prospects by way of their capacity to enact, or block, far-reaching public and social policy. In turn, this distinguishability renders the mechanism by which governments are chosen morally important. All else equal, we have a duty to partake in it given that the influence of government on the common good is far from negligible. Thus, if we ought to act as Good Samaritans toward society and help the common good, it seems that partaking of the mechanism that makes governments elected is essential. Even though voting is surely not the only way to affect government, it seems to me that it is the only way to choose it, and choosing a government is necessary before we can influence it.

Importantly, the nature of the government we choose can make a great deal of difference as to how badly we need to make sure we have the effective capacity to influence people in government. If good governance is possible without extreme vigilance on the part of the electorate, because the administration elected is prima facie fair-minded, then it seems to me that voting with care plays a big role in explaining this circumstance. I do not entertain the naive thought that vigilance is ever unnecessary, but I want to emphasize that the first, most basic step we can take to maximize the chances of good governance is to elect the right type of government— understanding this as a government whose policies and promises appear to be better to further the basic interests of the common voter than alternative electoral choices.[5]

It is undeniable that many ways to affect the common good exist besides voting. Insofar as we care to do something for the common good, we could think of the duty to vote as an instance of a broader "imperfect duty" (in Kantian language). For Kant, imperfect duties give as a wide margin of choice in how and when we should act to discharge them. Kant calls them "laxer" duties because of this flexibility. He differentiates them from "stricter" duties—such as the duty not to commit suicide or the duty not to lie—in that they don't always require us to *do* something. Imperfect duties admit of multiple means of fulfillment.[6] Moreover, Kant suggests that the duty to aid others is one example of the latter type of duty.[7]

So if we rely on his distinction between perfect and imperfect duties, we may be led to think that voting in order to help society is one of those duties that we are not required to fulfill because there are many other ways in which we can help society. But I want to show that one can see voting as a (non-optional) moral duty *despite* the fact that other activities besides voting have the power to affect the common good. Thus, I do not think that voting with care can be seen in the light of a Kantian imperfect duty. To this task of clarification, I now turn.

4.2. The Principle of Moral Inescapability

We don't need to deny that there are indeed many ways to further the common good in order to conclude that some of those ways may still be required of us (not by the law but by our conscience). An analogy will help to clarify this point: imagine that your good friend is using crutches, and you are both waiting for a bus to arrive. Your friend would benefit from your assistance to board the bus. The effort to help him board the bus would not be unduly strenuous for you. Your friend also happens to have a lot of credit card debt. While the bus is approaching, you hand him a check and say: "Take this money to pay your bills, but I'm not going to help you get onto the bus." Your monetary help is surely beneficial to your friend. However, in that moment he needs you to help him board the bus. In other words, the fact that your financial help is real and effective does not detract from your duty to help him with boarding the bus.

Voting provides us with a similar situation to consider. The quality of government significantly affects every person in society. Elections offer us a relatively easy way to improve society if we vote with minimal information and end up choosing decent governments. Other forms of contributing to the common good may be valuable and beneficial, but it is not clear that they let the individual off the hook when it comes to voting in order to contribute to the emergence of good governance. The reason why is that society needs its members to pick fair-minded leaders regardless of what else anyone else needs. To reinforce this idea, consider the following example.

You are walking down the street and witness a petty robbery. A thief has grabbed someone's wallet and run away. The victim, a woman walking in front of you, is now left with no money and is disoriented. To make the case more dramatic, imagine that the woman is a foreign tourist and has no one to turn to in the city, where she had planned to spend the night. The Kantian logic of imperfect duty dictates that you do nothing wrong by ignoring the woman's plight because, say, last week you helped a homeless person buy lunch. How many helpful things can one person be expected to do? You are in a hurry. But is this the right way to proceed? I would say that it does not seem to be. Doing something in this case would be easy since you are well equipped to offer aid: you happen to be right there and you have a wallet. For example, you could give the woman some change for a bus ride that will take her to her embassy.

But does this mean that you ought to help anybody who conceivably may need help? Of course not. However, you are in such a good position to help in *this* case. Sure, you can think that the two coins for the bus ride could be given to a charity organization of your choice, but how bad is it to forgo this particular chance of aiding that you happen to be so well-situated to act on? I argue that it would be impermissibly bad *given* your circumstances. Let's call this idea the *Principle of Moral Inescapability*. It says that *given* certain confluence of factors, aiding is the right and obligatory thing to do. In the case of the stranded woman, the confluence of factors includes how easy it would be for you to help given your proximity and possession of a wallet *and* how bad it would be for the woman to have to sleep in a park that night.

In the same vein, I submit that elections entail a particular confluence of factors that render participation in them morally inescapable, all else equal. First, they constitute a structure that situates us in a perfect position to render help easily. Assuming minimal efficiency and transparency, the machinery of elections emerges in front of you for you to vote, and vanishes shortly after the choice period is over. You do not need to create this structure; it is part and parcel of the democratic system. It exists automatically, at least, from your strictly individual perspective. Because of this basic fact of democracy, one could say that you happen to be well-situated to use elections to help society. Second, given the importance of the Governmental Salience Fact (GSF), we know that elections are not morally innocuous events. They are not because they establish and replace governments; and governments' actions affect people's lives in nontrivial ways. Thus, we can conclude that ignoring elections (ignoring the Governmental Salience Principle, more concretely) carries with it costs that we should not incur simply because we'd rather help in other ways besides participating in them.

It is not valid to say that I may want to contribute to the common good in ways other than or instead of voting, just as it is not a valid argument to refuse to help the stranded woman because you'd rather donate the cash to Oxfam. Certainly, it would be equally easy to donate to Oxfam, which may be why you should do so regardless of whether you help the woman. But the *Principle of Moral Inescapability* dictates that you are still required to aid the woman because she needs the help *now*, and you are *there*, able to provide it. John Locke referred to this type of duty in his *Essays on the Law of Nature* as a duty where "the outward performance is commanded" but where we are not continuously obligated to act except for "at a particular time and in a particular manner."[8]

Thus, unlike Immanuel Kant's notion of "imperfect duties"—which we can freely choose when to honor—"duties of time and place" are not optional. The occasion to act on them presents itself sporadically (like elections, by the way) in the sense that we have to find ourselves under circumstances that will prompt us to act (such as seeing someone in distress and in need of help). But when such circumstances unfold before us, the duty is perfectly obligatory. I propose to think of the duty to vote with care as a duty of time and place, to borrow Locke's language. The duty becomes stringent when elections offer us an easy way to contribute to aiding society by way of choosing decent governments or ousting indecent ones. Failing to act when this circumstance unfolds would be morally problematic, other things equal. Locke's duties of "time and place," one could say, are morally inescapable when the right circumstances come to emerge that justify action.[9]

In the case of the tourist example, the Principle of Moral Inescapability requires you to help the woman at the time in which she is robbed by handing her money so that she can return home— not by taking her home yourself, for example. The principle also requires you to help because the good of sparing the woman a homeless night trumps your cost (i.e., the two coins). By the same token, society needs your help now (child poverty, anyone?) and elections exist so that you can provide such help easily, your cost being no more than the acquisition of available information (If you'd rather avoid the lines at the polling booths, you can always send the ballot by post). To ignore this confluence of factors, I would say, is morally wrong. Even though there is always something immoral about knowingly ignoring a plight for help when helping would not be unduly costly for the individual, there is something especially morally condemnable about being indifferent toward a situation in which help is needed and the means to help appear in front of us almost automatically, rendering coordination costs nonexistent.

For example, if a troubled swimmer is asking for help but you doubt whether you will be able to engage in the rescue unless someone hands you a lifesaver, it would be especially wrong to decline to help if someone does hand you a flotation device. In the case of the tourist, the fact that there is a bus that she can take to her embassy relieves you of further efforts in helping her by

WHY IS VOTING SPECIAL? 139

coordinating with others how to do so. In a similar vein, elections render coordination costs null (there is no doubt as to whether the aid can be materialized technically). In a way, the mechanism for help is provided easily for you to take—it unfolds in front of you without any efforts on your part—which explains why it is especially wrong to decline to use it. In cases where the helping mechanism is easily available, the individual evinces an attitude that is ostensibly at odds with the spirit of Samaritan duty if he refuses aid. In the case of voting, failing to use elections to contribute to aiding society reflects cold indifference toward the fate of our fellow citizens, which, arguably, is a moral failing because caring would not cost much.[10]

Does all this mean that, in the case of voting, every individual citizen has a right against me that I vote to aid them? Someone may say this is implausible because having a duty toward millions is impracticable. That may be so, although I fail to see how so in the case of voting since the simple act of casting a ballot would be sufficient to discharge that duty to millions of other people. But if we are uncomfortable with that conceptualization, we can think that we, as individuals, have a duty to society as a collective group of people. We ordinarily think in these terms in the case of other familiar duties. For example, when we say that we have a duty to pay taxes, to obey the law, or not to pollute, we have society as a collective in mind. Not all these duties may be legally enforceable but they are nevertheless justice duties toward others.

4.3. The Collective Dimension of Samaritanism (Again)

At this juncture, it could be objected that I am using an incorrect analogy. My two coins will suffice to aid the stranded woman, but my vote will most likely *not* make a difference to the result of elections. Duties to aid people in need are not good tools to argue for the obligation to participate in collective activities such as elections.

Although intuitive, the foregoing idea is incorrect. Acting on duties toward other human beings does not always require the capacity to make a measurable difference on a state of affairs, as I argued in previous chapters. If that state of affairs is too difficult to modify by one single person, we may only be morally required to contribute to a larger collective activity that will have a discernible impact. In short, we may be required to join forces with others regardless of our individual powerlessness.[11] But most importantly, the example of the stranded woman can be modified to accommodate the objection in question and illustrate that Samaritan justice can still require us to act in concert with others toward a goal that is achievable only through cooperative activity. There is nothing normatively relevant about Samaritanism that makes it a one-person responsibility only. In other words, contributing to a collective activity that will have Samaritan results is perfectly consistent with the spirit of Samaritanism.

Consider the same woman, who has been robbed, but this time she needs an expensive train ticket to reach her embassy since the latter is in the capital, far away from your town. You may rightly feel that the whole train fare is too high for you to afford alone. However, other pedestrians, who witnessed the unfortunate episode, have a duty to contribute to helping the unlucky woman if doing so would not deter from their goals in significant ways (assume that donating two coins each will suffice to relieve the tourist). In this case, we may say that those physically close enough to the event and able to help at a relatively low cost have a duty to cooperate, on this specific occasion, to assist the woman in need.

Thus, the argument of moral inescapability canvassed in this section can be understood to involve the following logical steps:

1. Under circumstances X, person Y finds herself in need of help.

2. Under circumstances X, you are particularly well-situated to help person Y because doing so would not demand much strategic or logistical effort on your part, which means that
3. Under circumstances X, helping person Y is not unduly costly for you, and
4. The cost to you of helping person Y is less morally relevant than the harm that would accrue to her if you did nothing. In other words, your cost can be offset by the avoidance of suffering that your help would cause.
5. Therefore, under circumstances X, it would be morally condemnable for you to remain passive.

Applied to the case of considered voting, the preceding logical excursion would look as follows:

1. Under circumstances of transparent and fair elections, you are particularly well-situated to help society because you can easily participate of elections. Elections are mounted automatically in front if you and dismantled as quickly when the collective choice period is over. You don't have to preoccupy yourself with their functioning or organization.
2. Under circumstances of transparent and fair elections, voting with minimal information and a sense of the common good is not unduly burdensome, although it is not utterly costless.
3. Therefore, under circumstances of transparent and fair elections, it would be morally wrong for you to remain passive and not vote.

Note that, at this point, someone could (again!) remind us that elections are a collective activity, that the single act of voting will not influence them, and that, therefore, it is not morally required to vote in order to fulfill a duty of aid toward society. Voting, in this context, is *not* morally inescapable, the objection would say. But I already gave an answer to this objection in the previous chapter. The answer was that some duties of assistance can only be discharged by way of cooperation among several individuals, and that the need for a collective effort does not make our single contributions any less required, morally speaking. Furthermore, the fact that if enough people contribute, your help will turn out to be unnecessary, does not make your duty to participate in the concerted action any less stringent. If it did, none of the individuals equally well-situated to help would have a duty to help either, and cooperation would not be a requirement for *anyone*. Although everybody appears to have an equal claim to being exempted from a duty of aid, on further inspection, and from a morally neutral standpoint, it is more appropriate to think that nobody has a special claim to not contributing. Thus, the logical excursion justifying the collective duty of aid would be as follows:

6. Under circumstances X, person Y finds herself in need of help.
7. Under circumstances X, you are particularly well-situated to help person Y because doing so would not demand much strategic or logistical effort on your part. However, your single act of help will be insufficient to relieve the plight of Y.
8. Under circumstances X, other people around you, A, B, and C, are equally well-situated to help person Y, and are as well-situated to help as you are. None of their acts of help alone are sufficient to relieve the plight of Y, but together, A, B, C, and yourself can provide Y with what she needs.
9. Under circumstances X, joining forces with A, B, and C to help person Y is not unduly costly for you—as it is not for A, B, and C.
10. The cost to A, B, C, and yourself of helping person Y is less morally relevant than the harm that would accrue to Y if A, B, C, and you did nothing. In other words, your (collective) cost can be offset by the avoidance of suffering that your help would cause. [12]

11. Therefore, under circumstances X, it would be morally subpar for you to refrain from joining forces with A, B, and C to act in concert to help Y. The same applies to A, B, and C respectively.

12. The above holds valid even if it is true that the individual's participation is not causally necessary to produce the aid in question. The person's claim to being exempted from the obligation to join others in the collective effort is no stronger than any other individual's claim to do the same. Thus, it follows that everybody has an equally stringent duty to "jump in." In the case of voting, this means that, prima facie, all citizens have a duty to contribute to the common good of society with a considered vote.

Voting with care, then, is a duty—under circumstances evoking the foregoing logic—even if it *is not the only* way to contribute to the common good of society. The fact that we can discharge a duty of justice in many ways does not make any of those ways morally optional *under all circumstances*. Some of those ways may become morally required because of the particular circumstances in which the individual finds herself. In the case of voting, there is reason to believe that the apparatus of democratic elections that appears in front of us episodically renders our participation in them an act that would be morally wrong to avoid given how relatively noncostly our participation would be, and given how effective the collective act of voting can be for furthering an interest in justice. This does not negate the fact that other ways of making society better *also* exist.

Surprisingly, the libertarian position against the duty to vote reinforces my point that some acts may be morally required of us *even if the repertoire of contributions to the common good of society contains many additional options*. As elaborated in detail in the previous chapter, Jason Brennan, in his book *The Ethics of Voting*, claims that we have a duty to avoid voting badly—without

information and carelessly. The reason why this duty is so important is that we have a prior obligation not to participate in collectively harmful activities. Voting carelessly or incompetently is an
example of how we can contribute to a harmful collective enterprise because, when many individuals vote in this way, the result
can be the election of bad governments, which can enact policies
that will make society more unjust. Thus, we have a duty not to contribute to harming society by voting carelessly. So far, this rationale
makes perfect sense, so much so that it actually ends up supporting
my view that voting with care is morally special even if it is not the
only way to further the common good. Let me explain.

Voting badly *is not* the only way in which we can harm society.
We can also contribute to harming society by cheating on our taxes,
by founding a political party with a genocidal platform, by plotting
to assassinate public officials, and by convincing others to cast bad
votes at elections, among other things. So, if the duty not to contribute to harming society with a bad vote is stringent *even though*
many other ways of harming society exist, we should not worry too
much about the fact that a duty to vote with care is also stringent—
all else equal—even though there are other ways of helping society
besides voting with care. The defender of the duty not to pollute the
polls with bad votes surely does not think that, because there are
other ways of not harming society besides refraining from voting
badly, refraining from voting badly is *not* morally obligatory. He
argues *it is*.

In the same vein, voting with care is not the only conceivable way
to advance justice or protect the common good. But why should
that matter for thinking of it as a moral duty? Voting with care may
be morally special, and required, even though it *is not the only* avenue through which we can help society—in the same way as
refraining from voting badly is a moral duty even if it *is not* the only
way of avoiding harm to society.

In the preceding pages, I tried to substantiate the claim that
voting with care is a special form of aiding society (in concert

with others) but not the only one. Its specialness—which makes it morally obligatory, all else equal—resides in the fact that it is the only method engineered to *directly* cause the election, and affect the composition, of government—understanding that term as the cadre of politicians and bureaucrats that will gain the reins of power after the choice period is over. This particular function of elections, then, puts each eligible-to-vote citizen in a *unique, favorable* position to aid her society—by contributing to elect a fair-minded-enough governing coalition. Other forms of helping others are not, for this reason, less valuable—but they are not (collectively speaking) as effective when it comes to the *particular* goal of erecting a government. There lies the specialness of voting. We don't need to deny that there are multiple ways of helping people other than participating in elections. Many of those ways of providing aid will be preferable to voting depending on the objective we seek to contribute to by helping. But saying that *because* voting is not the only way of helping society it is not deserving of moral attention, is quite simplistic. In the hopes of driving this point home more clearly, I offer one last analogy that, like the others, highlights the collective nature of the obligation to help when doing so would be relatively easy—and when the larger goal behind the (small) contribution is important.

Imagine that scientists discover that people with your blood type have a higher chance of resisting a potent and dangerous virus that is affecting the population in your area and causing much human suffering. In the quest for a successful vaccine, scientists and doctors need to obtain blood samples from millions of people with your blood type in order to test the possible reactions to the virus, and have as much information as possible before they can come up with the antidote. Because of the relative urgency of this public health issue, the authorities have offered to visit the volunteers at home or at their workplace in order to draw the samples. This visit would cause an interruption to one's daily activities, for sure, and it would need to be coordinated beforehand. It would also require, in the story, that the would-be volunteers know in advance whether they are the right blood type (which means that, for those in doubt but willing to help, the effort of finding out falls squarely on them).

If you happened to be the blood type needed to test this vaccine, and donating a sample was not unduly onerous for you, I would say that you are morally obligated to contribute to this public health effort. It is true that many others will/might be doing the same thing—which makes your single contribution not essential for attaining the final goal of creating a vaccine—but refraining from participating simply because of this reason denotes cold indiffer- ence toward the plight of others—besides denoting a shameless willingness to free-ride on those individuals that will participate and help device the vaccine that will keep *you* and *your* loved ones healthy (your blood type privilege does not make you totally im- mune to the disease, by the way).

If you happened to be in doubt about your blood type, running to a lab to find out your type may impose some costs that you may not be able to bear—but it may also be a momentary inconvenience that is not likely to change your overall ability to donate (say, if the lab is not far away from your home and if your job is flexible enough to permit you a trip there). Bearing in mind the different degrees of difficulty that donating volunteers may experience in this story, it is not far-fetched to suggest that many people will be uniquely well-situated to contribute to this large public effort. This will be so because (*a*) they will have the right blood type; (*b*) they will know that they do or will find it not onerous to find out that they do; and (*c*) researching this blood type is the *only* way for scientists to create a vaccine for this *specific* ailment.

One could certainly think that the donor would act equally mor- ally if he decided to spend the time that blood type testing takes writing charity checks addressed at organizations that fight hunger instead. In fact, aiding in the effort of fighting hunger is a very laud- able act. What my example seeks to show is that it would not be laudable for the individual to *substitute* charity giving with blood donation *in this particular case*—when society is facing a danger that could be combated with the cumulative/collective help of certain people—i.e., people like him, with his blood type. This conclusion cannot logically entail that fighting hunger is therefore unnecessary or morally optional. What it entails is that donating blood is *neither* of those two things *now*. As I said before, this conceptualization of duties may mean that we ought to accept a more demanding picture of our duties of justice toward others, that is, a picture in which we are bound by more duties of help than we thought, or would like to admit.

In the same way as having the right blood type puts you in a good position to help others, elections position eligible citizens in a unique situation to help society because they automatically appear and disappear to make the collective choice of government possible for us. They are especially designed to elect governments in a way that no other mechanism is; and it is reasonable to suppose that many would-be voters will not experience undue burdens when voting and deciding whom to vote for. As individuals, these citizens may reason that others will step up and vote—rendering the formation of government possible and, so, they may decide to stay home and let others do the work. However, this mindset is morally condemnable because it violates a duty to lend a hand to others in need when doing so would not cost us much. Importantly, this mindset would fly in the face of the fact that no one citizen—all things considered—has a stronger claim to being exempted from the duty than any other, as already explained in previous sections of this book.

4.4. Lesser-Evil Voting

The duty to vote with care entails a concern with preventing injustice by ensuring that indecent and inept governments stay out of power, or lose power. We foster good governance—and aid society as Good Samaritans—when we prevent governments that would enact unjust polices from gaining power or from staying too long in power. As Cicero masterfully explained (last chapter), anyone that could easily prevent an injustice but does not care to do so could be considered as morally deficient as someone that does the injustice himself. If preventing or minimizing injustice is an important goal when aiding society, then it would seem to follow from my arguments for the duty to vote with care that one ought to vote for the lesser of two (or more) evils when elections leave us no other choice.[13]

A problematic corollary of the foregoing argument is that the call to vote for the lesser of two evils means that, for example, in a society where the two candidates running for office are a person who promises to exterminate group X and a person who promises to put members of group X in internment camps, the citizen should readily vote for the latter. Not voting at all would constitute a contribution to the mass abstention that may enable the genocidal candidate to win, which would have more disastrous results in terms of justice than massive internment camps. The implication that one ought to vote for a despicable electoral option to prevent an even more despicable electoral option from winning is certainly troubling. Here, considerations of moral integrity and dirty hands enter the picture when reflecting on what the right thing to do is.

Moral integrity is the idea that we have moral commitments to values, goals, and ideals that certain actions would obviously contradict and degrade.[14] For example, we may be staunch supporters of equal rights, and contributing to an electoral result that violates this ideal of equality hampers that commitment and degrades our character in so doing. It makes us the kind of person that added, however marginally, to the collective activity that enabled a state of affairs that is morally repugnant. Thus, by acting in a way that is clearly contrary to profound moral commitments that we hold, we also make our hands dirty by contributing to the larger effort that we find morally reproachable. How can acting in this fashion *ever* be a matter of duty?

I say that it *can* be a matter of duty because not acting and keeping our hands clean can usher in morally more reproachable consequences, which we are not disassociated from simply because we don't act. In the case of voting, the search for a clean conscience may result in immoral behavior. If our vote will contribute to the defeat of the realistically electable "lesser evil," however marginally, therefore electing the "more evil" candidate, then we force society to pay a high price for our clean conscience. Sometimes, our concern for feeling morally impeccable should give way to a concern for averting injustice, even if the alternative is less injustice, not the absence of it.

But what about less extreme cases in which the electoral options are not between a genocide-lover and a mass-imprisonment aficionado, but between two or more candidates that meet acceptable standards of decency? In more familiar situations like the latter, we may still face the lesser-evil dilemma if it is reasonable to believe that one of the candidates would be better for society than all the others—even though she or he is not the ideal candidate or the one we would like to see win (for example, because a fringe-party candidate would be even better for society but said candidate stands no realistic chance of winning). In cases like this one, are we morally obligated to vote for the lesser evil or should we give our vote to the unelectable, yet better candidate that we prefer on principle? Are we to vote our conscience or "dirty our hands" by lending support to a candidate that we think is less than ideal? This situation also tests our moral commitments because, if we really care about justice, shouldn't we favor only the alternative that best honors such principle? And if no such alternative exists—not even an "unelectable" one—ought we not to abstain instead?

The duty to vote with care that I defend in this book is a duty that does not depend on the behavior of others to be morally stringent. In other words, fulfillment of the duty to vote with care does not hinge on what other individuals do regarding that fulfill-ment. If they decide to ignore the duty, their behavior does not ex-cuse my doing the same thing. This is so because considerations of Samaritan justice are prescient regardless of whether a partic-ular individual believes that they are. They are prescient regard-less of any subjective judgment. Thus, one should act with a view to pursuing justice as if all other individuals were doing likewise. One should do what is reasonable to expect others to do under the assumption that they will understand that others will also be doing their share of justice-pursuing acts (but not more).[15] This reasoning entails that one acts consistent with the duty to aid society when one votes for the best candidate even if she is the candidate of a fringe party. For if one is to base one's discharge of the duty to vote with care on what others ought to do, it follows that the electoral option that is most consistent with justice *on principle* should be the one that justice-minded voters will support regardless of party and other "strategic" considerations. This reasoning is not at odds with the spirit of my arguments for Samaritan justice and elections. However, it is not the last word. Let me explain.

In a nonideal world, we have to be prepared for the real possi-bility that some people will not honor their duty to promote a just society the way we would. They may do so for two reasons, at least (ruling out mere indifference to justice): They may vote differently because they may think that practical considerations of political in-fluence, power, and electability matter in determining who can ac-tually win an election. Or they may simply view another candidate as the best option for society, their judgment being reasonable, at least. If we have reason to believe that a sizable majority will not vote the way we think justice demands but we still think that the views of said majority are preferable (because they are more con-sistent with justice) to other "electable" alternatives, and it is true that our most preferred option cannot win because not enough people will vote for it, then we discharge our duty of justice toward society if we vote for what we deem to be the lesser evil. It makes sense to believe this is the case since our primordial obligation toward society is to prevent injustice and bad governance, not to keep our hands utterly clean at all costs.[16]

Despite this call to action for the sake of justice, it is worth reflecting on the problem of voter dissatisfaction. This is a legitimate difficulty for anyone concerned with the quality and responsiveness of democratic governments. It is the democratic system of government that must offer appealing and worthy choices to the voter—it is not the voter's responsibility to always accommodate to the alternatives available if those alternatives consistently happen to be less than appealing or decent. The burden does not lie with the citizen but with the political class. The main raison d'être for democratic governments is to serve the people, not the other way around. The principle of popular rule, however differently implemented in real societies, recommends one unequivocal thing: that citizens choose delegates and magistrates that best represent their principled views. Those magistrates have a fiduciary responsibility to honor citizens' interests to the best of their ability, even if that entails not adhering exactly to the citizens' desires all the time. However, when electoral alternatives are consistently deficient in ensuring this correspondence, the citizens have a right to express their dissatisfaction with the situation. How else are they to do this other than by not taking part of the process that keeps producing the electoral options that are unpalatable?

Abstention is not a ready sign of discontent because silence is at best ambiguous. Political inactivity can be interpreted both as a sign of anger and as a sign of contentment. There is a better solution to the problem of how to express frustration with the electoral alternatives available: it is the blank vote. Although this instrument is much more common in compulsory voting systems than in voluntary voting systems, there is no reason why it could not be implemented in the latter. When the blank vote is an option—and citizens can formally vote for nobody—society can count the number of citizens that express their unhappiness at the polls. This is a much more powerful tool for change than simply staying home and hoping that someday a better candidate will appear in the electoral horizon. Now the question emerges, Is there a duty to express one's discontent *at the polls*? I don't think that there is such a duty save to the extent that expressing one's frustrations via the vote may help society become more just. But this is an indirect justification. I would say that one has a duty to vote for the lesser evil insofar as doing so is called for by the good of preventing injustice. However, when all we are faced with are equal evils, the duty to vote loses stringency, unfortunately.

4.5. Responsibility in Elections

If voting is morally special enough to justify a binding duty, we are left with the question of responsibility for not doing our duty. Is the individual voter morally responsible for injustice if she fails to vote with care and an unjust, or insufficiently decent, government is elected? We know that voting carelessly is an uncontroversial breach of duty, as the libertarian critics rightly argue, because it contributes to a collective harm against society. But the interesting question becomes: Is omitting to vote grounds for moral blame for contributing to the perpetuation of injustice and bad governance?

Here we need to distinguish two senses of responsibility. First, there is the responsibility to discharge a duty. This is a forward-looking concept of responsibility; it simply means that we ought to do our best to fulfill a duty. It is almost a tautology to say that we have a responsibility to fulfill a duty. Since duties are morally obligatory, it is clear that we ought to fulfill them (provided no other moral considerations dictate the contrary in particular cases). Thus, it is correct to say that the individual is responsible for fulfilling a duty, and when she fails to do so for no justified reason, she is blameworthy. But the foregoing explanation is not the only sense of responsibility there is. Another sense of responsibility is the sense related to being guilty for something happening as a result, or byproduct, of having neglected to discharge a duty. This sense of responsibility attaches moral blame for a *causal role* in bringing about an undesirable state of affairs. An example may flesh out the difference between the two types of responsibility more clearly.

Consider Peter, a father of two, who has a moral duty of care to ensure the welfare of his minor children. In situation A, Peter is careless toward his children, but the children are unharmed despite his negligence. In situation B, Peter is also careless, but his children get hurt as a result of his negligence. In situation A, Peter is not morally responsible for harming his children, although we could say that he committed a wrong by violating his duty of care toward them. It was his responsibility to do everything in his power to avoid putting his children at risk, and he failed at that. He was simply lucky that his children didn't suffer for it.[17] In situation B, Peter is morally blameworthy for ignoring his duty *as well as* for causing harm to his children. He was the causal agent in the emergence of a harmful result (his children getting hurt). He bears moral blame for that harm, which is different from the blame he bears for being a negligent father who violates a duty of care more generally.

In the case of voting, applying these notions of responsibility may be difficult because we know that voting as an individual act cannot bring about a discernible result by itself. In other words, it is not the case that the sole individual is causally responsible for bringing about the outcome of elections. His vote gets lost in a proverbial ocean of votes. But if this is the case, failing to vote, as an individual act, cannot be the cause of a result, either. If the outcome of an election is the establishment of an unjust government, those citizens that failed to vote cannot be said to be *causally* responsible for that result because each individual omission *did not* exert a discernible impact on the election.

It is clear that full individual causal responsibility does not obtain in the case of voting (or not voting) because of the very nature of large elections. And if this is the case, does it follow that moral responsibility for contributing to a morally subpar result (an electoral outcome that is undesirable from the perspective of justice) or for contributing to a valuable result (an electoral outcome beneficial to the common good) is off the table? I think the answer is negative.

I want to suggest that one can still bear moral responsibility for contributing, however marginally, to a state of affairs. The responsibility in question is not for the full-blown result that is only possible by the joint acts of many people but for the small contribution we made to such collective activity. Our responsibility is a small share of the total responsibility for that outcome.[18] In the case of voting with care, one can be held morally responsible for having added, however infinitesimally, to the collective activity that enabled a result that is morally valuable, such as the election of a fair-minded government. In this sense, one bears *some* moral credit for having contributed to a larger goal whose outcome is objectively good from the standpoint of justice. In chapter 3, (previous), I argued that our tiny, individual contributions to larger collective activities inherit the moral nature of those collective activities. The point I am making here is slightly different. I am saying that one's imperceptible contribution is still causally more effective than no contribution at all, and for that causal power, however small, one bears a slight moral responsibility.

In the case of failing to vote with care by abstaining from voting all together, we can think that the individual is also slightly responsible when the outcome of the election is objectively bad from the viewpoint of justice if we assume, as we should, that omissions can also have causal force in explaining why things happen. As we established in previous chapters, omissions can explain the emergence of states of affairs because, when we fail to act, we may also fail to prevent injustice or harm.

For example, when we omit to rescue the drowning swimmer in the pond while passing by, we fail to prevent harm from happening. If the swimmer dies, her death can be attributed to us in a morally relevant way because we could have intervened in the causal strings of events that led to the swimmer drowning, and we could have avoided by way of our actions the result that was to be expected. We did not initiate the causal chain that eventuated in the swimmer facing a serious risk of death. We did not put the swimmer in the pond. However, we can exert causal power not only by initiating causal chains but also by way of interfering, or not, with causal chains that are already taking course. In the case of the imperiled swimmer, it is undoubtedly true that my intervention and rescue can have a causal impact in the way in which events unfold. My intervention, once the swimmer is at risk, is the difference between her survival and her death. If I fail to act, my omission is causally relevant in explaining why she died. In that sense, I bear some degree of moral responsibility, which derives from my causal impact on her situation. As already explained in the previous chapter, omissions can be causally relevant, and therefore, also the stuff of moral responsibility.[19]

Unlike the case of the troubled swimmer, my individual failure to cast a considered vote does not cause by itself an electoral result. My individual abstention does not by itself explain the defeat of a certain electoral alternative that would be better from the standpoint of justice than the winning alternative. In other words, my failure to vote with care does not by itself fail to prevent injustice or harm. Rather, only when many citizens together fail to vote with care can we say that they fail to prevent injustice. In the case of voting and elections, we can only prevent injustice when *we act in concert*—no individual voter can prevent injustice *alone*.

But this collective dimension to voting is not problematic. We already know that voting with care has value because it is the act that, *together* with other acts of its kind, produces an outcome that we have reasons to value highly. The logic is the same for omitting to vote. Failing to vote with care is an act that, however negligible in its individual impact, contributes to increasing the risk of a result that can be undesirable from the standpoint of justice. When enough of us fail to vote at all, we are opening the door to a less-than-appealing state of affairs from the point of view of justice. We are opening the door to the probability that a less-than-just government is elected to power because we are failing to counteract any possible bad votes that will support such alternative. Thus, when the individual fails to vote, her omission—however small amid many others—contributes to allowing injustice.

Even though we cannot be held morally responsible for the totality of an electoral result as individual citizens since our impact on elections is infinitesimally small—either when we vote or when we abstain—we can still bear some moral responsibility for contributing to the emergence of an electoral result. We can call this approach to moral responsibility "contributory" in that it does not require that the individual's action be the main causal force in forging a result.[20] In simpler words, the "contributory" approach to responsibility does not require that the individual brings about an outcome by himself—without the help of others—to be the object of blame or moral praise. However, it does not let the individual off the hook for her minimal causal contribution to that state of affairs. On the contributory view of moral responsibility, we do not assume that for the individual to bear any moral responsibility at all, she should be able to make a clear and discernible difference on the world by way of her single action.[21] Instead, we only require that she contributes to a certain state of affairs to be the proper object of blame or praise. The moral nature of her individual contribution, as I clarified in chapter 3, is contingent on the moral nature of the larger activity to which the contribution adds, however modestly. If the larger activity is morally reprehensible, the individual contribution must be thought of in the same light.

So if we contribute to a genocidal master plan, to take an example already used in previous chapters, by donating a small amount of money to the cause, we are to blame for our contribution however ineffectual our donation will be in the grand scheme of genocidal things. This is so because genocide is immoral and we have as a matter of fact added to it. By the same token, if the larger activity is morally praiseworthy—say when enough people are trying to elect a justice-minded government by participating in elections—then our small contribution to the larger activity will inherit that moral positive quality, regardless of the fact that we cannot bring about justice by virtue of our own efforts only. Thus, either when we act or when we fail to act, despite the causal role of the individual being small, moral responsibility does not disappear from the normative picture simply because the person did not cause a result *by herself.* The fact that she causally contributed to that result morally matters.

But the contributory view of moral responsibility can be challenged in the specific case of elections. Since a high number of votes will end up being redundant—in the sense that they will have surpassed the threshold of votes needed to get a majority and win the election—it is not true that they will contribute *causally* to an electoral result. These votes are causally neutral or even superfluous, one could say. They don't add to a result, however minimally, because the result will have emerged *without* them.[22] It must be said that it is practically difficult to know whether one's vote will be, or was, part of the set of redundant votes in a given election since all votes get counted anonymously and are cast almost simultaneously. However, the moral issue seems to remain unaffected. If many votes did not causally contribute to the electoral result, however infinitesimally, then it would follow that the voters that cast them will not bear moral responsibility for the outcome of the election. In the same way, if a high number of people abstained from voting, but only a set of those abstentions enabled the victory of the alternative that is worse for society, not all the abstainers can be said to have causally contributed to that result; therefore, not all of them will bear moral responsibility for it.

On further inspection, however, the foregoing logic fails. Redundant votes and redundant abstentions are still the source of moral responsibility because of what I call the issue of "moral indistinctiveness" when *taking part* in a collective action or a mass abstention. In order to understand this idea better, let us focus on an illustrative, albeit macabre example.

Imagine five men torturing a prisoner. Each of the five torturers takes turns consecutively until all of the torturers have participated. When torturer 2 is doing his part, the victim loses consciousness. He dies, but the torturers believe he just fainted and continue with the abuse until torturer 5 is done. Can we say, on pain of ignoring a great evil, that torturers 3, 4, and 5 are free of moral responsibility in this situation? They may be free of *causal* responsibility, strictly speaking, because their actions were not necessary to cause the prisoner to die of pain. But can we say that the men are also free of moral blame? It seems hard to.

This conclusion, then, appears to reject the idea that causal agency, of any degree, is a sine qua non condition for moral responsibility. And if it is the case that causal agency is not always necessary for moral responsibility, we are, then, in the province of the first meaning of responsibility explained above with the example of Peter, the father who happens not to harm his children despite his negligence. That example highlighted the possibility that the individual defaults on a moral duty, but that his defaulting does not cause a prudentially undesirable state of affairs. In this type of case, I pointed out before, the moral failing on the part of Peter seems to be that he neglected to care for his children, putting them at high risk, even if no harm materialized eventually simply because of sheer good luck. Peter was oblivious to a type of behavior that is required by his role as a parent; he ignored a basic duty of care toward his children. In the same vein, we could say, torturers 3, 4, and 5 neglected a basic moral duty to respect human dignity that all people are bound by, even though their neglecting actions in particular did not end up causing the horrible death of the victim. The torturers did not have any causal impact, however shared, on the result, but their actions surely denote a certain (morally despicable) disposition of character. Not passing any type of moral judgment on the men strikes me as implausible.

As in the case of the second Peter, the negligent but lucky parent, moral blame is not paired with causal responsibility in the case of torturers 3, 4, and 5—but it is nevertheless the product of the individuals *choosing* to act in contradiction with a moral duty. This sense of moral responsibility allows us to attribute moral failure to a person evincing a certain character trait or disposition (as evident through her actions) that is morally reprehensible *in itself*. That is to say that this feature of character is worthy of criticism independently of what the person that possesses it manages to bring about onto others. He may occasion injustice, or that result may ultimately not unfold for reasons unrelated to his behavior but to the workings of fortune.

In the case of failing to vote with care by not voting at all, the individual reflects a specific attitude that is at odds with the spirit of the Samaritan duty of justice to aid society.[23] The abstaining behavior evinces cold indifference to the fate of her fellow citizens, which we could think as ailing if governed unjustly or at the risk of such evil depending on the electoral result to come. What type of person denies help when doing so would not detract from his individual goals?

It must be said now that citizens may fail to vote with care due to different reasons, not all of which may evoke the same degree of blame. Some of those reasons may not elicit any blame at all. This is so because failure to act as a decent Samaritan by voting with care may not always denote cold indifference to the needs of others. We can understand this idea better by reflecting on a duty to aid in general. One reason why a person well situated to help may fail to do so could be that he is not aware that help is needed. For example, someone driving on the way to work may be lost in his own thoughts and fail to notice the person in need of aid by the side of the road. In this case, the driver fails to discharge a duty of aid, but this failure is not culpable in the sense that the person does not (fail to) act out of indifference. In the case of voting, we could imagine cases in which citizens omit to vote because they are not aware that elections are plausible vehicles of justice for society. In other words, some non-voters may not be aware of how morally and practically significant elections, and therefore voting, are. In this type of cases, we are faced with failures to discharge a duty but no conscious knowledge that one is doing so.

However, it is plausible to think of cases involving unawareness as entailing some degree of negligence. Even though we cannot blame the person for singlehandedly choosing to ignore the plight of those he could help—since the person did not choose to ignore anybody, he simply did not realize help was needed—we can still wonder whether he *should have known*. The answer to that question, in turn, will vary depending on what we think is a blameworthy cause of negligence or unwitting lack of care.

For example, if the driver was texting on his cellular phone and that prevented him from noticing the ailing pedestrian on the side of the road, then we may have a reason to attribute moral blame to him for not stopping to help. It's true that he may have stopped if he had seen the pedestrian—so we have no basis to think of him as coldly indifferent—but he was nevertheless doing something *wrong* that prevented him from becoming aware that help was needed. The degree of moral blame for the act that thwarted his awareness is surely lower than the moral blame we would attach to him if he had shown that he is impermeable to the suffering of others—but it is blame nevertheless.

Imagine another example: A construction worker fails to notice that someone is passing by the construction site because he does not look before he moves a big piece of machinery, and ends up hurting the passerby. He surely did not intend to hurt anyone, but his lack of proper care—we assume it is reasonable to expect him to have looked around before moving—is certainly culpable and deserving of reprobation.[24] He should have known that it was necessary to look around in order to check for pedestrians before moving the machinery. This is a cognitive standard that it is reasonable to expect him to be able to meet if he is a construction worker. The fact that he did not meet the standard makes him blameworthy despite not having any ill intention to harm.

In a different version of the example, the construction worker turns around to look, sees nobody in harm's way, and proceeds to move, but, all of a sudden, a running pedestrian comes out of nowhere and manages to get hit by the careful worker. Assume that it was impossible to foresee the abrupt appearance of the rapidly moving pedestrian. Or, in the case of the driver on his way to work, imagine that he failed to spot the accident victim because a big abandoned truck laid right in front of her, rendering visibility of the ailing person impossible. In these last two cases, neither the construction worker nor the driver did anything wrong that prevented them from becoming aware that someone needed help.

The cases of the driver and the construction worker in their two variants illustrate that a failure to discharge a duty may be due to several reasons, not all of them equally culpable, and some not culpable at all. In the case of failing to vote with care, we can also resort to these categories of moral responsibility, at least theoretically. For example, the citizen that fails to vote because he simply cannot be bothered, even though he knows that elections have a significant impact on the nature of governance, illustrates the case of the coldly indifferent driver who cannot lose a minute to stop and help someone he sees and recognizes to be in trouble. This reaction should trigger the highest order of moral condemnation. It is plain disregard for others when doing something would not be costly.

A citizen can also fail to vote because, as suggested already, she is not aware of how much there is at stake during large elections. This citizen is a kind of "meta-uninformed" citizen. She probably does not know much about politics because she does not know that elections matter. In order to assess moral responsibility here, we have to look into the causes of her unawareness. Did she not have civics classes in school? Does she live in poverty and is it hard for her to take time to think about politics? Or has she been advantaged enough to be surrounded by many sources of reliable information, which she chooses to ignore? I am not sure we can have answers to all these questions in specific cases, but my aim here is to pose the theoretical question about moral responsibility during elections, not to assess every citizen's particular reasons for discharging or not discharging her civic duty. It is theoretically possible that many citizens fail to vote with care because they are not entirely familiar with the idea that the outcome of elections generally matters.

Another conceivable reason for failing to vote at all is the intention not to contribute to harm if one is not prepared to make an acceptably informed choice at the ballot box. As we already know very well, opponents of the duty to vote like Jason Brennan argue that it is indeed a duty not to vote in circumstances of ignorance or ineptitude. This position is highly intuitive. We may believe that when citizens are ill equipped to cast an informed and pro-social ballot, their paramount duty is to *not* vote rather than vote. If the individual cares for society, he ought to choose not to contribute to the harm of bad governance that is likely to occur when undesirable leaders and coalitions are elected as a product of misguided votes.

I wholeheartedly accept the possibility that many people are ill equipped to fulfill the duty to vote with care while at the same time being able to discharge the duty to refrain from voting badly. It certainly is easier not to do anything at all than it is to prepare oneself to cast a sufficiently informed vote. However, recognizing this empirical fact is not a problem for my position as I have defended it here. It is common to find instances in which individuals fall short of complying with well-justified ethical requirements. However, that failing does not overshadow the normative justifiability of those requirements.

For example, we normally accept the justifiability of a duty to keep our promises even though we know that, as a matter of fact, the world is full of people who consistently break their promises for no valid moral reason. Cases of promises broken for valid reasons are also common but pose no interesting counterexample: my views here do not deny the possibility that the duty to vote with care takes the back seat to other moral considerations of a more urgent nature in particular cases (i.e., a duty to care for the sick on election day, a duty to disassociate oneself from a patently abusive political system, a duty to uphold one's spiritual beliefs if they require that we withdraw from public life, etc.). I would say that the conscientious citizen that refrains from voting badly because she's unprepared to vote with care is still failing in a moral sense if his lack of preparation is due to no morally valid reason. This point brings us back to the possibility that there is a spectrum of moral blame behind a decision not to vote with care. Let me illustrate.

Imagine that the driver in the example above is inebriated. He spots the needy pedestrian on the side of the road but nevertheless makes the conscientious decision not to stop because he fears he will lose control of the car, his reflexes are weak, and he could run over the ailing person. One could think that this person is a responsible drunk driver that deserves much praise. But his behavior overall is not admirable because he should not have been driving under the influence of alcohol in the first place. The abstainer who rightly justifies his decision not to vote on his lack of competence deserves prima facie praise for being so mindful about the fate of his fellow citizens. However, on further inspection, that praise may turn out to be underserved if the reason for his incompetence is unjustified. Just as the conscientious driver's blame derives from his earlier decision to drink and drive, which, we assume, he could have avoided at no high cost to himself, the voter's unpreparedness is blameworthy in an important respect if it is caused by a lack of effort that he could have made at no high cost to himself.

We can think, however, of cases in which the ignorance resulting from that lack of effort is not blameworthy, or not equally blameworthy—i.e., if social disadvantage, for example, makes that effort too exacting. But ignorance and misinformation may be considered blameworthy even though the individual may have no control over the situation that causes them. For example, the citizen may be to blame for the situation that causes him to be unprepared to cast a considered ballot if he consistently neglected becoming informed in previous election cycles and the amount of information needed in this one seems overwhelming.

If a citizen has—with some degree of negligence—put herself in a position to be uninformed, that breach of judgment must bear on her obligation to vote. Avoidable negligence does not erase blame in the same way that circumstances beyond our control may. Lack of interest or simple indifference toward the fate of others—and society—that is not rooted in deeper causes related to disadvantage or inability to access truthful information evinces a character flaw that is morally reproachable—and makes the failure to fulfill the duty to vote with care all the more suspicious. As advanced before, the citizen that is unable to cast a careful vote due to his previous negligence in obtaining information about the election ought to refrain from voting randomly or irresponsibly. But this measure of caution is not laudable in the same way as we will not see the actions of the drunken driver who fails to stop to aid the troubled pedestrian as laudable—since the right thing to do would have been not to get inebriated. Damage control is not a source of moral praise if it turns out that the damage being controlled is of your *own* (avoidable) making.

Voter negligence, then, affects the moral duty to vote in a particular way: it interrupts its discharge for reasons of "major force" (a consideration informed by the higher duty to avoid harm to others) but it creates a second obligation to reverse the conditions of ignorance that forced that interruption. In simpler words, negligent, ignorant voters have a duty to become informed—they are not morally off the hook simply because they are ignorant. When it comes to what constitutes morally good behavior during elections, the citizen's moral failure would be obvious were she to commit the imprudence—and injustice—of casting an uninformed ballot. Refraining from doing this is a weighty duty—as Jason Brennan rightly argues. But we should not see the citizen's failure to vote simpliciter as a permissible consequence of a moral freedom (although we could see it as a permissible consequence of a *legal* freedom not to vote). If the unpreparedness behind the abstention is blameworthy, we should see the citizen's abstention as a culpable omission—even if her intention now is noble because she wants to minimize societal harm by staying out of the voting booth. The latter goal is morally good but it should not overshadow the earlier wrong of failing to add to the collective effort of helping society at a reasonable cost. One morally (and practically) good decision does not erase a prior wrong.

Now, we must emphasize how structural injustice assuages, or even erases, the moral blame for not voting. In the same way as we cannot expect a person to act as a Good Samaritan if the assistance needed would be unduly costly, or impossible, to provide, we cannot blame a non-voter that fails to vote because of reasons not related to a deficiency in moral character such as indifference or laziness. Structural poverty, which leads to lack of resources and information, lack of opportunity caused by discrimination, and vulnerability to laws that seek to suppress voting rights for some (albeit disguised as formally general) make voting more burdensome for citizens affected by these evils. Any convincing account of a moral duty to vote that seeks to be comprehensive enough cannot ignore these differences on pain of unrealistic simplification.

The foregoing conclusion speaks to a more general fact, namely, that moral responsibility for our behavior can be mitigated by circumstances (or states of mind) that render our control of life more feeble than it otherwise would be. Within the realm of the humanly possible, one can say that one's moral responsibility for things that happen to us is stronger the more control that we have over how our life develops. Nobody has total control of what happens to her, but my point is that some unchosen obstacles in life certainly render a person's capacity to "escape fate" more difficult. This is not the time to engage in a deep philosophical discussion of what constitutes true voluntary action, but it bears mentioning that, consistent with prevailing philosophical understandings of moral responsibility, my approach to the morality of voting takes seriously the multiple reasons that can render moral responsibility mute or weak (or strong, for that matter). In this sense, it would not be far-fetched to point out that socioeconomic background and educational level may act as mitigating or reinforcing factors of moral responsibility for our voting behavior because they may explain why, and if, our lack of information and political interest is solely due to our failure to care or to other impediments beyond our full control.

Relatedly, the fact that the individual moral responsibility of the non-voter may be affected by pervasive societal disadvantage grounds a duty on all non-disadvantaged members of society to contribute to the eradication of that disadvantage, to the extent that doing so will not relevantly harm others, and to the extent that a condition of relative privilege makes that contribution non-costly and effective (at least collectively). This duty to contribute to the eradication of disadvantage stems from the original duty of justice to help society via the vote. Let me explain.

Besides voting with care ourselves, we also rely on the judicious vote of others for good governance, or the minimization of bad governance, to occur. As explained at length in previous chapters and this one, voting is a collective endeavor. Because this is so, it follows that the duty to participate in the joint pursuit of justice must also entail doing what we can—if no high costs are involved—in enabling would-be voters to become (careful) voters. The more of those we can rely on, the more confident we can be that the collective activity of Samaritan aid that is performed though elections is actually fruitful.

What activities in particular are included in the duty to contribute to the eradication of disadvantage? The list is too long to describe here, which also explains why this duty does *not* prescribe a fixed number of concrete measures. However, it does, in the manner of an imperfect duty à la Kant, "suggest" a menu of options that the (relatively) privileged citizen is free to choose among. Examples include forms of political protest as well as personal contributions to educating others on important issues at stake in the election, among others.

Lastly, when thinking about moral responsibility and voting, one should bear in mind the possibility of the voter who votes with care, yet ends up contributing to the victory of what turns out to be a bad candidate and an unfair government. Officeholders oftentimes turn their backs on their electoral promises. Many of these cases are not easy to spot before the candidate in question becomes a public official, after winning. In cases of this sort, it seems only fair to adjudicate no blame on the voter, who, at the time of voting and collecting information, fulfilled the conditions for non-negligent action and met the cognitive standard expected from a good-enough voter.

But could the voter be held responsible for her casual contribution, however tiny, to a bad result? Strictly speaking, yes, but this case shows, again, that moral responsibility and causal responsibility part ways sometimes. An essential source of moral assessment of actions and attitudes is a person's intention and a person's reasonably careful (non-negligent) behavior. If the voter did not mean to contribute to injustice by voting, nor did she cast an uninformed ballot, the voter must be free of blame in the same way as the driver who did not spot the ailing victim due to a truck blocking his vision must be. The latter did not evince a morally inapt attitude such as indifference, nor did he act negligently while driving. Sometimes luck has an ironic way of influencing states of the world.

The possibility of the "chameleon candidate"—i.e., the candidate that reneges on her promises—shows that voting with care is not the only mechanism to protect society against injustice and bad governance. As I emphasized in the introduction to this book, I make no pretense of thinking that voting with care is a panacea.

However, voting is a necessary, yet non-sufficient, condition for good governance in the sense that it allows members of society to evict governments that have betrayed their trust as well as to elect those that might work for the common good because they are responsive to the people's needs.[25]

5

Self-Standing Arguments against a Duty to Vote and Why They Fail

This chapter will list the most effective arguments rejecting the idea that voting is an ethical duty under normal circumstances.[1] My responses to the arguments in question do not necessarily speak to my own case for the duty to vote, which I developed in more detail in other chapters already. Most of the responses that I provide in this chapter can stand on their own even if my particular thesis for a duty to vote ends up failing according to the judgment of the reader. I enlist these self-standing responses in a separate chapter because I want to show the reader that some of the most ubiquitous arguments *contra* the duty to vote are not solid enough, regardless of whether a successful argument *pro* the duty is ultimately plausible. One can show that argument X is not sufficient to disprove thesis Y, without that entailing that thesis Y is ipso facto true. Although I hope to have established that there is a moral duty to vote, I do not need to rely on that claim in order to show that many arguments against the duty fail to conclusively show that the duty *does not exist*.

In particular, this chapter offers detailed responses to two of the most powerful criticisms against a duty to vote. These two objections are what I call the "irrationality argument" and the "perfectionist argument." The irrationality argument should sound familiar to us already but I will tackle it in more depth here. It says that voting is irrational because it is ineffectual from the perspective of the individual, therefore, not morally required. The reasoning is that since the individual's vote will likely make no difference to the election's outcome, it makes no sense to think about the act of voting as a moral duty.[2] What type of duty is a duty that requires us to do something that will change nothing? The irrationality argument assumes that a necessary condition for rational action is the individual's capacity to make a non-negligible difference to a state of affairs when acting. Relatedly, it also implicitly assumes that duties can really only be morally binding if the individual that discharges them has the capacity to make a noticeable difference to a state of affairs *through her single action*.

The perfectionist argument, in turn, has it that viewing voting as a moral duty infringes on the freedom not to vote that citizens have in liberal democracies. This critique suggests that conceiving of voting as a moral duty entails a morally perfectionist view, that is, the oppressive idea that voting is surely a path to the morally "good life." Equating political participation with "the good life" has a strong pedigree in the civic republican tradition that we can trace back to Aristotle. One can see why anyone that places a high value on the ability to live life as she wishes would find a perfectionist account of the good menacing to freedom. The notion that voting is an example of a life well lived may strike some as an affront to the individual's capacity to decide for herself what makes a life good. The perfectionist position, the objection goes, imposes on the individual a rather narrow idea of moral character. It is based on the notion that the political life is superior to other pursuits, and so it does not leave much room for valuing personal virtues other than the ones needed to make for an "excellent" citizen.

In the pages that follow, I will refute the irrationality argument and the perfectionist argument against the duty to vote. I will show that the first critique, which is based on rational choice-inspired views on voting, is not correct in its predictions of irrationality. Voting can be perfectly rational. Because it can be, we could conceivably think of it as a nontrivial moral duty. Second, I will show that the moral duty to vote does not impinge on individual freedom in a way that morally matters. On the contrary, it can enhance freedom understood as something else than non-interference. The duty to vote does not have to be justified on a perfectionist view of morality that exalts the political life. Rather, it can be justified for very different reasons, not premised on the moral superiority of political participation over other human activities and goals.

5.1. Voting Is Irrational Because It Is Ineffectual

In his celebrated 1816 essay "The Liberty of the Ancients Compared to That of the Moderns," Benjamin Constant adumbrated the logic that many would use much later to criticize the act of voting as individually irrational. He said:

> The size of a country causes a corresponding decrease of the political importance allotted to each individual. The most obscure Republican of Sparta or Rome had power. The same is not true of the simple citizen of Britain or of the United States. His personal influence is an imperceptible part of the social will which impresses on the government its direction.[3]

Political scientists and voter behavior experts in particular have been preoccupied with finding a solution to the so-called "paradox of voting" for decades.[4] The literature has produced many persuasive explanations of why people may choose to vote despite the vanishingly small probability that their single vote will have an impact on the outcome of the election. Some of these solutions include the idea that people vote for expressive reasons (i.e., the same reasons that drive them to cheer for their sports team at a game);[5] to feel good about themselves as citizens (i.e., after carrying out the most basic act of citizenship one is supposed to feel satisfied with one's moral character);[6] and to avoid regretting the fact that one didn't vote (after learning that if one had done so, one could have swung the election in favor of one's preferred candidate).[7] These reasons all embrace what the literature dubs "consumption benefits" from voting. Consumption benefits are the opposite of "investment benefits." The investment benefits of voting are those linked to the outcome of elections. They are given by the difference in utility that the individual attaches to having her preferred candidate win over her non-preferred candidate. According to the classical rational choice model of voting, this benefit utterly hinges on the voter's ability to cast the decisive vote, that is, on her power to swing the election. Because this probability is close to zero in big elections, the expected investment benefits of voting are infinitesimally small as well.[8]

Consumption benefits, by contrast, are produced by the satisfaction that comes with performing the act of voting, but they are *not* contingent on the results of the election. The voter feels satisfied regardless of what the election brings, maybe out of a sense of having discharged an important civic duty, or out of a sense of having expressed one's moral and political positions in an election. The vast voter psychology literature today offers many arguments to grapple with the supposed irrationality of voting, and the detailed description of those arguments would call for an altogether different book.[9] What is important to take away from those arguments is that they all tend to highlight *non-instrumental* reasons for voting. That is to say, those arguments suggest that the voter is motivated to vote by consumption benefits, or "feel-good reasons"—not the result of the election.[10]

Although none of the foregoing accounts seek to answer the question of whether there is a moral duty to vote—since they are focused on explaining behavior not philosophy—it is easy to see how someone could avail himself of them to reject the idea that voting is a question of moral duty. In fact, authors sympathetic to the notion that voting is *not* a duty of any kind, just a freedom, have argued that the fact that voting does not make any instrumental sense from a personal point of view makes voting a nonstarter candidate for a moral duty. The reasoning is simple: if our vote can't make a difference, then it shouldn't be ethically mandated, or even recommended. If our actions do not have any visible consequences for us, or others, why should morality care at all? In this section, I will reject this conclusion. I will show that it is philosophically plausible to defend a duty to vote on grounds of the instrumentality of voting. One's vote matters even it does not matter in a *decisive* way by being able to determine the result of an election on its own. In other words, voting may not be futile even if it is not beneficial from a strictly individual viewpoint because a single vote will not swing an election. Let me explain in more detail.

The paradox of voting is indeed a paradox only if we hold on to a self-centric definition of rationality, whereby the benefits of voting are understood to be personal gains, strictly. As Anthony Downs explained in his seminal book *An Economic Theory of Democracy*, when the costs of voting are high and the individual benefits are almost nonexistent, rationality predicts abstention. But what about the possibility of voting to benefit others? Rationality may well entail caring for the well-being of third parties, not just our own. A poor mother is rational when she underfeeds herself to feed her starving child. An individual is not irrational when he donates money for facing the costs of his good friend's cancer treatment. There is nothing irrational about employing a means-end logic to further the well-being of those we care about or consider important. Rationality is not necessarily or only self-centered. Even though voting is a futile instrument for pursuing our self-interest narrowly understood, it may be an effective way of improving the well-being of others and the community's. The altruistic theory of voting suggests just this.[11] Let me explain.

When people vote altruistically—the theory of altruistic voting tells us—they act in the same way as someone who is buying a lottery ticket.[12] They know that the chance of their particular ticket being the winner ticket is vanishingly small, but they also know that if they happen to buy the winning ticket, the winnings will be formidable. Buying the ticket, despite the low chances of winning, is a cost-effective act because the results of that chance becoming a reality are very desirable. One cannot forgo the opportunity, however unlikely, given that the costs involved are small enough and the results may be incredibly good. Of course, when we buy a lottery ticket for ourselves we are acting with a self-centered sense of rationality in mind. But altruistic voters are not self-centered, at least not completely, although they are rational in a means-end sense of the term because they act with a particular end in mind

As Andrew Gelman et al. propose, altruistic voters act as if they were buying lottery tickets not only for themselves, but for many others.[13] They act as if they were buying a lottery ticket that—if a winner—will clearly benefit society. Voting, on this "altruistic account," is a form of charity. If acting rationally is understood as acting consistently with an objective we desire to attain, there is nothing irrational about acting so as to benefit others.[14] Rational objectives can be others-centered objectives.

Innovative accounts of altruistic voting sustain that others-regarding reasons can make casting a ballot perfectly rational—thereby contradicting the classical rational choice literature that which sees rationality only through the prisms of self-interest. These (relatively) recent accounts of benevolent voting sustain that voting is not irrational if the voter's goal is to promote the well-being of others. Since much is at stake in elections, generally, the tiny act of casting a ballot in an informed way can still have a beneficial impact for the common good. It is rational to vote, then, in that the individual perceives the impact of her vote to be potentially large enough (for others) that the utility or value of voting is well justified.

In actuality, the altruistic theory of voting tells us that the voter's objective when voting is mixed—it is *not* entirely altruistic. We can see this by taking a look at the mathematical formula that describes the shape of the voter's utility function under this theory. The utility function under the altruistic theory of voting is $Uv = p \, (Bs+\delta NBo) > C$, where p is the probability of one's vote being pivotal in the election (tilting it), Bs is the *personal* benefit that the individual derives from her vote, Bo is the benefit to *others* (society) from the vote, N is the number of voters that cast a ballot in the election, and δ is the "altruism variable" (it represents how much the particular voter cares to benefit others).[15]

The main feature that differentiates altruistic accounts of voting from classical, rational choice-based accounts of voting is the idea that the citizen cares about the benefits that accrue to others from the preferred electoral outcome. Under this assumption, B is a function of two types of different benefits, which are unequally weighted in the utility equation. These are benefits to oneself *and* benefits to others. We can understand "others" as the remaining population in general, or a majority thereof, who is affected by the result of the election and who the voter thinks will gain more than lose with the voter's preferred result. These altruistic assumptions, thus, transform the classical rational choice calculus of voting.

In the classical, rational choice-based voter utility function, there is no room for a benefit-to-others variable. This means that said function does not contemplate anything other than pure self-interest when voting. Since strictly individual benefits will be negative because the probability of our vote swinging the election is so low, and the costs of voting will be higher than said probability, the conclusion we draw based on the classical voter utility function is that it makes no sense to vote. By contrast, the altruistic dimension of the new utility equation indicates the psychological possibility—which is quite human—that people behave beneficently toward others and willingly undertake costs that will enable others to gain, if said costs are not terribly high.

It is important to remark that the new, altruistic voter utility function does not make of moral sainthood a central quality. When we talk about altruistic acts in discussions about voting, the costs borne by the beneficent individuals do not have to be unduly burdensome. In fact, the costs of voting, even informed voting, cannot be said to belong to the category of saintly acts. Altruistic behaviors like the one predicted by the altruistic theory of voting are cost-effective. When an act is cost-effective, it means that the end result may well justify the costs. Proponents of the new altruistic account of voting claim that their way of determining the utility that derives from casting a ballot is more in tune with actual voter psychology than the classical, rational choice view of voting because people will generally realize that the potential benefit of voting to help others far outweighs the cost of participating in elections. In other words, purely individualistic motivations may not reflect the entire complexity of human rationality when it comes to the act of voting. People do indeed vote with the welfare of others in mind.[16] Altruistic voting is a testament to the possibility that people vote with the goal of making an impact, not *despite* the fact that their efforts won't. Thus, on the altruistic account of voting, casting a ballot is still rational because it is instrumental. This means that, through the lens of altruistic voting theories, voting is an investment benefit—not a consumption benefit like traditional expressive and civic satisfaction theories of voting have proposed.

Opponents of the duty to vote have not acknowledged the force of the altruistic accounts of voting just described. Despite this curious omission, paradigmatic opponents of the duty to vote do address the question of whether voting would become rational if something important was at stake in the election—presumably for society, not just the voter.[17] They address this question when referring to the work of Derek Parfit and Brian Barry on voting. Let me elaborate further.

The question of voter rationality aimed at helping others was raised in the literature decades ago by Brian Barry and Derek Parfit, separately. Barry and Parfit use logic very similar to that used by later proponents of altruistic voting, and they conclude that, when the stakes in an election are sufficiently high, the cost of voting may be rationally compensated for by the potential benefit of our vote contributing to a desirable result. Parfit offers the following analogy to illustrate:

> It may be objected that it is irrational to consider very tiny chances. When our acts cannot affect more than a few people, this may be so. But this is because the stakes are here comparatively low. Consider the risks of causing accidental death. It may be irrational to give any thought to a one-in-a million chance of killing one person. But if I was a nuclear engineer, would I be irrational to give any thought to the same chance of killing a million people? This is what most of us believe . . . when the stakes are very high no chance, however small, should be ignored."[18]

Brian Barry, in turn, refers to voting as a *socially utilitarian* act. He explains that "If an act-utilitarian really gives full weight to the consequences for everyone that he expects will be affected, this will normally provide an adequate reason for voting. If I think that one party will increase the GNP by 0.25 percent over five years more than the other party, that for the utilitarian is a big aggregate difference. Are they *really* significantly more beneficial things one could do with fifteen minutes?[19]

Opponents of the duty to vote readily dismiss Parfit's and Barry's arguments. Jason Brennan does so by alluding to the all-too-classical view that, no matter how generous the voter is feeling, his single vote won't make a shred of a difference to the final outcome of an election. Brennan does not think that it is rational to vote for the sake of bettering the well-being of others, for the same exact reasons that he believes that voting to further our self-interest is irrational. Our vote can't make a difference to the result of the election and it is therefore also futile as a form of collective beneficence. He notes that "the point is that in any large-scale election, an individual vote does little expected good or bad in terms of its propensity to affect electoral outcomes. Even when the right outcome is worth a huge amount, individual votes for that outcome are worth close to nothing." Brennan adds that, in an election, "how we vote matters but how any one of us votes does not."[20]

It is true that the decisive power of one vote does not change simply because the voter has society's benefit in mind, but it is not so clear that such fact alone is sufficient to dismiss the moral force of a supposed duty to vote. We may be bound by a duty to contribute, however infinitesimally, to the realization of a collective goal (such as winning an election or not losing it by more than a certain margin, for example). This argument entails accepting that, even if the impact of our single vote is extremely low, it is greater than zero. Our vote may contribute to the emergence of a result even if it is not the vote that, in particular, breaks a tie and secures the election. In other words, being impactful does not mean being *decisive*. There are degrees of impactfulness, however infinitesimal. Simply because a contribution is small, even infinitesimally small, doesn't mean it is inexistent. And if it is not inexistent, it is not morally innocuous. And if it is not morally innocuous, then it is not irrational. I elaborate on this idea in the next section.

5.2. Non-pivotal Instrumentality

The foregoing account of rationality—which centers on instrumentality but not on pivotality (i.e., the capacity to tilt an election with one's vote) partly evokes Richard Tuck's arguments in his book *Free Riding*, which has made waves in the field of rational choice theory and voting studies in particular (Tuck does not concern himself with the duty to vote, only with the rationality of voting, that is why I say "partly").[21] Tuck argues that voting can be rational based on instrumentalist reasons, even if we openly acknowledge that the voter's impact is vanishingly small in the election at large. His book offers one of the most innovative retorts to classical, rational choice theory and its emphasis on decisiveness or the capacity to tilt the election with a vote. In order to understand what his thesis says, it may help to remember the ground zero assumption in the rational choice theory, namely, the idea that voting in large elections is irrational because the vote will get lost in a sea of votes, making no impact in the final result of the election. This means that the individual costs of voting will override the individual utility of voting, which is primordially determined by the probability that our vote is decisive. Tuck's book challenges that very same idea. He proposes that voting is *not* irrational if the voter intends to form part of a set of causally efficacious votes, which can, in theory, be responsible for determining the election as a group of votes. The causally efficacious set is composed of the votes that are causally necessary, strictly, to win the election.[22] The following is an apt explanation of Tuck's main argument by Brennan:

> Suppose that 10,000 people vote for A and 3,999 people vote for B. If so, 4,000 votes for A were necessary for A's victory; the other 6,000 were superfluous. The causally efficacious set of votes totals 4,000—these are the votes that won the election. The probability that a random voter's vote formed part of the causally efficacious vote is 40%.[23]

Tuck wants to argue that it is rational to vote because the voter may intend to be part of the set of causally efficacious votes, which is not the same as intending her single vote to determine the election. The voter's sense of instrumentality, thus, does not vanish, although it takes a different target. One objection to Tuck's line of thinking is that the individual's vote is not strictly needed because any one vote can form part of the set of votes that will help win the election. In other words, any person's vote could easily be replaced by the vote of any other citizen. If my vote can be replaced by any other person's vote to form part of the set of efficacious votes, then how is it rational to vote? I may as well stay home watching a good movie; somebody else will fill in for me surely. This discussion points to the phenomenon of "overdetermined causation." An example will illustrate what this term means.

If five people are needed to lift a car that is out of order and move it to the side of the road, and six do it, logic suggests that none of those six helpers was strictly necessary for moving the car because if any one of them had refused to help, the remaining five could have carried out the collective task without a problem. But this analysis of causation is not without controversy. To understand why, imagine the following situation described by Alvin Goldman.[24] Consider a firing squad with 10 members who all fire simultaneously at a victim and all hit the mark. The victim dies. Is it not bizarre to declare that none of the individual actions of the shooters had any influence on the outcome? Moral responsibility for the death of the victim is arguably contingent on the causal role of the shooters' actions. But if we conclude that none of the shooters can be seen as causally responsible, then we must also conclude that none of them can bear any moral responsibility whatsoever for the executed person's death. Yet the person is dead because he *was killed*.

The model of moral responsibility that undergirds the preceding counterintuitive conclusion requires that someone's role be absolutely necessary for a certain result to obtain. To attach moral responsibility for an outcome, the model requires evidence that, had the person acted differently, the same result would have *not* obtained. We can call this logic *counterfactual*.[25] It seems misguided precisely because it can absolve everyone who played a role in a particular event. When transferred to elections, this counterfactual model of moral responsibility suggests that the individual act of voting is morally relevant *only* when the citizen can determine the election because, absent her vote, the result would indeed have been different (a defeat or a tie).

But this notion of moral responsibility may not be the most appropriate to understand elections and other phenomena more generally. After all, all but a few elections are chosen by a margin of more than one vote. The counterfactual model implies that absolutely nobody's vote is a cause of the election's outcome because no particular individual vote is strictly necessary to determine the outcome of the election, "but surely some of the votes –at least those cast for the actual winner—exercised *some* causal influence toward the outcome."[26]

Tuck's argument suggests that decisiveness (i.e., the capacity to tilt an election with a single vote) is not the only type of causal influence that a person can have as a voter. I second this view and add that the moral value of voting is not therefore circumscribed to the power to swing or tie an election. By contrast, the classical rational choice theory proposes that absent the capacity to determine an election, there is no value in voting. This reasoning reflects a very narrow view of causal and moral responsibility altogether. Traditional rational choice theory considers the individual act of voting irrational because that theory relies on a particular view of causality, which only emphasizes the power to be decisive, that is, the power to tilt the election in which one is voting. However, that view of causality is not the only one available to assess rationality. One can act rationally even if one's vote is not decisive. One can simply act with a view to *contributing* to the emergence of an outcome even if it is true that one's contribution could be replaced with the contribution of someone else.

Brennan admits that Tuck is not concerned with the more philosophical issue of whether voting is a duty; but he adumbrates future efforts to build a case for conceiving of voting as morally obligatory based on Tuck's arguments—and he wants to dispel the possibility that anyone will try. Brennan thinks that no duty can be derived from Tuck's views because Tuck has an incorrect idea of rationality.[27] Here, I want to show the way in which Brennan's objections to Tuck ultimately fail—even if my arguments for voting are not based on Tuck's logic. Tuck does not have the wrong theory of rationality. Once I have shown this, it will become clear why Brennan's view of rationality is overall flawed, which will explain why his claim that voting is instrumentally futile, therefore irrational, fails to fly. Once we understand why Brennan's idea of rationality is defective (for which we need to understand Tuck's arguments), it will be easier to see how my arguments for voting also withstand Brennan's futility objection.

I believe that Tuck's reasoning provides a very ingenious and valid alternative to the classical rational choice perspective on voting, which almost invariably predicts rational abstention and rational ignorance (i.e., the conscious decision not to seek out information to vote responsibly because our single vote will not matter). I will show how Brennan's criticisms of Tuck's theory of rationality do not in fact reflect a flaw in Tuck's reasoning. On the contrary, they reflect Brennan's confusion.

In his book *Free Riding*, Tuck argues that the voter is perfectly rational if she votes because she thinks that her vote can be causally efficacious even if it is not decisive. In other words, showing that votes can be causally efficacious is sufficient to show that voting can be rational. Brennan's objection to this idea can be broken down into two different claims:

1. Tuck's arguments only work under the assumption that the potential voter "desires not merely that a good electoral outcome occurs but also desires that she be causally responsible for the outcome of the election."[28] In other words, Tuck assumes that voters care about being efficacious, but Brennan believes that this is unwarranted. A voter may care about a result but he may not care about contributing to its occurrence.

2. Even assuming that the voter will care about being efficacious in bringing about a given result, it is not clear that it will be rational for her to vote because (*a*) the probability of being part of the set may not be high enough, or may be unknown, and (*b*) voting has opportunity costs attached. This means that it is only rational for an individual to vote if the expected utility of her voting is "higher than the expected utility of other

available actions."[29] And so the expected utility of voting will depend on how likely it is that her vote will be part of the set of causally efficacious votes *and* on how much we value voting vis-à-vis other alternative actions we could be doing *instead* of voting. Brennan illustrates this point with the following example: "suppose that I value being causally efficacious at $50, I value watching the three *Godfather* movies on election day at $41, and the probability my vote will be in the causally efficacious set is less than 80 percent. If so, then, the expected utility of voting is less than the expected utility of watching the movies. If so, then it is not rational to vote, even though I care about being in the causally efficacious set."[30]

Brennan's summarizes his objections to Tuck in the following way: "Tuck can show that it is rational to vote provided 1) one *desires* to be efficacious, *but only* if 2) one has nothing better to do with one's time when one votes."[31] Let me explain why Brennan's reasoning fails in rejecting the efficacious-set logic that Tuck proposes. In so doing, my goal is not to defend a duty to vote primarily based on Tuck's rationale, although doing so would not be analytically misguided. My goal is, rather, to show the flaws in reasoning that detractors of the duty to vote usually evince, which are quite evident in Brennan's rejection of Tuck's views on voter rationality.

Brennan's first critique of Tuck's arguments is that Tuck unwarrantedly assumes that voters *care* about being causally efficacious. Taking this intention for granted reflects a mistaken conception of rational action, the argument is. One can desire a certain result, or state of affairs, but not desire to participate in bringing it about. Brennan's is an intuitive view because it is correct that people may desire things without desiring to act to cause them. For example, I may desire that global warming be reverted but may have no desire to stop driving my ecologically unfriendly Hummer vehicle. Or, I may desire for world poverty to diminish but may not desire to give my money to Oxfam or to any other charity organization.

Brennan thinks that assuming that a desire for a result and a desire to act to produce that result always travel together gets human rationality wrong. I posit that he may be right in a general sense but he's wrong when it comes to voter rationality in particular.

Brennan calls the theory of rationality that he imputes to Tuck "the theory of rationality as effectiveness."[32] He further explains that "Tuck thinks that if Xing is sufficient to produce a desired outcome then it is rational to do X."[33] This understanding flows from Tuck's assertion that "the essence of instrumental action is . . . that we do what is a means to an end, that is, what causes it."[34] On this view of rationality, an action is rational if doing it is one effective way to achieve a goal or desire. But this account seems to leave something out: opportunity costs, Brennan observes. What if the potential voter would rather stay home and watch mafia movies? Means-end effectiveness does not capture the totality of rational action. Tuck is being inattentive to alternative uses of one's time when contemplating one particular course of action. He would do well in adopting a revised theory of rationality, thinks Brennan. This improved understanding should suggest that a rational person will choose the course of action that he believes is the best way of achieving a goal—not *simply* an effective way of doing so. Brennan indeed dubs this new account "instrumental rationality." It "takes into account opportunity costs in decision-making because rational agents do not merely desire to be effective in securing their ends; rather, they want to economize among their goals."[35]

But Tuck's understanding of rationality does not ignore opportunity costs; it only assumes that those costs are acceptably low to make voting a rational course of action. Indeed, some political scientists and experts on voter behavior have argued that the costs of voting are sufficiently low to explain why a lot of people vote, despite rational choice theory's predictions to the contrary. There is the possibility that people simply do not care to make mental calculations involving opportunity costs on election day because the strictly individual benefits of voting are small and so are the costs. The idea is that minding opportunity costs and calculating benefits is a trivial exercise under circumstances like those offered by large elections. Or the costs of voting are so low that the individual voter may take an altruistic perspective and vote as if he was buying a lottery ticket (see the explanation of this new account of voting rationality given previously).

Following Brennan's critiques of Tuck, one could surely say that watching movies or going to vote are two alternative, opposing courses of action on election day. However, under circumstances we can imagine, people can watch movies and still do other things during voting day, especially if those other things are not all time-consuming because they will not require more than a small fraction of our time. What I am suggesting is that, when weighing courses of action against one another to assess the opportunity costs associated with them, one must bear in mind the *right* equivalence. We need to preserve some type of appropriate standard of comparability in the assessment of opportunity costs. If we don't do that, we risk being irrational in assessing the magnitude of those opportunity costs. Let me explain by using some fanciful, yet illustrative, examples.

I may not want to go to work today because the cost of missing an extraterrestrial landing in my terrace is too high. Extraterrestrial landings are not common, and missing one today may mean that I won't be able to witness one ever again in my lifetime. This is costly because the event in itself would be unforgettable and amazing. This (ridiculous) case suggests extreme irrationality, but less extreme examples also come to mind. For instance, I may prefer not to go shopping with my friend in the morning of the day in which I must make a midnight flight (even though I'm already packed and ready to go) because the cost of missing my flight is too high. In this more realistic example, it is not far-fetched to think that my obsession with arriving early to airports is causing my assessment of opportunity costs to be somewhat irrational. Objectively, it is reasonable to think that I will be able to catch my flight at midnight if

I go shopping in the morning. When assessing opportunity costs involved in two or more competing alternatives, we have to make sure that our assessment in itself meets minimal standards of rationality.

Thus, we may very well say that Tuck is not ignoring opportunity costs when he sustains that it is perfectly rational to vote in order to form part of an efficacious set of votes. He is simply assuming that the would-be voter engages in a rational comparison of opportunity costs when deciding whether to vote, and that her comparison, under normal circumstances, will tend to favor voting without an important loss to the voter. In simpler words, Tuck appears to assume, reasonably, that the act of voting leaves plenty of room for other activities, so that the opportunity costs of voting are low enough to be borne by the voter.

As advanced above, Brennan also sustains that for Tuck's arguments to make sense, it has to be true that the individual desires *at all* to be part of the efficacious set of votes that will determine the election. But Brennan's objection flies in the face of traditional rational choice predictions about voting. Anthony Downs, decades ago, offered the still-most-used calculus of voting to predict voter behavior. This equation stipulates that if the individual probability (p) of making a noticeable impact on the result of the election is high enough, and the individual costs are sufficiently low, then the voter will rationally bother to vote. Nowhere in the traditional rational choice calculus that (allegedly) predicts voting behavior does the variable of "actually desiring to make an impact" figure as relevant. Maybe it should, but Brennan, who fully adheres to the traditional rational choice account, should provide an explanation of why rationality requires the new variable now. But more importantly, Brennan should provide an explanation of why this new addition matters *at all*. The reason why someone may desire result X but may not desire to do what it takes to produce X may be that it is too costly or burdensome for him to act. As mentioned, I may desire a less polluted environment, but the cost of not driving my favorite highly contaminating car may be too high since I enjoy driving the vehicle so much. People can be too self-absorbed when it comes to actions that directly and immediately affect *their ways of life*. However, we have established that when it comes to voting, opportunity costs are not high enough to matter a great deal under circumstances we can all imagine. People vote all the time without their ways of life being significantly, or even modestly, altered. And if this is so, then it should also be the case that, provided costs are low enough, it is not illogical to want to exert influence with no great difficulty. Of course, we have no way of knowing if our vote will *actually* be part of the efficacious set of votes in the election. However, we know that the probability that our vote is in the efficacious set is higher than the probability that our vote is decisive by itself. This difference, alone, serves as an incentive to participate in the election. If someone objects that it is still improbable that our vote is in the efficacious set, this fact is not a devastating criticism for the following reason. No matter the low chances, it is cost-effective to vote for the sake of others in society given how relatively easy it is to do and how much is at stake during elections.

As I advanced in previous chapters, the voter behavior literature has proposed another reason why voting may be perfectly consistent with an instrumental logic even if the voter does not expect her vote to swing an election. For example, Gerry Mackie suggests that people may vote to increase their preferred candidate's margin of victory or to diminish her margin of loss.[36] Negligibility is not the same as futility, and that is why people may still have an incentive to act, however small their individual contribution to a larger outcome may be. In his "Contributory Theory of Voting," Mackie suggests that voters can rationally vote for the benefit of others by voting for the party that they think will most improve the situation of a majority, even if they know that their vote will not be decisive in the election. They may desire to strengthen the winning candidate's mandate by contributing to increasing said candidate's electoral margin of victory; or they may desire to weaken their non-preferred candidates' mandate by contributing to abridging, however infinitesimally, their preferred candidate's electoral margin of defeat.

We can understand the contributory logic in the language of sports: the individual player knows that her contribution may not determine her team's victory by itself but it may nevertheless contribute to a result that makes her team the winner. In the event that victory is not an option, the player's contribution may be motivated by an intention to diminish the disadvantage by which her team loses. Voting, on this account, is not like cheering for a team—as the expressive theory of voting has it—but like playing in it. It is instrumental, thus.

The objection most likely to emerge at this point is similar to the objection that doubters of the duty to vote offer against Tuck's arguments, namely, that it still doesn't matter what we do because our imperceptible vote will not make a valuable difference to the result of an election. But this objection starts from the wrong premise, namely, that actions that are not difference-making alone are irrational and morally trivial. I say that they are not irrational because they do exert an impact, however small; and because they exert an impact, they are not morally trivial. In this logic, there is no threshold of effectiveness (understood as difference-making power) that one should pass for one's vote to count as rational. Many actions are rational despite making a minimally small, even unnoticeable, difference. A contribution may be of value because it is larger than zero. Something, however small, is better than nothing.

But why is an imperceptible effect morally important? This question is different from the question of what motivates the individual to vote. An imperceptible, yet existent, contribution may be morally valuable because it is part of a larger set of acts that, all together, will have a perceptible impact that is of high worth in terms of justice or well-being. An example will clarify this idea.

Imagine a food drive to help poor children in a community's disadvantaged neighborhood. The drive asks every person willing to help to donate one can of non-perishable goods. It is quite evident that your donation alone is only infinitesimally useful for the larger enterprise of appeasing hunger, in the same way, we could argue, that a single vote is useless to win an election. However, we could think that your one donation is the right type of act because, together with many other identical acts, will lead to the morally valuable result we are collectively aiming for, which is to reduce hunger.[37] The act of donating a can of food is only marginally helpful, yet the larger set of similar acts is extremely impactful. This type of collective rationality—i.e., acting with a view to producing the larger collective outcome that takes shape when others act like us—may perfectly explain people's willingness to contribute despite being cognizant of how little impact they can exert alone. One person's single contribution, then, may be morally valuable because it indicates an *intention* to act to produce, in conjunction with others, a worthy result. In other words, an individual small act has value because it denotes a moral commitment to contributing to a state of affairs that we have independent reasons to prefer because of justice or some other noble good.

Tuck's "efficacious set rationale" and Mackie's "contributory rationality" refute classical choice-theory predictions that people will *not* vote because their votes are negligibly impactful individually. Normatively, these new approaches to voter rationality give us a basis for thinking that a moral duty to vote is not implausible simply because the agent does not act with a view to swinging the election. Of course, as mentioned at the beginning of this chapter, there are many non-instrumental (consumption-based) theories that explain why people vote. They are not inconsistent, necessarily, with the instrumental accounts described here. Different voters may evince different reasons for voting. Who said human motivation was to be explained by one simple rationale? If rational choice theory got something wrong, it is surely the idea that there is one "blanket cause" for action.

5.3. Voting Impinges on Freedom

In what follows, I challenge what I have called the perfectionist argument against the duty to vote. Proponents of the duty to vote, the objection goes, defend a narrow conception of what makes a life worthwhile. This narrow conception puts politics at the center of moral attention to the detriment of other meaningful activities that the individual may prefer over active citizenship. As mentioned, the tradition that sees politics as the fountain of the "good life" has a long pedigree in republican democratic theory. Republicans who value participation as infusing life with moral value are inclined to appeal to a broadly Aristotelian notion of human beings as social animals. They will claim that living together with one's fellow citizens is not something undertaken merely as a means for ulterior ends. Rather, it is a central component of living well. In this view, politics is more than a means to security, order, and justice. It is a reflection of the highest form of human association—one that is not for the sake of anything other than itself. For the classical republican tradition, and for those intellectually inspired by it, not all conceptions of the good are equal.[38]

We may find the exaltation of politics troubling. Why should we rely on such an incomplete notion of human flourishing? The freedom to decide how to live a worthwhile existence seems to be in danger when we are told that political engagement is a sure recipe for it. What if it is not for us? Moral perfectionism—i.e., the idea that certain ways of life are superior to others—is not a friend of freedom.

In what follows, I argue that we do not have to commit to a morally perfectionist view to defend a duty to vote. Relatedly, I also argue that the duty would enhance, rather than thwart, freedom. It would do so by protecting the polity, and each individual member of it, against domination by its political elite. Thus, even though it is trivially true that a moral duty may hamper individual freedom of choice because our conscience may require us to do that which we do not desire to do, the moral duty to vote has effects that, all else equal, tend to increase total freedom without sacrificing individual rights. For this reason, I believe that seeing voting as a moral duty does not jeopardize freedom in a way that morally matters.

If we do not feel at ease with the idea that political participation will make our life morally better, we do not have to accept that seemingly oppressive notion. However, that does not mean that we have to give up on the morality of a duty to vote. The freedom argument against the duty to vote sustains that seeing voting as a moral obligation does not respect individual freedom because it demands from people that they participate in the political life of their societies even if they do not place a high value on politics.

But what if a duty to vote actually fostered freedom instead of hindering it?

The idea that we can value politics for reasons other than moral virtue receives serious consideration by contemporary theorists in the neo-republican tradition, which sees political participation not so much as a sign of the "good life" but as an instrument of protection against tyranny.[39] Unlike classical, or Aristotelian, republicans, who tend to value political participation as part and parcel of a life worth living, "instrumentalist" republicans (also called neo-republicans) view participation as a means to an ulterior end. This end is freedom understood as non-domination, which means *not* being subject to the arbitrary will of another.[40]

In the neo-republican tradition, which draws centrally from Machiavelli's thoughts on republicanism as expressed in the *Discourses on Livy*, freedom as non-domination is understood as that state in which the individual's freedom is not dependent on the benevolence of a ruler, who may discretionally change his mind and crush us at any time.[41] When one is dependent on the benevolence of a ruler, one is really at his mercy. This type of power is possible because the ruler is not accountable to the citizenry; he has not been elected by citizens to protect their interests and does not try to do so in order to be able to remain in power. His tenure does not depend on the choices that citizens make at elections. Therefore, the leader may be good to the people, if she so desires, but she may change her mind at no considerable cost to herself. Living with the possibility that this happens at any time is living under domination by another. It is clear, then, why we can minimize domination under republican forms of government, in which the people have the power to place and remove leaders via elections and can hold them accountable for their actions and breaches of trust.[42]

Minimally fair republican institutions exist in many corners of the world. In the West, for example, it is presumably true that we don't live in domination of the type admonished against by the classical republicans. Why should we justify a duty to vote on the basis of a kind of freedom that we already enjoy, then?

The real test of freedom as non-domination is the *effective* ability to make government accountable for what it does or fails to do. That is, what makes us free in the sense of freedom as non-domination is the knowledge that rulers work for us, and that, if they are good to us, it is not because they discretionally chose to be benevolent toward us but because they would lose their position of power if they weren't so. In other words, what makes us free in the logic of republican political theory is the fact that we control our representatives via the *threat* of ending our support for them and causing them to lose their grip on power, or never gain it in the first place. It is this ability that we have as citizens that renders their power over us *conditional instead of arbitrary*.

The foregoing reasoning, then, must entail that one enjoys freedom as non- domination when rulers do not systematically ignore, or are indifferent to, our plight and predicaments without facing a considerable cost—even if they are not outright cruel toward us. After all, the principles of republican government prescribe accountability of rulers not only when the latter blatantly abuse citizens, but also when they are oblivious to their interests and needs. The raison d'être for governments under the republican philosophy of government is to serve the people because the people have given (figurative) consent to justify the functions of government. Because of this consent, the governed retain the power to judge the work and character of their representatives and may change who controls the machinery of political power if they deem it necessary. Thus, governments that are indifferent to the needs and concerns of the represented, and pay no price for it, are in a significant way taking away that control that should ultimately rest in the hands of the governed. Living in non-domination, then, should require living under sufficiently *responsive* governments that act on the people's demands and that the citizenry can punish if they fail to carry out the tasks for which they were chosen—even if they are not patently abusive in the way in which a tyrant could be.

A responsive government in the sense that matters for this discussion does not pay heed to popular preferences simply because they are the people's. Some preferences may be immoral and unworthy of being acted upon (for example, as when some citizens may prefer to see others discriminated against or eliminated). However, a responsive government acts to protect and meet objectively important interests that it is reasonable to impute to citizens in all societies, such as an interest in equal opportunity, in safety, in a minimally good quality of life, in a decent level of income, in peace, in basic rights, and so forth. It is true that not all individuals will want and need the same things all the time, but it makes sense to focus on the notion of social primary goods, which are goods that we can surmise all rational human beings will want to have access to regardless of all other things they may want in life.[43] I think it is appropriate to stipulate that rational individuals will have a basic interest in unobstructed access to this type of goods.

Unresponsive governments are governments that do not respond satisfactorily (if at all) to the interest that citizens have in accessing social primary goods. Thus, a focus on responsiveness is not necessarily a focus on popular preferences per se, although it should be clear that leaders that constantly contradict people's preferences cannot be said to be responsive—unless the people are wrong about what they need and want *absolutely* always, which is not highly plausible. Citizens in modern-day liberal republics can still live in a state of domination when their representatives ignore their needs and don't suffer high costs for doing so. When this happens, it means that citizens are unable to keep their representatives accountable for what they fail to do. We don't have to look at undemocratic societies, only, to make sense of how subtler forms of domination may affect us. I propose that domination in its contemporary form does not only have the face of the authoritarian, unquestioned prince, but can also take the shape of the unheard, forgotten democratic citizen.

In recent decades, many countries—and the United States especially—have experienced increasing representational inequalities. Representational inequality is just one of the symptoms of larger inequality, but it is worth focusing on it because of its relationship with domination as entailing political powerlessness. Representational inequality happens when politicians and public officials pay much more heed to some segments of the population than they do to others because the latter do not vote frequently enough to count as constituencies that need to be catered to in order for candidates to gain a seat in government.[44] People that do not vote, or hardly vote, make it easier for politicians to bypass their concerns when legislating or enacting policy. Chronic non-voters make it more likely that their interests will be ignored by the ruling class at little political cost.[45] Much of this inequality derives from the fact that the representatives elected will cater to the needs of voters much more efficaciously than they will to the needs of non-voters. In other words, voters are much better represented than non-voters.[46]

In practice, voters usually tend to be the more educated, those with a higher income, and those belonging to no ethnic or racial minorities. In other words, they tend to be more advantaged than non-voters.[47] These differences explain why falling turnout rates in the United States and other democracies are seen by many as a cause of worry: lower participation rates means more unequal participation because voters and non-voters are not evenly distributed in society.[48] If certain groups systematically abstain from voting, politicians may ignore their interests and instead attend to the interests of groups that are known to turn out to vote more reliably. Since democracy is based on the principle of political equality and the promise that each interest must have the same chance of being considered, socially uneven electoral participation calls into question a central component of democracy.[49]

Some theorists are doubtful of the impact that representational inequalities may have on the quality of democracy. Jason Brennan, for example, suggests that if voters vote with the common good in mind, non-voters will *not* be ignored since the altruistic mindset of voters means that citizens will not forget to protect the interests of those that do not show up to vote.[50] This logic validates the conclusion that we have no real reason to worry about disparities in turnout and, consequently, no real reason to defend a duty to vote. However, this line of thinking is oblivious to the real political incentives that move politicians to act. It is true that altruistic voting exists and should be fostered (something that I defend in this book) but Brennan's arguments disregard real-world dynamics that explain how politics work. It may be possible to have people vote altruistically, but it may not be possible to have politicians govern for the common good *regardless of who actually votes*. Policy outcomes are not just a result of what voters want; they are also a result of what politicians do. I explain in what follows.

For decades now, there has been well-established empirical evidence that questions the thesis that inequalities in turnout do not matter. Who votes and who doesn't has important consequences for who wins office and, consequently, for the content of public policies and laws. Instead of using a demand-side focus—whereby researches look at what voters want from their representatives—many political science studies examine the supply side of politics—parties, policies, laws—and find that elected officials and representatives appeal to those citizens who actually turn out to vote.[51] For example, a study finds that center-left parties adopt more leftist platforms in countries with a higher turnout since, in order to win votes, these parties need to attend to the concerns of many voters that in low-turnout countries would not vote.[52] By the same token, if parties expect the socially disadvantaged to abstain from voting on a systematic basis, they will have no strong incentives to address their needs and concerns. In particular, the findings suggest that when turnout is noticeably unequal (which generally implies that the least advantaged abstain from voting much more than the more advantaged do) politicians whose fates depend on popular support will not bother to appeal to the interests of non-voters in the formulation of public policy. Voters and non-voters might diverge only slightly in their preferences (although their needs and priorities may not be the same) but if parties consistently seek to address the median voter rather than the median citizen, these differences could accumulate over time and translate into worryingly different policy outcomes.[53]

For example, research shows that, for the United States, the more underrepresented the poor are among the voters of a state, the less generous its welfare spending will be.[54] Similarly, other political science work shows that members of the US Congress do not allocate resources simply according to need but rather tend to direct them strategically to high-turnout areas within a district.[55] The relationship between turnout disparities and unequal policy outcomes also obtains cross-country. For example, research shows that high-turnout countries redistribute income more.[56]

It is reasonable to believe that acceptable levels of income equality are valuable because they reflect that the less advantaged members of society will enjoy minimally decent access to social goods such as education, healthcare, a dignified living standard, and job opportunities, among others. Relatively equal, or not too unequal, policy outcomes indicate that the interests of those at the bottom of the income hierarchy are not being ignored by the political class. In other words, they indicate that officeholders are acceptably responsive to the needs and demands of the least fortunate in society (or those that are not wealthy and powerful *only*).

Let me return now to the idea of freedom as non-domination. I argued that citizens can experience domination in non-authoritarian, democratic systems if public officials fail to pay heed to their concerns without incurring serious political costs for doing so. What the literature and findings previously described suggest is that when citizens do not count for rulers—even in democratic contexts—their freedom from hardship, from poverty, and from social exclusion is at risk. Differently put, citizens' freedom to have their interests considered by the political class is in jeopardy when representatives do not care equally about all citizens. Thus, voting contributes to securing and increasing freedom as non-domination because it sends public officials the signal that they will be held accountable for the policy outcomes produced during their tenure. This means that they will incur costs for not attending to the needs of voters—a fact that gives voters *control over their representatives*. Having control over the fate of rulers—as opposed to just hoping that they will act benevolently toward us without much recourse if they don't—is what defines freedom as non-domination.

Someone may object that it is not the duty to vote but the voting in itself that is doing the work of reducing domination here. But I answer that, because the duty is morally obligatory, this means that, all else equal, it will translate into more frequent voting. Thus, it may be true that voting per se is a source of non-domination, but the duty to vote strengthens this quality because it means that, under circumstances we can imagine, everybody will vote, not just those inclined to do so because it is fun, entertaining, or socially expected in one's group. Thus, the point I want to press is that there is a distinct power that the duty to vote—not just the mere act of voting—possesses when it comes to the alleviation of domination as I understand that term here. This is the power to make voting more common among eligible citizens, which, logically, will mean that the fight against domination will be more effective.

6

Voting and Collective Rationality

Final Thoughts

The received wisdom opposing Samaritan duties as morally obligatory is that the average bystander has no obligation to intervene to avert or minimize harm affecting others. This understanding, however, also has it that *if* the bystander voluntarily (and benevolently) decides to intervene, she has a duty to avoid carelessness in her efforts.[1] It is this latter part—demanding competence *if* one decides to help—that has motivated the defiant position toward voting as a common citizenship requirement, encapsulated in the writings of critics such as Brennan, Lomasky, Somin, and others. In their view, one does not have a duty to vote *at all*, but *if* one decides to vote, one must do so competently—that is, with information and knowledge of the alternatives. If one decided that helping via the vote is not worth it, or that it is not fun or interesting compared to other ways of spending one's time, then there would be nothing ethically worrisome about the choice not to intervene (by casting a ballot)—even if it would be possible for the would-be voter to vote competently. In this view, failing to vote because of reasons unrelated to lack of competence—such as a desire to spend one's time doing something else instead of voting or a lack of care for what happens in elections—is perfectly acceptable. In other words, there are no reasons to *blame* someone who fails to vote because he did not feel like doing so; voting is *morally optional*. Taking the trouble to vote well is, moreover, supererogatory. It is a nice gesture toward others—in the same way as it is a nice gesture to go out of one's way and risk our safety to rescue another person seriously imperiled. But it is in no way expected from us. Because it is not, we are surely to be commended for doing it—who wouldn't commend the passerby who puts someone else's safety before her own? Voting with care, then, is a source of moral praise, but not voting at all is not a source of moral reproach. The gist of this conclusion, which we can attribute to the position rejecting the duty to vote with care, is that voting judiciously is a sacrifice that should not be expected from anyone but should surely be applauded if eventually done. This conclusion, moreover, rests on the assumption that voting with care is too costly (maybe too time-consuming for the personal benefits it causes) or difficult (not everybody can do it right; *special* preparation is needed) to be thought of as a regular duty *instead of a heroic act*.

In this book, I argued that the duty to vote must actually be a duty to vote with care. If the outcomes of elections matter—in terms of justice and the well-being of citizens—then asking people to vote for the sake of voting without regard to the nature of their vote is not only irresponsible but also morally wrong. But I am also convinced that the abstainer should not get a pass for not voting if it would have been comparatively easy for him to do so minimally well. The ability to vote with care entails, centrally, that the would-be voter be acceptably free of structural impediments to voting, which include, among other things, disabling poverty, political measures designed to discourage voting, overtly confusing electoral rules, weak or inexistent civic education, public officials' unresponsiveness to citizens, and (partisan) propaganda campaigns in the media designed to manipulate the average voter's understanding of basic issues at stake in the election. These requirements are a tall order under the circumstances in which we live, but, as I argued in the book, the defiant position that has gained so much ground in the last years is completely oblivious to them—and to the possibility that many of these structural variables that contribute to voter misinformation and voter disinterest are alterable. Instead, critics mentioned throughout the book assume that voter misinformation and voter apathy are the result of individual-level cognitive failures prompted by laziness or lack of intellectual capacity or both. I am not ready to deny the existence of the latter deficiencies, but nor am I ready to assume, without question, that democracy is doomed because voters are *naturally* inept.

Against Jason Brennan's view that we can classify voters into unbiased experts (vulcans), ignorants (hobbits), and fanatics (hooligans), I suggested that the distinctions should be more fine-grained. Voters are not just highly educated and rational, hotly passionate about politics in ways that cloud their judgement, or completely incompetent. A large number of citizens are mindful of the need to become acceptably informed about important issues before the election, but they may still be confused and overwhelmed by the contradicting messages existing in the media. Many of these people are responsible, regular voters even if they do not possess formal expert knowledge on economics or political science. They may neither be irrationally biased against or in favor of a position. They are not fanatics because politics is not an absolute priority for them—and they are not belligerent about their views. Many of them are quite dedicated to "getting it right" by investigating different perspectives in an objective a way as possible. I called them "Moderately Interested Voters" (MIVs), for lack of a better term. They are not "experts," but they are acceptably smart and motivated during the election period.

Relatedly, one must call attention to another fallacy in the position against the moral duty to vote. Even though competent voting entails possession of information and rationality, we should not equate the expertise needed to be a good voter with expertise in other (professional) activities. Opponents of my views do this frequently. It is not uncommon to hear that if we expect doctors to treat the sick, then why don't we expect the experts to vote—not just anyone who happens to be around? Sometimes doctors are replaced with plumbers in the analogy.[2] Even though becoming a doctor is admittedly more difficult than becoming a plumber, the argument is meant to suggest that political expertise is complex, not everyone can acquire it relatively fast, and those that do not have it are completely unable *to do* the practice in question on pain of committing grave mistakes. Imagine someone without a medical degree performing an operation on a patient. He could kill him. Or someone with no idea of how pipes work meddling with the plumbing installation of a home. He could cause serious flooding. These are terrible costs to bear, and how could anyone deny that only surgeons should operate on people and only plumbers should change pipes?

But voting is different. Although not everybody may possess the knowledge necessary to vote smartly at all times, this knowledge is not terribly difficult to acquire since it does not entail extreme depth and extensive breath of information. As Aristotle suggested, and many contemporary political scientists have argued more technically since then, political expertise by the regular citizen requires mostly the ability to assess the real skill and competence of candidates and public officials as well as the general (non-technical) nature of their ideological positions and proposals. Moreover, regular citizens are equipped to assess the *ethical ends* of policy—even if the technical and causal theories escape them. Questions of moral value are not understandable only by the highly educated. For example, one can understand that lower taxes on the rich and higher taxes on the middle class may be unfair—even if one does not fully understand the economic effects that will make this so because one never took a course in macroeconomics. Likewise, the average voter can conceivably understand that permanent wage stagnation in the face of inflation calls for correction because it harms working people—even if they are not familiar with the basics of labor economics.

Not everybody is minimally competent to vote smartly, but citizens do not need the equivalent of a medical degree or a professional plumbing license to do so, either. Elevating the political knowledge required of common citizens to vote responsibly to the

level of complex technical knowledge is not only empirically unnecessary but also morally unjustified. The equivalence is incorrect
because the common citizen does not need technical knowledge
to perform the essential activity of governing. The doctor and the
plumber, in contrast, need technical knowledge in order to perform surgical operations and plumbing restorations, respectively.
Citizens in representative democracies, however, are not in charge
of policy formulation and legislation *themselves*. The main role of
citizens is to monitor the performance of their representatives—
not to *do the job* of their representatives. The monitoring demands
a minimal level of skill, but it does not demand highly complex
technical knowledge. When shopping around for a good doctor,
we may need the competence required to understand what our ailment is and what reviews and evaluations about the doctor that we
have come across mean. We may also need to understand what the
doctor's educational credentials say about her expertise and ability.
However, if we had to know about medicine as much as the doctor
does, then why would we need a doctor in the first place? The case is
not vastly different regarding political candidates for public office.

What about the argument that my views erroneously presuppose that citizens will happily agree on how to resolve controversial
issues of justice? The accusation that I'm disregarding ineradicable differences in how people view justice does not bite strongly
enough. In any case, the critics of the duty could be thought guilty
of the same problem. They never give a definition of what voting
for the common good entails other than the strictly epistemic
requirements of cognitive rationality (understanding causal
mechanisms in economics and social science more generally) and
information about the candidates' platforms. I go a step further
than this merely epistemic approach to careful, judicious voting: I
argue that we can rely on a procedural—yet morally illuminating—
mechanism to know how a judicious voter should ponder about her
electoral decision. Judicious voters should make a conscious effort
to think about the alternatives available from the perspective of all

possibly affected parties, not just their own. This exercise does not guarantee perfect, or even large, consensus on questions of justice and morality more broadly. However, it makes it more probable, and, I sustained, it is sufficient for the purposes of discharging the duty to vote with care.

One of the arguments for my case in favor of the duty to vote is that abstaining from voting is an omission with moral meaning. In the same way as it is morally wrong to contribute to injustice with an incompetent vote (per the no-duty-to-vote position), I argued that it is morally wrong to contribute to injustice with an abstention when we know that the accumulation of considered votes could very well override the collection of incompetent or immoral ones. The immorality of partaking of collective activities that have larger, undesirable results is not controversial —and this is independent of how causally powerful an individual contribution is. In the same vein, it should not be controversial to see the morality of partaking of collective activities that have larger, desirable outcomes, and which do not impose an undue burden on the contributor.

Critics like Brennan fervently sustain that it is immoral to vote incompetently *however* imperceptible *our single* vote is. This is because associating our agency with a morally suspicious collective outcome is wrong. It is immoral to contribute to the collective achievement of bad governance via elections—even if, and despite the fact that, a single bad vote makes no difference to the electoral outcome in question. Following this reasoning, it is also clear why it is wrong to donate to Nazis and racists even if doing so would not advance their cause in a perceptible way because the money we give, as single individuals, is too little. Contributing to a morally suspicious cause is wrong, period.

But if it is true that what matters in condemning bad, careless voting is *not the* individual impact of one vote on the election (that will be negligible) but its *association* with an immoral collective activity, doesn't it follow that demanding individual effectiveness from single (good) votes is inconsistent and confused? Brennan takes pains to argue that contributing to injustice with incompetent votes is wrong regardless of how individually effective those single votes are in isolation from each other, yet he opposes a moral duty to vote with care because, among other things, single votes get lost in a proverbial ocean of votes, rendering each one of them causally powerless in determining the election. This seems inconsistent. I would say that, if one is to oppose bad voting on moral grounds, one cannot oppose (morally obligatory) good voting differently. Moreover, if one is to recognize that the accumulation of immoral, yet individually negligible, acts (such as voting badly) *does* lead to harmful states of affairs, then, by the same logic, one should be willing to recognize that the cumulative impact of moral (yet individually negligible) acts (such as voting with care) also leads to beneficial states of the world. And if this is so, arguing that it is a duty to refrain from voting badly but that it is *not* a duty to vote judiciously is inconsistent if the claim is based on the importance of the capacity to exert change *individually*.

In the book, I sought to highlight a central claim. This is the simple idea that voting is a *collective* exercise in power. It makes little sense to analyze it through the lens of the traditional rational choice approach that sees rationality based on the *individual's* capacity to make a discernible and measurable difference in the world. There is nothing irrational or wasteful about wanting to take part in a collective enterprise that will have a noticeable impact on a particular state of affairs such as the justice of society and the well-being of our fellow citizens. Indeed, if we care about contributing to shape big trends in society, voting in important—and not so seemingly important—elections may be a more effective way to help others than many endeavors *not* causally connected with how government is chosen. As I explained in detail in previous parts of this work, government is a powerful entity with the practical capacity to affect people's quality of life in significant ways—which sets it apart from most other human organizations. The caliber of the people that populate the institutions and channels of power that make legislation and policy formulation possible can make a difference to justice, then. Because of this influence, the mechanism that gets public officials elected is not impermeable to moral analysis—and the alleged duty that makes this mechanism effective is also central to this analysis.

I argued that, under the right circumstances, casting a careful vote is morally obligatory because there is no excuse that may help us escape this requirement. Elections are a necessary mechanism to enable collective action in the choosing of political authority. They make it possible for society to summarily record and collect citizens' preferences on candidates and to return a result shortly after. Imagine if the counting was made informally by some citizens going around private homes and asking people whom they prefer, and then, coming up with an estimation of who the winner is. Besides discrepancies in the estimation among volunteers doing the counting, the process would not be sufficiently accurate because of lack of time and perfect mobility on the part of the surveyors. Elections solve this problem. They exist to resolve a collective action difficulty in *deciding* who will govern us. Additionally, elections do not present the average private citizen with any burden related to their setup. All the citizen has to do is wait for them to take place and appear at the appropriate voting location (non-automatic voter registration may add a considerable degree of burden for some— that is why, in tune with the just-mentioned, society should provide for automatic registration for all eligible citizens).

The nature of elections as collective action solvers and the fact that they do not impose undue costs on citizens in terms of their functioning mean that the average citizen is in a propitious position to help society by participating in them. This statement makes all the more sense in the background of what I just said, namely, that helping to choose government is morally significant because of what government can do for, or against, its citizens. Neglecting to take part of the collective endeavor of choosing government is, therefore, morally inexcusable if it is true that the costs of participating are small. We may prefer to spend our time helping others in other ways, and many of those ways may not be political at all, but ignoring the morally salient nature of participating in elections is wrong, I sustained, because elections achieve a goal that no other activity can achieve—and this goal is *uniquely* important. We may perhaps have duties to help others in non-political ways also, and this may mean that morality is more demanding on us that we would like to admit, at first. However, this realization does not entail that voting is morally optional under the right conditions.

To the argument just canvassed, the following objection usually is made: The fact that elections are a collective activity must mean that no particular person's help is strictly needed to make them effective. In other words, no one particular citizen's Samaritan help will be necessary since elections will throw up a result regardless of whether any one citizen votes or not. This is so because each individual vote is too imperceptible to make a decisive impact on the election. And if this is so, why make the duty to participate in elections a binding one? Does it make sense to ask from people that they do activities that have no capacity to change *things by themselves*? This question is recurrent for the critics of the alleged duty to vote; and their answer is always a resounding no. But their answer underscores a series of contradictions in their own thinking and in how they interpret common-sense morality.

First, most forms of non-electoral help to society also entail the "problem" of low individual impact. Give to charity? I bet you won't end global, or even domestic, poverty alone. Give to cancer research? I bet your money will not alone cause the cure to be discovered. Volunteer to teach inner-city kids? I bet your time will not be sufficient to significantly, or even marginally, improve educational standards for underprivileged children. Thus, most non-political ways of helping society are not ostensibly more effective than voting, *individually*. But it was the charge of individual ineffectiveness that took a central role in the defiant position against the duty to vote and in the related argument that other ways of helping may be preferable.

Second, we don't need to be maximizers of good results (or social utility) in order to discharge a duty to help society. Not even the original proponents of utilitarianism as a doctrine that prescribes a personal duty to make conscientious efforts to increase the welfare of others demands this from us. As was noted in chapter 1, the duty to help in general is a duty to contribute, even marginally, to larger activities that will maximize total welfare as a result of the accumulation of many people's acts. There is no evidence, to my knowledge of the utilitarian philosophy, that the duty to help others prescribes actions that have noticeable effects on the world *on their own*. Critics may say, "But we are not in the business of defending utilitarians anyways!" Well, they do claim that altruistic actions must have discernible instrumental effects, by which they mean that those actions must alter, by improving, the world *by themselves*. But I am replying to them that, on any reasonable account of what it means to be effective, it doesn't *only* mean that you have to be effective *alone*, in isolation from the contributions of others.

Third, the fact that we don't need to be effective alone means, also, that the duty to intervene as a Samaritan is no less stringent *only* because we need many other people to intervene in order to bring about the sought-after result. Recall the image of the passenger under attack in a busy subway car. The attacker could easily be restrained by the collective intervention of a number of spectators—but not by any *single* one acting alone. Does this mean that all bystanders are off the hook morally? No. Rather, it means that none of them in particular has a stronger claim than any other to be relieved of the duty. This conclusion explains why they all have a duty to coordinate, or initiate a coordination effort, with all the others in order to effect the rescue. Voting judiciously offers an apt analogy to this example, but the situation is even simpler since there is no need to coordinate anything in the presence of elections. Elections do the coordinating for us. Because this is the case, the moral inescapability of the duty to help by voting becomes even easier to see than it may be in the case of the subway attacker.

Lastly, in the book I addressed the issue of overdetermined causation. Overdetermined causation unfolds when we seek to contribute to a final outcome, but our single contribution ends up being causally inert since the outcome is achieved with independence of our action. For example, if we need six people to move a broken-down car away from the middle of the road, but seven people help lifting the vehicle, we could say that the efforts of the seventh person were superfluous in the sense that they were unnecessary. Likewise, if we need a certain number of votes to win the election, but the winner receives more, the votes above the winning threshold have no causal impact, therefore, no moral relevance, either.

But the conclusion of moral irrelevance does not follow in the case of voting for various reasons. First, there is no way of knowing ex ante which votes will be unnecessary. Because of this, we could say that all of them are equally relevant morally. After the election is over, we could still decide that the votes cast last were unnecessary, therefore morally trivial. But how does this observation help us in determining ex ante who is obligated to vote and who is not? Inherent problems of fairness and collective action lie deep inside this question. Second, overdetermined causation in voting does not entail the moral irrelevance of some votes, for another reason: we should not see causal effectiveness only through the lens of *decisiveness*—understanding this term as a voter's power to tilt the election with her vote. Marginal contributions to the result of elections may have the power to help decrease or increase the margins of victory or defeat, something that the voter may rationally desire to see happen.

This book argued that it matters *how* we vote; it not only matters *that we vote*. It matters that we vote with a view to improving the lot of others, and of society more generally, although this others-oriented view does not imply self-effacement. One can worry about other people's well-being without, for that reason, forgetting about one's own (although this view rules out instances in which improving our well-being may require unfair or immoral acts that would decrease the well-being of others). But the idea that the content of our choice at the ballot box matters significantly may give us some pause. After all, the skeptic's position regarding the duty to vote is that too many people are incompetent and, so, they may harm democracy by voting because they may choose bad governments. The way they vote (i.e., badly or non-smartly) is a problem. It matters. Based on this reasoning, the skeptic may believe that universal voting rights are not always a great idea. Epistocratic forms of government—whereby only the qualified can participate in collective decision-making are, in this view, more consistent with justice than democracy.

The fact that outcomes matter should not give the skeptic a reason to prefer non-democratic decision-making procedures on the grounds that they *may* produce more just outcomes than democratic ones. The skeptic tells us that we have not tried all types of conceivable epistocracies and that some types of effective, benevolent schemes whereby the knowledgeable have more political power than the rest may be plausible (and certainly, that they are morally justified).[3] But why is the idea that just government by the knowing is empirically plausible more credible than the idea that regular citizens may get better at making smart and moral decisions at the voting booth? [4] In other words, why is the argument that some knowledgeable people may be better at understanding and fighting for other people's needs than those people themselves more empirically valid than the argument that regular people may get better at obtaining and understanding political information if given the right tools? At best, these two arguments deserve the same degree of empirical plausibility. Cases where the not so knowledgeable can blindly trust the experts with fair protection of their rights without worrying about injustice or abuse are very rare in history; but I do know of cases in which regular citizens (many of them) vote judiciously or with the interest of society at heart, even if it is true that citizens also vote in harmful ways. As I said before in the book, the knowledgeable are as likely as others to have their own ideological and self-interested biases, and those biases may (and have) driven many of them to behave unjustly toward society and others, despite their superior cognitive performance and credentials.[5] In this book, I defended a duty to behave as a good Samaritan via the vote, but I never said, or implied, that Samaritanism is necessary because the regular citizen does not know best what her true interests are or will not be motivated to protect those interests. The duty to be a Good Samaritan via the vote is a duty for the regular citizen (and everybody else) to counteract the unjust selfish impulses of others (including the experts) when making decisions about life in common.

Notes

Chapter 1

1. For this general approach see Geoffrey Brennan and Loren Lomasky, "Is There a Duty to Vote?," *Social Philosophy and Policy*, 17 (2001): 62–86; Anthony Ciccone, "The Constitutional Right to Vote Is Not a Duty," 23 Hamline Journal of Public Law & Policy, 2002; H. B. Mayo, "A Note on the Alleged Duty to Vote," *Journal of Politics*, 2 (1959): 319–323; Michael G. Colantuono, "The Revision of American State Constitutions: Legislative Power, Popular Sovereignty, and Constitutional Change," 75 California Law Review, 1987.
2. In this book, I will be using "duty" and "obligation" interchangeably unless I indicate otherwise.
3. Another, somewhat more trivial, example of a case in which a freedom may entail a duty is the obligation to report a crime when doing so would not be dangerous to us. It would not be far-fetched to suggest that failing to report a crime that we witnessed, when doing so would be non-costly, is indicative of a type of indifference that is morally suspicious, especially if the crime is likely to occur again when authorities go unnotified, thereby causing (avoidable) harm to others.
4. For two particularly prominent examples of the literature that sees voter incompetence as the greatest threat to democracy today, see Ilya Somin, *Democracy and Political Ignorance* (Palo Alto, CA: Stanford University Press, 2013) and Jason Brennan, *Against Democracy* (Princeton, NJ: Princeton University Press, 2016).
5. Somin, *Democracy and Political Ignorance*.
6. See, among others, Bryan Caplan, *The Myth of the Rational Voter: Why Democracies Choose Bad Policies* (Princeton, NJ: Princeton University Press, 2007), and Hans-Herman Hoppe, *Democracy: The God That Failed* (New Brunswick, NJ: Transactions Publishers, 2001). The latter presents a critical approach similar to Caplan's but, paradoxically, is not referenced by Caplan in his book.

7. Peter Singer, "Famine, Affluence and Morality," *Philosophy and Public Affairs, 1* (1972): 229–243.

8. Avoiding bad governance entails a repeated, sustained institutional response in the form of good-enough policy. People vote for governments that will (or will not) enact adequate and fair-minded measures to assuage injustice. It is *that* individual action (i.e., the act of voting) that my reasoning equals to Samaritanism, not the institutionalized, governmental response to injustice.

9. Anna Stilz, *Liberal Loyalty* (Princeton, NJ: Princeton University Press, 2009).

10. See Jeremy Waldron, "The Principle of Proximity," NYU School of Law, Public Law Research Paper No. 11-08, 2011.

11. Christopher Kutz, *Complicity* (Cambridge: Cambridge University Press, 2000).

12. Eric Beerbohm, *In Our Name* (Princeton, NJ: Princeton University Press, 2012).

13. John Rawls, *A Theory of Justice* (Cambridge, MA: Harvard University Press, 1971), 115.

14. Thomas Christiano, *The Constitution of Equality* (Oxford: Oxford University Press, 2008), 249.

15. John Rawls defines "social primary goods" in this way in *A Theory of Justice*, 79. I think that the concept is helpful and I'm only using it here to illustrate the notion of basic necessities (including rights and liberties) as opposed to luxuries.

16. Mill says: "But the exercise of any political function, either as an elector or as a representative, is power over others. Those that say that the suffrage is not a trust but a right will scarcely accept the conclusion to which their doctrine leads." John Stuart Mill, "Considerations on Representative Government," in *On Liberty and Other Essays*, edited by John Gray (Oxford: Oxford University Press, 2008), 354.

17. Ibid., 355.

18. For this argument and analogy, see Jeremy Waldron, "Votes as Powers," in *Rights and Reason: Essays in Honor of Carl Wellman*, edited by Marilyn Friedman et al. (New York: Kluwer Academic Publishers, 2000).

19. Ibid., 48.

20. Ibid., 48.

21. The power-of-attorney analogy that Waldron offers is really an analogy between the right to vote and familiar powers of private law such as making a gift, completing a sale, making a will, making a contract,

forming a corporation, etc., but he also points out that the right to vote can effectively be analogized to forms of "public law powers." Examples of public law powers include a police officer's legal power to arrest, an official's legal power to issue a license, a judge's legal power to impose a sentence, etc. The core of the idea of a private or a public power is that the individual(s) exercising them can affect the distribution of rights and duties in society. There are examples of public and private law powers that are only effective when exercised collectively (by at least more than one individual). For instance, the opening of a joint checking account distributes power among more than one person; it is an example of a (simple) collective private law power. The verdicts of a jury, or an appellate court, are examples of public law powers exercised collectively. Voting in elections is, then, a collective public law power exercised by many individuals at the same time.

22. Hannah Arendt, "On Violence," in *Crises of the Republic: Lying in Politics; Civil Disobedience; Thoughts on Politics and Revolution* (New York: Harcourt Brace Jovanovich, 1972), 232.

23. Jason Brennan, *The Ethics of Voting* (Princeton, NJ: Princeton University Press, 2011) and "Polluting the Polls: When Citizens Should Not Vote," *Australasian Journal of Philosophy, 87* (2009): 535–549.

24. Geoffrey Brennan and Loren Lomasky, "Is There a Duty to Vote?" and *Democracy and Decision: The Pure Theory of Electoral Preference* (New York: Cambridge University Press, 1993).

25. Morris Jones, "In Defense of Apathy: Some Doubts on the Duty to Vote," *Political Studies, 2* (1954): 25–37.

26. This summary is primarily based on Jason Brennan's account and Brennan and Lomasky's account.

27. In delineating these structural factors, I follow Nick Clark, "Explaining Political Knowledge: The Role of Procedural Quality in an Informed Citizenry," *Political Studies, 3* (2016): 61–80.

28. We can trace this idea back to Anthony Downs's seminal book *An Economic Theory of Democracy* (New York: Harper, 1957), in which he makes the argument that voting is irrational and therefore a paradox because the individual costs of doing it surpass the individual benefits. I elaborate more in the next chapter.

29. Jeremy Bentham, *An Introduction to the Principles of Morals and Legislation* (Middletown, DE: First Rate Publishers), 1–2 (chapter 1).

30. Ibid.

31. Jon Stuart Mill, "Utilitarianism," in *On Liberty and Other Essays*, 137.

32. In fact, the classical utilitarians reckoned that single individuals had limited power to affect the welfare of large numbers of people. See Judith Lichtenberg, "The Right, the All Right and the Good," *Yale Law Journal*, 92 (1983): 552. Generally, they believed that the actions of people had a narrow scope when it came to its effects on others. In Mill's words: "The multiplication of happiness is, according to the utilitarian ethics, the object of virtue: the occasions in which any person (except one in a thousand) has it in his power to do this on an extended scale—in other words, to be a public benefactor—are but exceptional: and on these occasions alone is he called on to consider public utility; in every other case, private utility, the interest or happiness of some few persons, is all he has to attend to." See John Stuart Mill, "Utilitarianism," 149.

33. David Hume, "Of the Original Contract," in *Political Essays*, edited by Knud Haakonssen (Cambridge: Cambridge University Press, 2006), 197.

34. The term "collective activity" denotes a different meaning than a fortuitous accumulation of acts by many people. A collective activity entails awareness that the acts contribute to a shared purpose, whereas an accumulation of acts does not entail a shared purpose: The result that is beneficial for all is a byproduct of individual intentions, strictly. For example, if gas prices are high and drivers take to carpooling in order to save money, the decrease in air pollution due to fewer cars on the road can be thought of as an unintended consequence of many individual goals fortuitously converging. In contrast, if high pollution levels motivate drivers to minimize use of their cars, the resulting improvement in air quality can be viewed as a collective activity because it was brought about by a shared purpose—that of decreasing pollution for all of us. I will not elaborate on this distinction save to say that voting can be seen as a collective activity in the light of a shared purpose—that of securing just governance, even if we don't all agree on what concrete policies good governance requires. For the concept of joint intentionality, see Michael Bratman, *Shared Agency: A Planning Theory of Acting Together* (Oxford: Oxford University Press, 2014).

35. However, the conceptual idea seems to have been quite obvious to Bentham: "When an action, or in particular a measure of government, is supposed by a man to be conformable to the principle of utility, it may be convenient, for the purposes of discourse, to imagine a kind of law or dictate, called a law or dictate of utility: and to speak of the action in question, as being conformable to such law or dictate." Bentham, *Introduction to the Principles of Morals and Legislation*, 3.

36. As will become clear in subsequent chapters, this is part of Jason Brennan's main argument in *The Ethics of Voting*; see, especially, chapter 3.

37. Singer, "Famine, Affluence and Morality," presses this point, although he later retracts it and offers a less demanding theory.

38. Phillip Pettit and Michael Slote, "Satisficing Consequentialism," *Proceedings of the Aristotelian Society*, 58 (1984): 139–176.

39. Martin Luther King Jr. "Civil Right No 1: The Right to Vote," *New York Times Magazine*, March 14 (1965): 26–27, reprinted in *A Testament of Hope: The Essential Writings of Martin Luther King, Jr.*, edited by James Washington (New York: HarperCollins, 1991).

40. Martin Gilens and Benjamin Page, "Testing Theories of American Politics: Elites, Interests Groups and Average Citizens," *Perspectives on Politics*, 12 (2014): 564–581; Alan Monroe, "Public Opinion and Public Policy: 1980–1993." *Public Opinion Quarterly*, 62 (1998): 6–28.

41. When defining "responsiveness," empirical political scientists mainly study the degree to which legislation and policy formulation at the executive level reflect the preferences of voters (average or aggregated in some way). However, from a normative perspective, there is the valid question of whether focusing on preferences alone is advisable, since preferences may be irrational, uninformed, or simply not indicative of what is good for citizens, that is, of their objective interests. However, I suggest that both "preferences" and "objective interests" must be taken into account when thinking about government responsiveness. It is plausible that citizens' preferences be at times mistaken, but it is not plausible that routinely ignoring them will be in the citizens' interest. As a general norm, respecting the people's preferences (short of those that Ronald Dworkin called "external" for entailing immoral desires regarding the lives of others; see Ronald Dworkin, *A Matter of Principle* [London: Clarendon Press, 1985], 335–372) reflects a predilection for thinking that the agent knows what is best for her better than anyone. On the other hand, we should be ready to allow representatives to discern when certain preferences may be detrimental to the interests of the represented or of society as a whole. In other words, we should give them the space to act as "trustees"—not mere "delegates" of the people (see Hanna Pitkin, *The Concept of Representation* [Berkeley: University of California Press, 1969]). In this book, I take no definitive position on what theory of representation must accompany an argument for the duty to vote with care. However, I content myself with suggesting that a happy medium between the unreflective honoring of popular preferences and

the wholly independent acting of elected officials is preferable to either of the two opposite poles.

42. See, classically, Anne Phillips, *The Politics of Presence* (Oxford: Oxford University Press, 1995).

43. Yascha Mounk, *The People versus Democracy* (Cambridge, MA: Harvard University Press, 2018).

44. See Martin Gilens, "Inequality and Democratic Responsiveness," *Public Opinion Quarterly*, 69 (2005): 778–796.

45. See, for example, Christopher Achen and Larry Bartels, *Democracy for Realists: Why Elections Do Not Produce Responsive Government* (Princeton, NJ: Princeton University Press, 2016); Ian Shapiro, *The State of Democratic Theory* (Princeton, NJ: Princeton University Press, 2003); Jane Mansbridge, *Beyond Adversary Democracy* (Chicago: University of Chicago Press, 1983).

46. Phillip Pettit, *On the People's Terms: A Republican Theory and Model of Democracy* (Cambridge: Cambridge University Press, 2013).

47. Yves Cabbane, "Participatory Budgeting: A Significant Contribution to Participatory Democracy," *Environment and Urbanization*, 16 (2004): 27–46.

48. Mill, "Considerations on Representative Government," 210.

49. As subsequent chapters will show, this ideal of impartiality is loosely based on a moral contractualist logic whereby justice calls us to think in terms of what others could find acceptable, not just what is acceptable *to us*. See, for example, Thomas Scanlon, *What We Owe to Each Other* (Cambridge, MA: Harvard University Press, 2000). However, this logic does not require familiarity with complex theories of ethics. As mentioned, political science studies show that many voters already vote with the common good in mind—thus approximating the spirit of my arguments for impartiality here.

50. Brennan, *Ethics of Voting*, particularly chapter 2.

Chapter 2

1. For paradigmatic examples of this literature, see Carole Pateman, *Participation and Democratic Theory* (Cambridge: Cambridge University Press, 1970); Benjamin Barber, *Strong Democracy* (Berkeley: University of California Press, 2004).

2. Thomas Christiano, *The Rule of the Many: Fundamental Issues in Democratic Theory* (New York: Westview Press, 1996), 3.

3. Regarding this question, see the debate between proceduralist and instrumentalist accounts of democratic value. This literature is much more varied and abundant than I can explain here.

4. My aim in this chapter (and book) is not the defense of political participation all across the board. However, my arguments should not be taken to imply that "too much" participation is detrimental to democracy or good governance. My approach is not mistrustful of civic engagement, but I do not think that democracy requires as much participation as possible on the part of the individual citizen because such demand would be unacceptably burdensome. I focus on voting, in particular, as a mechanism for helping society and our fellow citizens attain just governance because I reckon that it is not unwarranted to think of it as a moral demand under circumstances we can imagine (i.e., the system is responsive and it is not dangerous to vote).

5. A problem with Kutz's emphasis on intention alone is that it does not apply well to cases of causal contribution without discernible intention. Examples of this sort are cases of causal contribution to harm that result from the collection of many private acts that were uncoordinated (that is, *not* committed in the framework of a common project or activity). For example, air pollution due to the driving of non-environmentally friendly vehicles does not necessarily signal a conscious intention to harm. Rather, it reflects a careless lack of attention, which, if repeated by millions, will result in collective harm. In turn, I am sympathetic to Beerbohm's approach to moral complicity for injustice and to his (perfunctory) suggestion that political participation (to promote justice) should be seen as a redeeming mechanism—besides being a practical way to exert change (see his book *In Our Name*). However, my view of the duty to vote is not grounded in a (backward-looking) duty to avoid complicity for wrongdoing but in a (forward-looking) *duty to aid* society. Additionally, Beerbohm errs in disregarding an important variable that, I reckon, influences assessment of moral responsibility and complicity for injustice, namely, the distance between the people and its representatives; and the former's incapacity to always render the latter faithful to popular wishes and needs. One of the most underexplored aspects of democratic politics in the philosophical literature is that the represented do not always have the agency needed to justify collective responsibility for wrongdoing, especially if the institutional mechanisms for monitoring their representatives in-between elections are malfunctioning or downright broken. I think that political *representation* may weaken claims of collective responsibility for state injustice. Prevalent

accounts of collective responsibility assume that citizens are *invariably* morally implicated in the deeds of their state because of the relationship that exists between democratic citizenship and the state's policies. However, the nature and functioning of representative institutions—and the inability that citizens may experience in monitoring and punishing public officials other than via elections—must play a role in our assessment of complicity for state injustice. Furthermore, even though the non-voluntary acceptance of state benefits cannot constitute a strong claim against duties to obey the law, the fact that citizens are coerced into supporting the state on pain of legal sanctions must debilitate claims of moral fault for wrongful state acts. Beerbohm does not expand on this line of criticism, which I think is quite powerful. Unfortunately, I cannot develop this line of thinking here.

6. Brennan, *The Ethics of Voting*, 4.
7. Being a Good Samaritan does not require that we bring the person being assisted to an ideal state of health, nor that we bring the society being helped to an ideal (perfect) state of justice. It just requires that we minimize/avert harm or injustice respectively. Because of this, it follows that we have a moral duty to vote as Good Samaritans even if the electoral result we support is decent but not ideal (because there is no ideal alternative to choose from or because the ideal alternative is non-electable). From this it also follows that my arguments for Samaritanism in elections are consistent with viewing lesser-evil voting as moral, and perhaps required—although my arguments would also be consistent with a duty to support the non-electable, yet ideal, alternative, if existent, so that it becomes electable by virtue of the collective support received. I expand on this issue in chapter 3.
8. I take the term "decent Samaritan" from Judith Thompson's "In Defense of Abortion," *Philosophy and Public Affairs*, 1 (1971): 47–66. Thompson originally distinguishes this term from "Good Samaritan" to denote the idea that some acts of help may be much less demanding than the help that the Good Samaritan in the biblical story provided to the ailing victim.
9. Jason Brennan, "Polluting the Polls: When Citizens Should Not Vote," *Australasian Journal of Philosophy*, 87 (2009): 535–549 and *The Ethics of Voting*.
10. Jason Brennan fashions this argument in particular but the other theorists associated with the no-duty position would agree with it, I believe.
11. James Fishkin, *The Limits of Obligation* (New Haven: Yale University Press, 1982).
12. Joel Feinberg, "The Moral and Legal Responsibility of the Bad Samaritan," *Criminal Justice Ethics*, 3 (1984): 67.

13. For a similar approach to the duty to prevent harm and rescue, see Arthur Ripstein, "Three Duties to Rescue: Moral, Civil, and Criminal," *Law and Philosophy, 19* (2000): 751–779.

14. Ibid., 768.

15. Allan Buchanan, "Justice and Charity," *Ethics, 97* (1987): 561 .

16. Ibid.

17. Cicero, *On Duties*, Book 1.

18. Mill, *On Liberty*, 15.

19. Not all non-doings amount to omissions (identifiable failings to act). It makes little sense to think that, because we were sleeping last night, we omitted to save street dogs from being run over by cars, for which we should be blamed. Not all absences of action have moral repercussions or amount to something. Sometimes, not acting amounts to a nothing-event. However, other times, such as when harm is directly in front of us, we are aware of it, and could avert or minimize it with no great difficulty, it is reasonable to think that a failure to act is blameworthy because it signals violation of a positive duty of easy aid. This conclusion, thus, challenges the argument that positive duties are only owed to those with whom we are related by reasons of contract, promising, role-based responsibilities of care, or familiarity such as family and friendship—but not to strangers. This may seem as a conclusion by fiat, but so is the conclusion that positive duties of aid are not universally owed to all humans. Philosophical arguments depart from some unquestioned foundational premises, and in this case, the disagreement seems to relate to the nature of a foundational premise. In (implicit) defiance of universal, unqualified, positive duties of assistance, Robert Nozick, *Anarchy State and Utopia* (New York: Basic Books, 1974), claims that we count omissions as causing harm only when we are convinced, a priori, that the omitting individual had a duty to do something to prevent or assuage the harm or suffering. Thus, our assessment of the causal effect of the omission is moralized. I don't think Nozick's point is detrimental to my argument in this chapter insofar as it points to an assumption that I'm not reticent to refute, and this is the assumption that we are normally bound by universal (non-special) duties of easy assistance towards strangers. Because we are, counting an omission to aid as causing undue harm is not incongruent or mistaken.

20. Joel Feinberg, *Harm to Others: The Moral Limits of The Criminal Law* (Oxford: Oxford University Press, 1984), 173–175 and John Kleining, "Good Samaritanism," *Philosophy and Public Affairs, 5* (1976): 390–393.

21. I elaborate more in detail on this duty subsequently.

22. As originally theorized by Anthony Downs in *An Economic Theory of Democracy*.

23. See Tracy Isaacs, *Moral Responsibility in Collective Contexts* (Oxford: Oxford University Press, 2011).

24. Ibid., 9.

25. Eric Beerbohm, *In Our Name* (Princeton, NJ: Princeton University Press, 2014), 231–322.

26. I take and adapt this example from ibid.

27. Judith Thompson has argued that there are "minimally decent" Samaritans, "good" Samaritans, "very good" Samaritans, and "splendid" Samaritans. See her "A Defense of Abortion."

28. Jeremy Waldron, "A Right to Do Wrong," *Ethics*, 92 (1981): 21–39.

29. Virginia Held, "Can a Random Collection of Individuals Be Morally Responsible?," *Journal of Philosophy*, 67 (1970): 471–481.

30. In this respect, see Laura Valentini, "Social Samaritan Justice: When and Why Needy Fellow Citizens Have a Right to Assistance," *American Political Science Review*, 109 (2015): 735–749 for a different view of the distribution of duties to help others. Valentini claims that, because many people may be in an equal position to help an imperiled victim, no one of them has a duty to do so. For this reason, she argues that we should understand duties of Samaritan aid (to help the troubled) as duties that the state owes to its citizens but that private citizens carry out in its name (just as prosecutors carry out the state's duty to incriminate the guilty, for example) when no other institutional forms of assistance can step in (such as firefighters, to name a few). Valentini errs in drawing this conclusion because the fact that there are multiple bystanders involved only means two things: (1) that the bystanders may have a duty to coordinate among each other the rescue and (2) that every one of them has a duty not to be indifferent to what the others will do or are doing, especially if the rescue requires cooperation and collective action. Valentini also argues that duties of Samaritan rescue cannot be universal (owed to humanity) but only special—binding towards fellow citizens. This argument is highly counterintuitive because natural duties of justice are feasible among strangers. Her conclusion is also strange because it denies, from the outset, that individuals may have any duties whatsoever to initiate or attempt the coordinating of efforts to help others in need in the absence of *one's* state institutions. For example, if I am vacationing in a foreign beach and spot a swimmer in distress, do I have a duty to help a foreign state in its rescue functions by throwing a lifesaver to the drowning person? From Valentini's arguments strictly,

it is not clear that I have. Denying that one has duties of aid to other individuals qua individuals contradicts the all-too-sensible intuition that duties of aid are, in principle, universal. The debate on whether justice is circumscribed to domestic affairs is too big to be discussed here. It suffices to say that a duty of Samaritan justice to vote is not a special duty that binds us to our fellow citizens *because* we share something special with them. If voting were to be done in districts that straddled countries, for example, my arguments for the Samaritan duty to vote with care would be equally strong. It should be noted that the fact that we share common institutions with our fellow citizens means that we are effectively *only* able to cooperate with them in elections. But this ability is a matter of practical reality—not of principle, in my view.

31. Derek Parfit, *Reasons and Persons* (Oxford: Oxford University Press, 1984), 70.

32. There is a difference between coordinated collective action and spontaneous collective action. The former implies the existence of a common goal that drives cooperation. The latter entails the accumulation of individual actions without a common goal. In this case, there is no cooperation per se but many spontaneous actions coexisting. There is a spectrum of "tightness" in collective action depending on how clear and official a common goal may be. Generally, voting should be seen as a case of (loosely) coordinated collective action whose goal is the achievement of good governance (even if there is disagreement as to what that entails; see last section for elaboration on the point).

33. We will not be required to make up for the contributions of individuals that fail to fulfill their duty to act, however. We are only morally required to do our fair share of aiding. That means, as I see it, that we are only required to do the amount of work that would be needed if everyone cooperated on an equal basis. We are required to do that which would lead to the sought-after outcome (the possibly best outcome) if everyone contributed the same amount. I take this intuition from Derek Parfit's *Reasons and Persons*, 30–33. Liam Murphy in "The Demands of Beneficence," *Philosophy and Public Affairs*, *22* (1993): 267–292 takes Parfit's reasoning as central to justifying a "principle of limited compliance" (i.e., the idea that we are not required to make up for the lack of compliance of others with a moral duty). The spirit of Murphy's principle of limited compliance is consistent with my formulation of the Samaritan duty of justice to help society via the vote. Samaritan duties are binding insofar, and *because*, they do not require large sacrifices from the individual. This logic also applies to cases in

which there is no free riding in cooperation but where circumstances are such that, even if cooperation was perfect, each individual contribution to the activity would have to be too large for the common effort to have an effect.

34. See Brennan and Lomasky, "Is There a Duty to Vote?" for a refutation of the generalization argument for the moral duty to vote. Jason Brennan in *The Ethics of Voting* also evokes it to rule it out as ineffective. Here I am distinguishing my reasoning from the generalization rationale.

35. See ibid.

36. Brennan and Lomasky make this point by resorting to the following example (see their "Is There a Duty to Vote"): a society where nobody wants to be a farmer would cease to exist because people would not be able to get food. Does this mean that people have a duty to become farmers, then? They say, of course not. But this example poses a mistaken analogy. Farming is a market activity done for profit. Making people become farmers goes against freedom of occupational choice, which is a basic right in liberal democracies. But we do make everybody pay taxes and serve jury duty, for example, and nobody seems to find strong normative objections to this. These duties do not have to be grounded on the (Kantian) generalization logic. We may just think that requiring from everybody that they pay taxes and serve as jurors secures two important public goods, namely, national financial health and a fair administration of justice. Voting poses a similar possibility for argument.

37. See, for the American case in particular, Vanessa Williamson, *Read My Lips: Why Americans Are Proud to Pay Taxes* (Princeton, NJ: Princeton University Press, 2016). Williamson's book argues and shows that Americans are better informed about taxes, and more morally in support of paying them, than is traditionally assumed. She also argues that Americans are willing and proud to pay taxes because they don't see them as the price to pay for received benefits by the state but as a sign of civic commitment to society at large. More Americans believe that there is greater than zero chance that Elvis Presley is alive than that it is OK to cheat on one's taxes, Williamson remarks.

38. Amartya Sen refers to the foregoing sense of collective rationality as the logic of "commitment" in "Rational Fools: A Critique of the Behavioral Foundations of Economic Theory," *Philosophy and Public Affairs*, 6 (1977): 317–344 I adopt his term here.

39. Parfit, *Reasons and Persons*, 77.

40. However, the rational choice perspective could advocate voting in this case since a small number of voters means that my individual capacity to tilt the election is higher if I vote.

41. Steven Finkel, "Personal Influence, Collective Rationality and Mass Political Action," *American Political Science Review, 83* (1989): 885–903, argues that they do so by focusing on generalization arguments that ground moral commitments (i.e., what would happen if everyone did that?) and by believing, mistakenly, that for a collective result to come about, all without exception must contribute.

42. Amartya Sen, *The Idea of Justice* (Cambridge, MA: Harvard University Press, 2011), 194.

43. Brennan, "Polluting the Polls," 539.

44. As will become clear in chapter 5, even though votes can be redundant when it comes to reaching the threshold needed to win an election, those votes may not be instrumentally futile. As Mackie argues (in "Why It's Rational to Vote," in *Rationality, Democracy, and Justice: The Legacy of Jon Elster*, edited by Claudio Lopez Guerra and Julia Maskivker [Cambridge: Cambridge University Press, 2015], 21–49), people may vote with a view to narrowing a candidate's margin of loss or to widening her margin of victory. In this way, for example, the winning candidate's mandate can be strengthened or weakened correspondingly. Richard Tuck in *Free Riding* (Cambridge, MA: Harvard University Press, 2008) also claims that people may vote with a view to forming part of the set of votes that will be needed to tilt the election (to pass the threshold) even if they know that their vote will not be decisive in the election. In general, even though many votes will end up being redundant in an election, there is no way to know in advance which ones. Thus, it makes sense to think that all votes are equally important instrumentally, at least in the face of uncertainty.

45. Yet elections are not the only way to achieve good results. Furthermore, according to Bernard Manin in *The Principles of Representative Government* (Cambridge: Cambridge University Press, 1997), elections have an "aristocratic" (and thus inegalitarian) character. Some have recently suggested that (a return to) lottery, not elections, would be a more "democratic" procedure to select our representatives. See Alex Guerrero, "Against Elections: The Lottocratic Alternative," *Philosophy and Public Affairs, 42* (2014): 135–178. Random sampling also resonates with the ideal of justice as impartiality. I don't think that recognizing these points would compromise the validity of the main argument here. In a democracy via lottery,

the accent would be put on the moral duty of democratic citizens to serve (which already applies to juries), rather than to vote.

46. Judith Lichtenberg, "The Demandingness of Negative Duties," Ethics, *120* (2010): 564.

47. For a classical elaboration of the view that individuals are to be held morally responsible for what they do as opposed to what they fail to do or prevent, see Bernard Williams "A Critique of Utilitarianism," in *Utilitarianism: For and Against*, edited by Bernard Williams (Cambridge: Cambridge University Press, 1973).

48. The baseline is met via the fulfillment of some basic requisites for a person's well-being. The literature on justice refers to these requisites as fundamental human interests. See, as an illustration, Thomas Scanlon, "Preference and Urgency," *Journal of Philosophy, 72* (1975): 655–669. These are interests that all individuals can be reasonable said to share on grounds of their humanity. They are essential because they are necessary for the achievement of ultimate life goals. Health, a minimum of income, and education are examples of these basic requisites for well-being.

49. Joel Feinberg: *Freedom and Fulfillment* (Princeton, NJ: Princeton University Press, 1992), 5. Feinberg defines harm in this sense as the "thwarting, setting back, or defeating of an interest." *Harm to Others*, 33. I submit that the harm entailed in failing to vote well adversely affects the interest that society as a collective body has in being governed fairly. It also affects the interests of individual citizens in enjoying the fruits of good governance.

50. The reader may refer to the discussion on opportunity costs in chapter 5.

Chapter 3

1. See Scanlon, *What We Owe to Each Other*, for use of the term "rejectability."

2. Generally, reasoning on the basis of impartiality is in the tradition of Kant's categorical imperative, which tests principles of conduct by their hypothetical acceptability from all points of view. Kant views public reasoning as shared reasoning from the *standpoint of everyone*, and he sees this type of perspective as fundamental to the public justification of the state and its coercive laws (see, among others, Kant's notion of "public reason" as elaborated in his famed 1784 essay "What Is Enlightenment?" His logic for the notion of public reason, however, is more generally derived from his defense of the categorical imperative as a test for ethical action; see his *Groundwork of the Metaphysics of Morals*, written in 1785). The impartiality

rationale that I am invoking for defining what good voting entails is also in the tradition of J.-J. Rousseau's distinction between the private reason and the public reason of an individual, where the latter constitutes reasoning from the perspective of everyone in the community (see his *On the Social Contract*). In the contemporary philosophical literature, the conceptualization of impartiality that I have in mind when I think of a considered vote could be thought to evoke Thomas Scanlon's standard of fairness as elaborated in *What We Owe to Each Other*. Discussions of justice as impartiality also include, but are not limited to, Brian Barry *Justice as Impartiality* (Oxford: Oxford University Press, 1995) and Thomas Nagel, *The View from Nowhere* (Oxford: Oxford University Press, 1986). I'm well aware of the fact that these accounts of impartiality do not present a monolithic front. Here I only take ethical contractualism as a premise for understanding justice in an admittedly general way. I believe that despite their obvious differences, these accounts share a common respect for the morality of taking into account other people's views when it comes to finding social solutions that will pass the muster of justice. I am hesitant to include John Rawls's conception of justice as epitomized by his famed "original position" device because of the powerful argument that his ideal is ultimately not an example of impartiality but of reciprocity-based, or mutual advantage-based, conception of justice (Barry makes this point in *Justice as Impartiality*). For reasons of space, I cannot deal with this point in the book.

3. Robert Goodin, *Reflective Democracy* (Oxford: Oxford University Press, 2003), 15.

4. For references on this empirical literature, see chapter 5 here.

5. Bryan Caplan, *The Myth of the Rational Voter* (Princeton, NJ: Princeton University Press, 2007); Illya Somin, *Democracy and Political Ignorance*; Brennan, *The Ethics of Voting*.

6. Phillip Tetlock, *Expert Political Judgment: How Good Is It? How Can We Know?* (Princeton, NJ: Princeton University Press, 2005); Arthur Lupia, and Matthew McCubbins, *The Democratic Dilemma: Can Citizens Learn What They Need to Know?* (Cambridge: Cambridge University Press, 1998); Arthur Lupia, "How Elitism Undermines the Study of Voter Competence," *Critical Review*, 18 (2006): 217–232; Mackie, "Why It's Rational to Vote"; Samuel Popkin, *The Reasoning Voter: Communication and Persuasion in Presidential Campaigns* (Chicago: University of Chicago Press, 1994).

7. Benjamin Page and Robert Y. Shapiro, *The Rational Public: Fifty Years of Trends in Americans' Policy Preferences* (Chicago: University of Chicago Press, 1992). The authors conclude that aggregated American opinions on

public issues and policies are stable, coherent, and make sense in terms of available information. They find that public opinion on identifiable issues changes in predictable ways in response to changing events, and opinion changes are sensible adjustments to new information and conditions.

8. Robert Shapiro and Yaeli Bloch-Elkon, "Political Polarization and the Rational Public," paper prepared for presentation at the Annual Meeting of the American Political Science Association annual presentation, 2006, available here: http://themonkeycage.org/Shapiro%2520and%2520Bloch.pdf.

9. Brennan, *Against Democracy*, chapter 2.

10. Ibid., chapters 1 and 2.

11. Rawls, *A Theory of Justice*, section 14.

12. However, this approach does not assume the existence of an uncontested and eternal "moral truth." The universally valid criteria are given by concerns that everyone can accept, not by an externally construed or objectively discovered truth, so, no need for "moral" experts. Each citizen can make a contribution.

13. See Goodin, *Reflective Democracy*.

14. Thomas Scanlon, "Contractualism and Utilitarianism," in *Ethical Theory: An Anthology*, edited by Russ Shafer-Landau (London: Wiley Blackwell, 2013), 557.

15. See chapter 2 for the pertinent references supporting this point.

16. Barry, *Justice as Impartiality*, 69.

17. In this respect, my understanding of impartiality or fair-mindedness is different from impartiality theories of morality that rely on the neutral spectator imagery (see, for example, David Hume's "judicious spectator" or Sidgwick's "point of view of the universe"). The latter are oblivious to considerations of self-interest because the neutral observer is disinterested and, for that reason, often criticized as inhumanly demanding.

18. Thomas Scanlon, "Contractualism and Utilitarianism," 557.

19. Rousseau, *The Social Contract*, Book IV, chapter I.

20. Barry, *Justice as Impartiality*, 70.

21. Ibid.

22. Phillip Pettit, *On the People's Terms: A Republican Theory and Model of Democracy* (Cambridge: Cambridge University Press, 2008), 248. Pettit is basing his explanation of this approach to the common good on Adam Smith's *The Wealth of Nations*, as presented to the world in 1767.

23. Pettit, *On the People's Terms*, 249.

24. The explanation that follows is primordially based on Pettit's account in ibid., 249–251.

25. Ibid., 249.

26. *On the Social Contract*, Book II, chapter 3.

27. Robert Goodin, "Institutionalizing the Public Interest: The Defense of Deadlock and Beyond," *American Political Science Review*, 90 (1996): 331–343.

28. This is the spirit of James Madison's (and the Federalists) writings in arguing for the ratification of a new constitution of the United States in the 1780s. However, it would be inaccurate to associate Madison with the most contemporary and elaborate theories of pluralist power in political science.

29. See, classically, Robert Dahl's *Who Governs?* (New Haven: Yale University Press, 1961). Some argued that the pluralist wave of theorists in the 1950s and 1960s saw the relationship between groups and the state too simplistically. "Neo-pluralists," by contrast, don't assume that the state is a neutral umpire mediating between the demands of different interest groups. Rather, they assume that it is relatively autonomous and will defend sectional interests. The enormous political science literature on the functioning of democracies in the last two decades reflects this trend.

30. J. S. Mill, "Considerations on Representative Government," 245.

31. John Dewey, *Intelligence in the Modern World: John Dewey's Philosophy*, edited by Joseph Ratner (New York: Modern Library, 1939), 402.

32. J. S. Mill presented several (and sometimes conflicting) rationales for political participation. One of them was the educational benefits of civic engagement understood, roughly, as the intellectual advantages that putting one's mental abilities to work for the sake of public affairs would cause, by voting, performing jury duty, or serving as a public official. See "Considerations on Representative Government," 247–250.

33. Ibid., 255.

34. J. S. Mill, *Later Letters*, letter 1186, in *Later Letters 1848–1873*, edited by Francis Mineka and Dwight Lindley, vol. 16 (Toronto: University of Toronto Press, 1972), 1340.

35. See John Rawls, "Justice as Fairness: Political Not Metaphysical," *Philosophy and Public Affairs 14* (1985): 223–251 and *Political Liberalism* (New York: Columbia University Press, 1991).

36. Micah Schwartzman, "The Completeness of Public Reason," *Politics, Philosophy, and Economics, 3* (2004): 192.

37. For example, some citizens may support generous welfare state programs based on their religious beliefs (say, Catholic doctrine and the duty to help the poor). Other citizens may equally support the welfare state based on a secular understanding of the requirements of social justice. More on this possible distinction in the following pages.

38. Rawls made this modification to his view after criticism that his notion of public reason was too constraining and incompatible with the motivation of many actual citizens. See Rawls, *Political Liberalism*, 241–242.

39. This is what the critical literature on public reason refers to as the "asymmetry objection." Defenders of the public reason doctrine as traditionally conceived suppose that disagreements on questions of political justice will be less frequent and less deep than disagreements on questions of religion and further philosophies of life. Thus, there is an asymmetry in attributing probabilities to these two types of disparities. See Jonathan Quong, *Liberalism without Perfection* (Oxford: Oxford University Press, 2010). Quong argues that the asymmetry objection can be overcome. In what follows, I challenge his view in important respects even though I do not abandon the public reason doctrine in its general form.

40. I take this useful description of Rawls's notion from Quong, *Liberalism without Perfection*, 194–195. Rawls alludes to it in *Political Liberalism*, 53–57.

41. However, as it will become clear shortly, the burdens of judgment should also entail disagreement on questions of justice—not only comprehensive doctrines.

42. The political science literature on voting behavior and religion/religiosity is enormous to cite here, but for a start, see Yilmaz Esmer and Thorleif Pattersson, "The Effects of Religion and Religiosity on Voting Behavior," in *The Oxford Handbook of Political Behavior*, edited by Russell Dalton and Hans-Dieter Kinglemann (Oxford: Oxford University Press, 2007).

43. Christopher Eberle. *Religious Conviction in Liberal Politics* (Cambridge: Cambridge University Press, 2002); Gerald Gaus and Kevin Vallier, "The Roles of Religious Conviction in a Publicly Justified Polity: The Implications of Convergence, Asymmetry and Political Institutions," *Philosophy and Social Criticism*, 35 (2009): 51–76; David Reidy, "Rawls' Wide View of Public Reason: Not Wide Enough," *Res Publica*, 6 (2000): 49–72.

44. Schwartzman, "The Completeness of Public Reason"; and Gerald Gaus, *Justificatory Liberalism: An Essay on Epistemology and Political Theory* (Oxford: Oxford University Press, 1996).

45. There are other objections to the public reason literature in general but I do not have the space here to explain what those are in detail. The inconclusiveness and indeterminacy objections are clearly the most relevant to my arguments for the fair-minded voting standard, and so, I provide an answer to them as applied to my case for careful voting in this section. Note, however, that I will also address, briefly, the insincerity objection to public reason, namely, the idea that, if justificatory considerations are expanded beyond shared beliefs, the reasons for accepting them will be insincere, therefore illegitimate. I will argue that expanding the range of reasons that we can offer others for acceptance does not entail, necessarily, being dishonest.

46. For a forceful formulation of this critique and a solution to it, as explained below, see Gerald Gaus, *The Order of Public Reason* (Cambridge: Cambridge University Press, 2010).

47. In *Political Liberalism*, Rawls describes how a reasonable balance of values will lead to the acceptance of abortion rights, but this conclusion has been challenged on the basis of the inconclusiveness objection. See Schwartzman, "The Incompleteness of Public Reason," 194.

48. For this example, see Quong, *Liberalism without Perfection*, 204–205.

49. Quong calls this type of disagreement "substantive" as opposed to "foundational." The latter is characteristic of indeterminacy cases. See *Liberalism without Perfection*, 201–209.

50. A variation of this example is given by Quong, *Liberalism without Perfection*, 204.

51. Quong, *Liberalism without Perfection*, 208.

52. Thomas Cristiano presents the division between general policy *goals* and concrete policy *means*; and he argues that it is the citizens' duty to worry about the first but not worry about the second since doing so may require a level of expertise that is not realistic to expect from them. See his "Rational Deliberation among Experts and Citizens," in *Deliberative Systems: Deliberative Democracy at the Large Scale*, edited by John Parkinson (Cambridge: Cambridge University Press, 2012).

53. Gerald Gaus, "Does Democracy Reveal the Voice of the People? Four Takes on Rousseau," *Australasian Journal of Philosophy*, 75 (1997): 156. Gaus attributes this view to Fred D'Agostino in "The Idea and the Ideal of Public Justification," *Social Theory and Practice*, 18 (1992): 143–164.

54. The paradigmatic proponent of this view is Gerald Gaus. See, among other works, the *Order of Public Reason*. Other proponents of the ideal include Paul Billingham, "Convergence Justifications within Political Liberalism: A

Defence," *Res Publica 22* (2016): 135–143 and Kevin Vallier, *Liberal Politics and Public Faith: Beyond Separation* (Oxford: Routledge, 2014).

55. Robert Goodin, "Institutionalizing the Public Interest," *American Political Science Review, 90* (1996): 331.

56. My emphasis on fair-mindedness means that my position deviates from a strictly formalist approach to correct voting. For example, Richard Lau and David Redlawsk in "Voting Correctly," *American Political Science Review, 91* (1997): 585–598, argue that to vote correctly is to cast a ballot that is consistent with your (previously) expressed preferences and values (if you had full information). But how is this correct in more than a formal, morally empty way? From Lau and Redlawsk's account it follows that, if your preferences are for genocide, and you don't vote for the genocidal candidate because you don't know there is one, then you don't vote correctly. This is highly counterintuitive because it is so devoid of any substantive argument concerning what it really means to vote well.

57. Kevin Vallier, "Convergence and Consensus in Public Reason," *Public Affairs Quarterly, 25* (2011): 272.

58. Paul Billingham, "Convergence Justifications within Political Liberalism," 145.

59. Contrary to the traditional consensus in the public reason literature, it is conceivable that people find it easier to agree with each other based on their comprehensive doctrines than on justice-based reasons, strictly. For example, an egalitarian will differ from a Nozickean libertarian in her views on progressive taxation to fight poverty, but a secular egalitarian may find agreement on this front with a religious person who bases her support of progressive taxes on Christian doctrine.

60. Micah Schwartzman, "The Sincerity of Public Reason," *Journal of Political Philosophy, 19* (2011): 375–398.

61. Convergence-based models of political justification, then, entail less demanding and more realistic standards of moral and cognitive reasoning. Unlike the idealized constituency in the traditional Rawlsian model, which imposes strict standards of evidence evaluation, convergence models like Gaus's assume that not everybody will reason following those standards most effectively. However, as long as their views are intelligible, they should be accepted in the debate. Very roughly, Gaus proposes to understand justification in terms of an individual's existing beliefs and inferential norms. This form of relativism does not ultimately mean that any set of beliefs must therefore be justified, however. For development of this standard, See *Justificatory Liberalism*, chapter 3.

62. I adapt this example from Gaus, *Justificatory Liberalism*, chapter 9.

63. Ibid., 289–292.

64. Billingham, "Convergence Justifications," 143.

65. Vallier, "Convergence and Consensus."

66. Mill, *Considerations on Representative Government*, 254–255.

67. It should be noted that several studies show how researchers' preconceived ideas about the capacities of average citizens undermine studies of voter competence. See Lupia, "How Elitism Undermines the Study of Voter Competence."

68. John Dewey, *The Public and Its Problems* (New York: H. Holt, 1927), 208.

69. Aristotle, *The Politics*, Book 3, chap. 11, 1282a18. Aristotle's line of reasoning here is consistent with the "Protagoras myth," namely, the idea that political wisdom is equally distributed among citizens, even if dormant. See Helene Landermore, *Democratic Reason* (Princeton, NJ: Princeton University Press, 2011), 55.

70. Lupia and McCubbins, *The Democratic Dilemma*.

71. Tetlock studies "political judgment" in regular citizens and shows that when evaluating and predicting, political "experts" fare hardly better than "laypeople" and are generally outperformed by statistical regressions. See Phillip Tetlock, *Expert Political Judgment*. See also Robert Talisse, "Does Public Ignorance Defeat Deliberative Democracy?," *Critical Review*, 10 (2004): 455–463.

72. Tetlock, *Expert Political Judgement*. See also Gerald Gaus, "Is the Public Competent? Compared to Whom? About What?" *Critical Review*, 20 (2008): 291–311.

73. Tetlock, *Expert Political Judgment*, 69.

74. Friedrich Hayek, "The Use of Knowledge in Society," *American Economic Review*, 35 (1945): 519–530.

75. For example, Samuel Brittan argues that macroeconomic models are of little use to predict economic outcomes. Similarly, Nassim Taleb claims that financial models have no predictive value at all. In the same vein, a study by Karlyn Mitchell et al, found that the performance of financial models in predicting the Treasury bill rate was indistinguishable from a random walk, and at times worse than random. See Samuel Brittan, "It Is Time to Jettison the Forecasts," *Financial Times*, December 9 (2007), cited in Gaus, "Is the Public Incompetent?," 300–305, Nassim Taleb. *The Black Swan: The Impact of the Highly Improbable* (New York: Random House, 2007); Karlyn Mitchell and Douglas Pearce, "Professional Forecasts of Interest Rates and Exchange Rates: Evidence from the Wall

Street Journal's Panel of Economists," *Journal of Macroeconomics, 29* (2007): 840–854.

76. Michael Reich, Ken Jacobs, and Annette Bernhardt, "Local Minimum Wage Laws: Impacts on Workers, Families and Businesses," Institute for Research on Labor and Employment, IRLE Working Paper No. 104-14, March 2014, Dale Belman and Paul J. Wolfson, "The New Minimum Wage Research," W.E. Upjohn Institute for Employment Research, *Employment Research, 21* (2014): 4–5.

77. David Card and Alan Krueger, *Myth and Measurement: The New Economics of the Minimum Wage* (Princeton, NJ: Princeton University Press, 2015).

78. Phillip Converse, "The Nature of Belief Systems in Mass Publics," *Critical Review, 18* (1964): 1–74.

79. Samuel Popkin, "The Factual Basis of Belief Systems: A Reassessment," *Critical Review, 1* (2006): 233–254.

80. UK pollster *Ipsos Mori* interviewed 11,527 people in 2015 and constructed a 14-country Index of Ignorance. The United States is the second most ignorant country on the ignorance list, after Italy. Even though the experiment finds that all country populations get facts wrong, there is considerable difference between those at the bottom and those at the top. See the index construction at https://www.ipsos-mori.com/Assets/Docs/Publications/Index-of-ignorance-calculation.pdf.

81. For a magnificent overview of this literature, see Richard Lau and David Redlawsk, "Advantages and Disadvantages of Cognitive Heuristics in Political Decision Making," in *Controversies in Voting Behavior*, edited by Richard Niemi (Washington, DC: CQ Press, 2011).

82. Arthur Lupia and Matthew McCubbins. *The Democratic Dilemma: Can Citizens Learn What They Need to Know?* (Cambridge: Cambridge University Press, 1998).

83. Popkin, *The Reasoning Voter*; Larry Bartels, "Uninformed Votes: Information Effects in Presidential Elections," *American Journal of Political Science, 40* (1996): 194–230; Paul Goren, "Core Principles and Policy Reasoning in Mass Publics," *British Journal of Political Science, 31* (2001): 159–177.

84. Popkin, *The Reasoning Voter*.

85. Lupia and McCubbins, *The Democratic Dilemma*; and Lupia, "How Elitism Undermines the Study of Voter Competence."

86. Lupia, "How Elitism Undermines the Study of Voter Competence."

87. Paradoxically, Jason Brennan argues that "most citizens have good and reasonable intuitions about political competence. The average citizen can give a reasonable account of the difference between a good and a bad juror, between a well-informed and an ignorant voter, between an incompetent and a competent member of parliament or between a competent and an incompetent district attorney" (*Against Democracy*, 225). But Brennan argues immediately that even though "the average citizen is probably able to produce a good theory of political competence . . . they may be incompetent at applying their theory. . . . The empirical literature on voter irrationality and ignorance does not say that voters have bad standards but rather that they are bad at applying their reasonable standards" (ibid.). In finishing that phrase, he cites *only* Bryan Caplan's work to substantiate his conclusion. Nowhere in his book does Brennan mention and expand on a wealth of empirical work by political scientists and political psychologists that challenges the idea that most voters are not capable of applying their theories of competence when they vote. This is the literature on cognitive shortcuts and heuristics led by authors such as Lupia and others, who have made huge strides in showing that, despite the lack of deep expertise on political questions, a sizable number of regular voters can rely on secondary knowledge that makes up for their lack of expertise. They can rely on cues and variables that give them the knowledge they need to assess candidates despite not knowing much about the substance of their platforms. It is this literature that offers the most compelling case against Brennan's arguments against the average voter, and he should at least indulge in it more than he does. Saying that most voters are not competent enough to use the cognitive heuristics in question effectively will not do in the absence of a more formal analysis of the literature. Importantly, his assertion that most voters are capable of identifying who is an expert and what expertise requires in a public official is utterly consistent with the possibility that they are also capable of using cognitive heuristics satisfactorily in order to vote. After all, if a citizen can identify a competent candidate, why can't he vote for him on those grounds? Additionally, the worry that most voters cannot follow heuristics seems to be partly unfounded if one is to focus on how public opinion behaves in the aggregate. As mentioned before, Page and Shapiro, in *The Rational Public*, survey the policy preferences of Americans from the 1930s to 1990 and show that voting about broad and important issues changes sensibly in response to events and to changing government policies.

88. Mackie, "Why It's Rational to Vote." See also Tuck, *Free Riding*, for the argument that people may vote to form part of the set of needed votes to tilt the election favorably.

89. Furthermore, the fact that the contribution is so imperceptible may explain why people may not bother to do any calculus of rationality and vote out of other reasons such as civic virtue, expressive motives, or simply entertainment (more on this in chapter 5 ahead).

90. The rational ignorance thesis also assumes a dubious premise to start with: that people know their votes don't matter individually. In Jeffrey Friedman's words: "Voters who know that their votes are unlikely to matter should not only fail to inform themselves politically; they should also fail to vote. The fact that voters vote, along with the polls showing that they think their votes do matter, indicates that the premise of rational ignorance theory is false. See Friedman, "Ignorant: Yes, Rational: No," at https://www.cato-unbound.org/2013/10/18/jeffrey-friedman/ignorance-yes-rational-no.

91. See Caplan, *The Myth of the Rational Voter*.

92. As Friedman ("Ignorant") remarks, part of the evidence is on page 74 of Somin's book, *Democracy and Political Ignorance*, where it emerges that 70 percent of American voters think that their individual votes "really matter." See also David E. Campbell, *Why We Vote: How Schools and Communities Shape Our Civic Life* (Princeton, NJ: Princeton University Press, 2008), 52, where he says that a citizen participation study shows that 89 percent of voters say that influencing government policy is either a very important or a somewhat important reason for having voted. This view is inconsistent with the knowledge or awareness that one's vote is infinitesimally influential among millions of others.

93. Stephen Bennet and Jeffrey Friedman, "The Irrelevance of Economic Theory to Understanding Economic Ignorance," *Critical Review*, 20 (2008): 195–258.

94. Alan Abramovitz and Steven Webster, "All Politics Is National: The Rise of Negative Partisanship and the Nationalization of U.S. House and Senate Elections in the 21st Century," prepared for presentation at the Annual Meeting of the Midwest Political Science Association, Chicago, Illinois, April 16–19, 2015.

95. James Druckman, Erik Peterson, and Rune Slothuus, "How Elite Partisan Polarization Affects Public Opinion Formation," *American Political Science Review*, 107 (2013): 57–79; John Zaller, *The Nature and Origins of Mass Opinion* (Cambridge: Cambridge University Press, 1992).

96. John Zaller and Stanley Feldman, "A Simple Theory of the Survey Response: Answering Questions versus Revealing Preferences," *American Journal of Political Science, 36* (1992): 9.

97. Ibid.

98. James Druckman and Lawrence Jacobs. *Who Governs? Presidents, Public Opinion and Manipulation* (Chicago: University of Chicago Press, 2015).

99. Santiago Olivella and Joseph Uscinski, "The Mediating Impact of Conspiracy Thinking on Climate Change Attitudes," prepared for the "Suspect Science: Climate Change, Epidemics, and Questions of Conspiracy" conference, September 17–19, 2015, at the Centre for Research in the Arts, Social Sciences and Humanities, University of Cambridge, Cambridge.

100. Aaron McCright and Riley E. Dunlap, "Anti-reflexivity: The American Conservative Movement's Success in Undermining Climate Science and Policy," *Theory, Culture & Society, 27* (2010): 100–133.

101. Amelia Sharman, "Mapping the Climate Sceptical Blogosphere," *Global Environmental Change, 26* (2014): 159–170.

102. Michael Graetz and Ian Shapiro, *Death by A Thousand Cuts: The Fights over Taxing Inherited Wealth* (Princeton, NJ: Princeton University Press, 2005).

103. Again, critics of the duty to vote seem to utterly ignore the vast literature on interest group behavior and policy outcomes that political scientists, mainly, have produced since the 1950s (and even before). A classic piece for anyone minimally familiar with this literature is Arthur Bentley, *The Process of Government: A Study of Social Pressures* (Chicago: University of Chicago Press, 1908). More recent works include Fred Mc Chesney, *Money for Nothing: Politicians, Rent Extraction, and Political Extorsion* (Cambridge: Cambridge University Press, 1997); Glenn Parker, *Congress and the Rent-Seeking Society* (Ann Arbor: University of Michigan Press, 1996); Martin Gilens and Benjamin Page, "Testing Theories of American Democracy: Interest Groups, Elites and Average Citizens," *Perspectives on Politics, 12* (2014): 564–582.

104. Jeffrey Drop and Wendy Hansen, "Purchasing Protection? The Effect of Political Spending on U.S. Trade Policy," *Political Research Quarterly, 57* (2004): 35.

105. For a good overview of the growth and functioning of lobbying groups in Western Europe, see Jeremy Richardson, "Government, Interest Groups, and Policy Change," *Political Studies, 48* (2000): 1006–1025.

106. For more elaboration on the disparity, long discussed among political scientists, between concentration of benefits and diffusion of costs,

see "Roderick Kiewiet and Andrea Matozzi, "Voter Rationality and Democratic Government," *Critical Review, 20* (2008): 313–326.

107. Using data from the National Elections Survey, Abramovitz and Webster show that, in the last two decades, the United States has seen sharp increases in party polarization, which leads voters to have increasing negative opinions of the opposing party and their supporters. Increases in party loyalty, moreover, may lead to less flexible ways of processing information that is not favorable to one's ideological position as well as increasing the instances in which elites manipulate information to broaden the gap between the already polarized parties. Robert Shapiro and Yaeli Bloch-Elkon, "Political Polarization and the Rational Public," paper prepared for the Annual Meeting of the American Political Science Association, 2006. "With highly divided and ideological political parties, political leaders may have increasingly less compunction about attempting to manipulate or even deceive. Such leaders surely deserve our scorn" (ibid., 24).

108. Political polarization and ideological conflict are magnified by a media model that thrives on conflict (ibid., 24) and the public can selectively reinforce their polarized views by only attending to the media outlets that confirm their opinions. However guilty the voter seems for this, one cannot ignore the influence of the media dynamic that purposely incentivizes polarization.

109. Nick Clark, "Explaining Political Knowledge"; Gordon Stacey and Gary Segura, "Cross-National Variation in the Political Sophistication of Individuals: Capability or Choice?," *Journal of Politics, 59* (1997): 126–147.

110. Christopher Elmendorf and David Schleicher, "Informing Consent: Voter Ignorance, Political Parties and Election Law," *University of Illinois Law Review, 213* (2013): 363–432.

111. Clark, "Explaining Political Knowledge."

112. Michael Carpini and Scott Keeter, *What Americans Know about Politics and Why It Matters* (New Haven: Yale University Press, 1996).

113. Ignacio Sanchez Cuenca, "The Political Basis of Support for European Integration," *European Union Politics, 1* (2000): 147–171.

114. They measure economic inequality with by using the Gini coefficient. See Kimmo Gronlund and Henry Milner, "The Determinants of Political Knowledge in Comparative Perspective," *Scandinavian Political Studies, 29* (2006): 386–406.

115. Gronlund and Milner use data from the Comparative Study of Electoral Systems (CSES) based at the University of Michigan (1996–2002 wave of

data). They find that in more egalitarian countries (where redistributive policies are more abundant) there is more dispersion of political knowledge among the different educational categories in the CSES data, in comparison with less egalitarian countries. This means that educational level has a lesser effect on voter competence in countries with more redistribution.

116. Paul Howe, "Political Knowledge and Electoral Participation in the Netherlands: Comparisons with the Canadian Case," *International Political Science Review*, 27 (2006): 137–166.

117. William Galston "Political Knowledge, Political Engagement, and Civic Education," *Annual Review of Political Science*, 4 (2001): 217–234.

118. Ibid., 219.

119. Somin, *Democracy and Political Ignorance*.

120. Benjamin Page, "That Same Old Song: Somin on Political Ignorance," *Critical Review*, 27 (2015), 378.

121. Talisse, "Does Public Ignorance Defeat Deliberative Democracy?"

122. Gronlund and Milner, "The Determinants of Political Knowledge." For a similar argument, see Jose Maria Maravall, "Accountability and Manipulation," in Adam Przeworski et al., eds., *Democracy, Accountability and Representation* (Cambridge: Cambridge University Press, 1999).

123. As I argued at the beginning of the book, the duty to vote with care loses stringency if the political system is completely immune to change via elections due to its authoritarian nature (albeit offering a democratic facade). In cases like these, the interesting question becomes whether there is a duty to rebel or to resist extreme injustice. I cannot deal with this important issue here, for doing do necessitates much more space than I have.

124. Here I follow Benjamin Page and Martin Gilens, *Democracy in America? What Has Gone Wrong and What We Can Do about it* (Chicago: University of Chicago Press, 2017). To their classification, I would add a fourth category: civic education reforms. Research shows that civics as a subject has been systematically phased out of American high-school classrooms for decades now, which explains, in large part, why many individuals are clueless about basic facts of government design and functioning as well as why they are not as interested in political participation as previous generations. See William Galston, "Civic Education and Political Participation," *Political Science and Politics*, 37 (2004):263–266.

125. With an admittedly American focus, Gilens and Page do a wonderfully detailed job of explaining each of these three types of reform. When it comes to the first type, they tell us that there are already examples of reforms that have reduced the power of campaign donors, thereby reducing the dependence of elected politicians on special interests. They explain the case of the Connecticut Clean Elections Program and its real effect on the quality of policy directed to the common good. (See *Democracy in America?*, 183–185). They also explain that electoral reform laws include, for example, automatic registration, making election day a holiday, eliminating gerrymandering, eliminating single-member districts, and allowing for proportional representation, which affords a larger spectrum of views to disenchanted voters. Reforms to prevent deadlock, in turn, entail reform of the rules that shape discussion and policy formation in governmental institutions such as the Senate or Parliament, the Supreme Court, and the executive. The idea is that when gridlock is less common, responsiveness increases and voter apathy decreases.

126. Mathias Benz and Alois Stutzer, "Are Voters Better Informed When They Have a Larger Say in Politics?," *Public Choice, 119* (2004): 31–59.

Chapter 4

1. Jason Brennan in *The Ethics of Voting*, chapter 2, forcefully formulates this critique.

2. Lisa Hill and Jason Brennan, *Compulsory Voting: For and Against* (Cambridge: Cambridge (University Press, 2014), 200.

3. See Jose Antonio Chebub and Adam Przeworksi, "Democracy, Elections and Accountability for Economic Outcomes," in *Democracy, Accountability and Representation*, edited by Susan Stokes et al. (Cambridge: Cambridge University Press, 1999).

4. J. S. Mill, "Considerations on Representative Government," 217.

5. We could say that the moral saliency of government springs from its capacity to affect justice so powerfully. Relatedly, we can say that governments are morally salient agents because they are part of what Rawls called the "basic structure of society," which is supposed to be the first object of justice. Rawls takes the basic structure to be the "political constitution and the principal social and economic arrangements of society" (Rawls, *A Theory of Justice*, 7). In particular, the basic structure is supposed to secure what Rawls calls "background justice," that is, conditions of fair

access to basic social goods despite inequalities in wealth and opportunity that are passed through generations. John Rawls, *Political Liberalism* (New York: Columbia University Press, 2000), 265–268). Governments are essential actors in securing background justice because they can make or block policy and legislation that will affect citizens' enjoyment of rights and opportunities. Thus, the moral saliency of governments is due to an empirical fact (i.e., their power to affect people's life-conditions) as well as a related normative assumption (i.e., the expectation that they are primary avenues for securing background justice *because of* that power).

6. For Kant, perfect duties are negative duties not to do something (i.e., to refrain from killing) and imperfect duties are positive duties to do something (i.e., to aid others). Kant bases this distinction on his basic principle of morality, which holds that permissible actions are those that can be willed to be universal laws of action without any logical contradiction. For Kant, the failure to discharge a perfect duty results in the contradiction of a universal law. Imperfect duties, by contrast, do not involve logical contradictions that spring from willing a certain act into a universal maxim. They do involve the contradiction of an important human inclination or need, however. See Immanuel Kant, *Foundations of the Metaphysics of Morals*, translated by Lewis W. Beck (Indianapolis: Bobbs-Merrill, 1959), 420–426.

7. Jon Stuart Mill also refers to "imperfect duties." He defines them as "those in which, though the act is obligatory, the particular occasions of performing it are left to our choice, as in the case of charity or beneficence, which we are indeed bound to in practice, but not toward any definite person, nor at any prescribed time." See *Utilitarianism*, 185.

8. Locke's examples include relieving the troubled, helping the hungry, and consoling the distressed. See John Locke, *Essays on the Law of Nature* (Oxford: Oxford University Press, 2002 [1663]), 123.

9. Samaritan considerations of justice are not invalidated only because there is no fixed (sustained) correlativity between specific duty holders and specific right holders. This correlativity emerges given the right circumstances, as Locke's description of his duty of "time and place" suggests.

10. In the *Ethics of Voting*, Brennan claims that we could see participation in the market via one's job or work as a mechanism to fulfill our civic duty that is as valid as voting or participating in politics. One can surely contribute to society by creating goods and services that others want. But if it is true that one can fulfill one's civic duty by merely holding a job that is in some relevant sense wanted by others, it follows that morally suspicious market activities that others demand constitute a legitimate discharge of

duty. Is being Hitler's personal cook a good example of how someone may fulfill his civic duty to society? Is selling cigarettes a valid contribution to helping others? Of course, many market activities are beneficial to society (paid doctors surely are an example) but it is a stretch to provide a blanket definition of what is a valuable contribution that relies on the notion of *market demand*. Just because others want it doesn't mean it should exist or is valuable. More generally, it is somewhat odd to equate civic duty with profit or pay.

11. We will not be required to make up for the contributions of individuals that fail to fulfill their duty to act, however. We are only morally required to do our fair share of aiding. That means, as I see it, that we are only required to do the amount of work that would be needed if everyone cooperated on an equal basis. We are required to do that which would lead to the sought after outcome (the possibly best outcome) if everyone contributed the same amount. I take this intuition from Derek Parfit's *Reasons and Persons*, 30–33. See also Liam Murphy, "The Demands of Beneficence."

12. At this point an important caveat is in order. In reality, voting can prove costly for some individuals due to the ill-intentioned efforts to make voting difficult by many public officials, who may not benefit by an increased turnout, necessarily. Thus, we see, in the United States, for example, a host of voter suppression measures, such as the requirement to show ID at the voting station, which burden the poor disproportionately. The poor, in turn, tend to vote liberal or Democratic, which some non-liberal officials in power attempt to discourage (in an unconstitutional fashion). Voting taxes in the Jim Crow era were an example of this type of voting suppression measures. In cases of this sort, in which voting is unacceptably burdensome for the individual, we may have reason to relax the requirement to vote (although we may have reason to believe there is a duty to fight this type of injustice if one is not too powerless or disadvantaged to do so).

13. It follows from this logic, though, that if the electoral options are all equally evil and morally condemnable, the duty to vote with care loses stringency as elections cease to be a mechanism to foster justice or minimize injustice. Perhaps, depending on how costly and difficult other options to fight injustice are, citizens may have a duty to try those. However, citizens do not have a duty to fight against invincible moral monsters that may jeopardize their life and security.

14. Williams makes this point a central pillar of his philosophical work. See, for example, Bernard Williams, "Integrity," in *Utilitarianism* and Bernard Williams, *Moral Luck*.

15. See, again, elaboration of the idea that there is a fair share of aid-giving that each individual is obligated to undertake but this share does not become larger under conditions of general non-compliance with the moral duty. In other words, if others behave immorally and ignore their duty, that does not make my duty more stringent than already is, or more encompassing (i.e., requiring me to do more).

16. The system of ranked voting solves the problem of lesser evil voting and it avoids vote-splitting (i.e., the situation when a candidate with low prospects of winning takes away votes from a candidate who is well-situated to win). Ranked-choice voting is a method of voting allowing voters to rank multiple candidates in order of preference.

17. Nagel's concept of "moral luck" encapsulates this sense of randomness. See Thomas Nagel, *Mortal Questions* (New York: Cambridge University Press, 1979). Relatedly, see Alfred Mele, "Ultimate Responsibility and Dumb Luck," *Social Philosophy and Policy*, 16 (1999): 274–293.

18. See Isaacs, *Moral Responsibility in Collective Contexts*, for an argument defending this understanding of the relationship between responsibility for an individual contribution and responsibility for a total outcome.

19. As elaborated in the previous chapter, we must remember that if we take too much of a lax view of what an omission is, we can say that everything that we don't do is causally relevant in explaining reality. We must we weary of concept-overstretching, then.

20. This approach is not to be confused with Mackie's contributory approach to voter rationality, although it is predicated on the same logic, to wit, that of marginal contributions to a larger outcome.

21. For an approach emphasizing this line of reasoning, see Alvin Goldman, "Why Citizens Should Vote: A Causal Responsibility Approach," *Social Philosophy and Policy*, 16 (1999): 201–217.

22. This issue evokes, again, the problem of overdetermination touched on in chapter 3.

23. Whether she will be part of the set of abstentions that enable a result or not.

24. This example is an adaptation from an example provided by Rudolph Clarke in *Omissions: Agency, Metaphysics and Responsibility* (Oxford: Oxford University Press, 2015), 162–164.

25. I referred to institutional mechanisms that can help in this regard in chapter 1.

Chapter 5

1. Arguing for a duty to vote does not amount to arguing for the notion that the duty is especially stringent compared to other obligations that may conflict with the duty to vote in particular situations.

2. Jason Brennan says: "In this section, I examine arguments that claim we should vote because each individual vote has significant value in terms of its expected impact on the quality of governance. These arguments fail because individual votes in fact have vanishingly small instrumental value in terms of their impact on the quality of governance." *The Ethics of Voting*, 17. Brennan and Lomasky also adopt this approach: "if the inconsequentiality of voting renders it unimportant with regard to our own self-interest whether one bothers to cast a ballot, then, that inconsequentiality also infects the claim that one is producing some public good through exercising the franchise." "Is There a Duty to Vote?," 67.

3. Benjamin Constant, *On the Liberty of the Ancients Compared to That of the Moderns* available at https://oll.libertyfund.org/titles/constant-the-liberty-of-ancients-compared-with-that-of-moderns-1819.

4. For the original formal elaboration of this paradox, see Downs, *An Economic Theory of Democracy*.

5. Lomasky and Brennan, *Democracy and Decision*.

6. William Riker and Peter Ordeshook, "A Theory of the Calculus of Voting," *American Political Science Review*, 62 (1968): 25–42.

7. This is the "minimax regret" thesis offered by John Ferejohn and Morris Fiorina in "The Paradox of Not Voting: A Decision Theoretic Analysis," *American Political Science Review*, 68 (1974): 525–536. The problem with the minimax regret idea is that it is consistent with the objection that the individual should abstain because he could get killed going to the polls.

8. The classical rational choice-account of voting offers the following utility calculus for the act of voting: $U_v = B.p - C$, where B is the *personal* benefit that the individual derives from her preferred alternative winning the election, p is the probability that her vote will be decisive in the election (will tilt it or determine it), and C is the individual cost of voting. Since p will always be infinitesimally small but C will be some positive number, the utility of voting for the individual will be negative. That is, voting will not be worth the cost and effort to the voter.

9. For an instructive summary of this literature, see Andre Blais, *To Vote or Not to Vote: The Merits and Limits of Rational Choice Theory* (Pittsburgh: University of Pittsburg Press, 2000).

10. An original contribution to resolving the voting paradox further adds that rational choice theory calculations may not be applicable to the act of voting: "It may well be that both the costs and the suitably discounted benefits of voting are so low that it is simply not worth being rational about it." Brian Barry, *Sociologists, Economists and Democracy* (Chicago: University of Chicago Press, 1978), 23. John Aldrich "Rational Choice and Turnout," *American Political Science Review*, 37 (1993): 439–450, offers a similar view, although it is not as emphatic as Barry's. Aldrich argues that the rational choice model still applies to voting since people operate in its framework, but they make many mistakes in calculating benefits and costs. This discussion revolves around the benefits *to the voter* from voting. But rationality can also be understood in terms of others-regarding benefits, as I will explain subsequently in this chapter.

11. The rational choice literature, and the literature that challenges it, both agree on the idea that self-interested reasons for voting are not effective instrumentally because of the imperceptible impact of one individual vote. The costs of voting are always greater than the personal benefits derived from one vote. The situation changes when the motivation is altruistic because the benefits may be much larger than the costs, as I will explain shortly.

12. Richard Jankowski, "Altruism and the Decision to Vote: Explaining and Testing High Voter Turnout," *Rationality and Society*, 19 (2007): 5–34; James Fowler, "Altruism and Turnout," *Journal of Politics*, 68 (2006): 674–683; Andrew Gelman, Aaron Edlin, and Noah Kaplan, "Voting as a Rational Choice: Why and How People Vote to Improve the Wellbeing of Others," *Rationality and Society*, 19 (2007): 293–314.

13. See the previous footnote, and Gelman "Vote for Charity's Sake," at http://www.stat.columbia.edu/~gelman/research/published/charity.pdf.

14. We should we wary of the problem of concept-stretching. Understanding rational action as anything that we do to further a goal that we have is too lax an understanding of rationality. For example, if I believe that I have to dance naked in the rain to communicate with extraterrestrial beings, and I dance naked in the rain, can I be said to be rational? Unlikely. My explanation of the altruistic theory of voting does not endorse this type of concept stretching. It only endorses the widely accepted assumption that rational goals are not only or narrowly selfish. Besides this conceptual

expansion, the new view of rationality does not have to present any major differences in the traditional assumptions of what makes human action rational. For a start, the tools to assess the rationality of goals are the same. Rational goals may be said to be goals that are not based on delirious reasoning but on sound factual information and adequate understanding of causality. Rational action may also be said to be instrumentalist action, in the sense that there is a causal connection between a person's acts and a result (means-end rationality). It is this condition that consumption accounts of voting do not meet. On those views, the voter attains personal satisfaction but she doesn't act with a view to impacting an outcome, however marginally or imperceptibly. In other words, her satisfaction is unrelated to the consequences of her act on the world.

15. Gelman et al., "Voting as a Rational Choice," propose this easy exercise to illustrate the rationality of altruistic voting. We start from the classical rational choice theory calculus of voting $U_v = B.p - C$, where B is the *personal* benefit that the individual derives from her preferred alternative winning the election, p is the probability that her vote will be decisive in the election (will tilt it or determine it), and C is the individual cost of voting; p will be proportional (close) to $\frac{1}{N}$ where N is the number of voters (that actually cast a ballot) in the election. Under this assumption, it is clear that p will be infinitesimally small, always smaller than C, so the rational choice prediction of irrationality seems to make sense. However, if B contains some dimension pertaining to the benefit to other voters (to society, to the common good), B will be a function of N. This means, mathematically, that the bigger the group of voters that we care to benefit, the more benefit that we will derive from voting for what we think is the right alternative for society. In other words, it is not irrational to vote. Here is the simple mathematical proof: $1 / N.N - C$ (the two Ns cancel each other out). If C is relatively small (even counting informational costs), it is evident that voting is not irrational at all (C remains a negative number, which means that the benefits of voting overshadow its costs). Finally, for a moment, imagine that we can add another variable, D, to the modified calculus of utility. The D variable, introduced by Riker and Ordeshook, represents the individual satisfaction derived from discharging a civic like voting. If it is not far-fetched to think that altruistic voters will also derive an individual benefit from fulfilling what they see as a duty, then, it is even more clear why voting may be perfectly rational. For the argument that voters derive personal benefit from the fact of complying with civic duty, see Riker and Ordeshook, "A Theory of the Calculus of Voting."

16. Extensive political science research confirms that the common good and the good of the country are powerful motivators for voting. See Ronald Kinder and Roderick Kiewiet, "Sociotropic Politics: The American Case," *British Journal of Political Science 11* (1988): 129–161; Carolyn Funk, "The Dual Interest of Self-Interest and Societal Interest in Public Opinion," *Political Research Quarterly 53* (2000): 37–62; David Sears and Carolyn Funk, "The Limited Effect of Self-Interest on the Political Attitudes of the Mass Public," *Journal of Behavioral Economics, 19* (1990): 247–271. But see how Dennis Chong, Jack Citrin, and Patricia Conley, "When Self-Interest Matters," *Political Psychology, 22* (2001): 541–570 find that pro-social priming in voter surveys weakens but does not eradicate self-interest when personal stakes are clear. They also find that when personal stakes are not so clear, pro-social voting is common. For a comprehensive review of the studies that confirm socio-tropic tendencies in voters, see Mackie, "Why It's Rational to Vote." Many years ago, Jeremy Bentham adumbrated the existence of pro-social voting even though he must have been referring to anecdotal evidence to prove it. To justify universal suffrage, he argued: "according to a . . . supposition, the truth of which has, it is presumed been proved,—on the part of the electors—at any rate, on the part of the majority of them—there does exist the disposition to contribute towards the advancement of the universal interest, whatsoever can be contributed by their votes." Cited in Hanna Pitkin, *The Concept of Representation* (Berkeley: University of California Press, 1969). Pitkin cites Bentham from "Plan of Parliamentary Reform," in *Works*, edited by John Bowring (Edinburgh: William Tait, 1843).

17. I'm taking as examples of the paradigmatic no-duty position the following works: Jason Brennan's book *The Ethics of Voting*, and Geoffrey Brennan and Loren Lomasky's seminal article "Is There a Duty to Vote?"

18. Parfit, *Reasons and Persons*, 74–75.

19. Brian Barry, "Comment," in *Political Participation*, edited by Stanley Benn (Canberra: Australian University Press, 39).

20. Brennan, *On the Ethics of Voting*, 20.

21. Tuck, *Free Riding*.

22. To understand what an efficacious set of votes is, go back to the Roman republic. This is how elections worked in ancient Rome, where a roll call of voters would be taken in sequence until one candidate had enough votes to be guaranteed victory. In this process, the last person to vote for a candidate causes that candidate to be elected. So the crucial fact about voting is that one vote can indeed make a difference. For this explanation, see

David Runciman, "Why Not Eat an Éclair?," review of Tuck's *Free Riding* in *Boston Review of Books*, 30, 2008.

23. Brennan, *The Ethics of Voting*, 29.

24. Goldman, "Why Citizens Should Vote."

25. As Goldman does in his article (ibid.).

26. Ibid., 205.

27. Brennan, *The Ethics of Voting*, 29–33.

28. Ibid., 29.

29. Ibid., 31.

30. Ibid. Brennan shows how he calculates the utility of voting here: $U_v = \mathcal{P}Um$ where $\mathcal{P}$ is the probability that my vote will be in the set of efficacious votes and Um is the personal benefit that I derive from forming part of that efficacious set of votes.

31. Ibid., 31. Brennan also adds a third criticism: it is possible to be efficacious in other ways than voting. I deal with this view in chapter 3. I sidestep it for the moment to concentrate on theories of rationality in voting strictly speaking, and on whether they may give rise to a moral duty to vote.

32. Ibid., 32.

33. Ibid.

34. Ibid. The language belongs to Tuck, *Free Riding*, 54.

35. Brennan, *The Ethics of Voting*, 33.

36. Gerry Mackie, "Rational Ignorance and Beyond," unpublished manuscript available at http://pages.ucsd.edu/~gmackie/documents/RationalIgnoranceAndBeyond.pdf.

37. This logic is proposed and defended by Parfit in *Reasons and Persons*, 68–75.

38. For example, Hannah Arendt looks kindly to ancient models of democracy such as the ones in place in Greece and, later, Rome, and emphasizes political involvement as the mark of a meaningful existence: "without mastering the necessities of life in the household, neither life nor the 'good life' is possible, but politics is never for the sake of life. As far as the members of the polis are concerned, household life exists for the sake of the good life in the polis." Hannah Arendt, *The Human Condition* (Chicago: University of Chicago Press, 1978), 37. Similarly, Michael Sandel defends an Aristotelian understanding of politics that links political participation with excellence of character and valuable virtues: "The strong version of Republicanism, going back to Aristotle, finds the intrinsic value of political participation in a certain vision of human flourishing. Sharing in the governance of a political community that controls its own fate calls forth

distinctive human capacities—for judgment, deliberation, and action—
that otherwise would like dormant." See Michael Sandel, "Reply to Critics,"
in Anita L. Allen et al., eds., *Debating Democracy's Discontent: Essays on
American Politics, Law, and Public Philosophy* (Oxford: Oxford University
Press Online), 325.

39. Phillip Pettit, *Republicanism: A Theory of Freedom and Government*
(Oxford: Oxford University Press, 2012).

40. The classical republicans were a diverse group of political writers, including, among others, Machiavelli and his fifteenth-century Italian
predecessors; the English republicans Milton, Harrington, and Sidney;
Montesquieu and Blackstone; many Americans of the founding era such
as Jefferson and Madison; and some later observers such as Tocqueville.
These writers were all committed to the political ideal of a *res publica*,
where this was understood roughly as a community of citizens governed
by a shared system of law in which no one person or group holds personal
mastery over any other. As I said before, many of these republicans can also
be associated with instrumentalist republicanism, since their arguments
contain both classical as well as consequentialist views of political participation. However, the distinction between the two strands of valuation can
be made. The classical republicans were concerned with proposing and
defending institutions and practices that would cultivate civic virtue, understood as the virtues that might lead the individual to live a "good life."
They were also concerned with avoiding those institutions and practices
that would encourage dispositions inimical to virtue understood through
the lens of civic excellence. Instrumentalist republicans, in turn, are emphatic about the role of institutions in preserving freedom understood as
absence of domination by the powerful over the weak. Their concern is
not so much with virtue for virtue's sake. I owe this explanation to Francis
Lovett, "Machiavelli, Civic Virtue, and the Problem of Stability," delivered
at the American Political Science Association's Annual Meeting, 2013.

41. For an explanation of the republican ideal and the notion of freedom
as non-domination, see Pettit, *Republicanism*; Steven Wall, "Freedom,
Interference, and Domination," *Political Studies*, 49 (2001): 216–230;
and Thomas Wartenberg, *The Forms of Power: From Domination to
Transformation* (Philadelphia: Temple University Press, 1990).

42. Here I am using the term "republican" to mean government predicated on
the idea that political authority springs from the consent of the governed,
which usually goes hand in hand with some type of division of powers
and political accountability to keep rulers in check. As a general example

of the ideals that inspire republicanism in this sense, see James Madison, *Federalist* numbers 10 and 39. This sense of republican government may or may not accept the idea that politics is essential for a good life; see the distinction between classical and instrumentalist republicanism discussed previously.

43. Rawls writes, "The primary social goods, to give them in broad categories, are rights, liberties, and opportunities, and income and wealth" (*A Theory of Justice*, 79). He immediately adds, "A very important primary good is a sense of one's own worth, but for simplicity I leave this aside until much later" (ibid.).

44. Jan Leighley and Jonathan Nagler, *Who Votes Now?* (Princeton, NJ: Princeton University Press, 2014).

45. In their cross-country comparative study, for example, Mueller and Strattman found that increased political participation has a positive impact on income equality. The more citizens abstain, the greater income inequality will become. Dennis Mueller and Thomas Strattman, "The Economic Effects of Democratic Participation," *Journal of Public Economics*, 87 (2003): 2129–2155.

46. John Griffin and Brian Newman, "Are Voters Better Represented?," *Journal of Politics*, 67 (2005): 1206–1227.

47. Arend Lijphart, "Unequal Participation: Democracy's Unresolved Dilemma," *American Political Science Review*, 91 (1993): 1–14.

48. This empirical regularity prompted Herbert Tingsten in *Political Behavior: Studies in Election Statistics* (London: Arno Press, 1975), 230 to formulate the "Law of Dispersion," which postulates that the differences in electoral participation among social groups are smaller if the overall participation rate is higher. In a much more contemporary fashion, Amin Shafer constructs an "index of electoral equality" that shows how much people with lower education levels and lower income differ from the more educated and the richer in their predisposition to vote in an array of democracies. See Armin Schafer, "Republican Liberty and Compulsory Voting," Working Paper No. 11/17, Max Planck Institute for the Study of Societies, Cologne, 2011.

49. Robert Dahl, *Democracy and Its Critics* (New Haven: Yale University Press, 1989), 114–115.

50. Jason Brennan refers to his logic as an argument against what he calls the "demographic argument" for compulsory voting. He explains the latter in *The Ethics of Voting*, chapter 2, as well as in Brennan and Hill, *Compulsory Voting*, chapters 3 and 4. Brennan's use of this argument signals a degree of

simplification that no political scientist with minimal knowledge of how politics work would consider valid.

51. See Kim Quaile Hill and Jan E. Leighley, "The Policy Consequences of Class Bias in State Electorates," *American Journal of Political Science, 36* (1992): 351–365; Stephen Shaffer, "Policy Differences between Voters and Non-voters in American Elections," *Western Political Quarterly, 35* (1982): 496–510, Griffin and Newman, "Are Voters Better Represented?"

52. Jonas Pontusson and David Rueda, "The Politics of Inequality. Party Mobilization and Left Parties in Advanced Industrial States," *Comparative Political Studies, 43* (2010): 675–705. For a quite complete survey of this literature, see Schafer, "Republican Liberty and Compulsory Voting," 11–14.

53. James Avery, "Does Who Votes Matter? Income Bias in Voter Turnout and Economic Inequality in American States from 1980 to 2010," *Political Behavior 37* (2015): 955–976; James Galbraith and Travis Hale, "State Income Inequality and Presidential Election Turnout and Outcomes," *Social Science Quarterly, 89* (2008): 887–901.

54. Hill and Leighley, "The Policy Consequences of Class Bias"; and Evan Ringquist, Kim Quaile Hill, Jan Leighley, and Angela Hinton-Andersson, "Lower-Class Mobilization and Policy Linkage in the U.S. States," *American Journal of Political Science, 39* (1995): 75–86.

55. Paul Martin, "Voting's Rewards: Voter Turnout, Attentive Publics, and Congressional Allocation of Federal Money," *American Journal of Political Science, 47* (2003): 110–127.

56. Alberto Chong and Mauricio Olivera, "Does Compulsory Voting Help Equalize Incomes?," *Economics and Politics, 20* (2008): 391–415. Chong and Olivera find that countries that have compulsory voting laws in effect have higher rates of income equality than those where voting is voluntary; but they argue that higher turnout generally means more equality regardless of the existence of mandatory voting laws.

Chapter 6

1. There is a distinction to be made between the English-speaking world, on the one hand, and continental Europe and many Latin American counties, on the other. In the latter group, the law many times recognizes an enforceable duty of easy rescue and penalizes (when possible) the indifferent bystander. In the former group, it is traditionally harder to find examples of this scenario. Questions of negligence assessment and penalty are complicated and cannot be dealt with here. I have not argued for compulsory

voting laws in this book, but a debate around whether legal compulsion to make people vote is normatively justified would be, following the approach I laid out in this book, naturally related to a discussion about whether enforcing (some) Samaritan duties of justice is justified in general.

2. See Brennan, *On the Ethics of Voting*.

3. Brennan, *Against Democracy*, 211–222.

4. Even defenders of epistocratic systems of government can accept that people's political knowledge can improve. See, for example, Claudio Lopez Guerra, *Democracy and Disenfranchisement: The Morality of Electoral Exclusions* (Oxford: Oxford University Press, 2014). Lopez-Guerra argues that the right to vote should not be seen as a universally obvious right for everyone. Instead, we should focus on which institutional system best serves the goal of justice, first. In this vein, he ingeniously suggests that we select a representative sample of the population (and disenfranchise everybody else who was not selected by the random procedure) and educate those selected via their participation in political deliberation that would last a few days so as to prepare them to exercise the right to vote in elections in responsible manner. Although I disagree with Lopez-Guerra's arguments for disenfranchising most members of society, I agree with him that the uninformed can become sufficiently informed via access to the proper knowledge tools.

5. In *Against Democracy*, Jason Brennan argues that the best model for an epistocracy today is a system of universal suffrage with an epistocratic veto, whereby nobody loses the right to vote but a council of "cognitively elite" members is legally able to veto legislation that is at odds with justice. It appears that his arguments against democracy do not weigh enough here to justify doing away with universal voting rights, perhaps—as he hints at very briefly—because people would not enjoy being stripped of their right to vote. Brennan argues that the epistocratic veto system is analogous to judicial review, which, despite some objections, can be reasonably be seen as consistent with democracy. However, judicial review in the United States is a great example of how ideologically biased and politically self-interested the knowledgeable can be. For example, the Supreme Court of the United States decided *Brown v. Board of Education*, which made racial segregation in schools and public facilities illegal, but it also upheld infamous decisions that legalized racial discrimination and exclusion before that—as when it ruled in *Plessy v. Ferguson*, which institutionalized the "separate but equal" doctrine allowing segregation and discrimination based on race to be construed as legitimate and legal in the first

place. Although it is true that the American Supreme Court has gotten more partisan in the last decade than it ever was, the reality of this day and age is that many fear that a conservative majority in that high court may promptly rule against previously established decisions defending rights such as abortion rights and gay rights, among others. In line with this fact, political science research shows how avidly Supreme Court justices defend causes that they personally or politically identify with (regardless of partisan identification). See Lee Epstein et al., "Do Justices Defend the Speech They Hate? An Analysis of In-Group Bias in the Supreme Court," *Journal of Law and Courts*, 6 (2018): 237–262. Other political science research suggests that in instances where the issues in a case have a clear political dimension, such as employment discrimination cases or business regulations, personal and partisan biases can distort judicial decision-making. See Lawrence Baum, *Ideology in the Supreme Court* (Princeton, NJ: Princeton University Press, 2017) and Tracey George and Lee Epstein, "On the Nature of Supreme Court Decision Making," *American Political Science Review 86* (1992): 323–337. Based on the evidence that there is bias in judicial decision-making, I think that it is not at all clear that a system of parliamentary sovereignty, in which the law made by parliament is the last word—such as the one in place in England, New Zealand, and Australia—is inferior to a judicial review system such as the one in place in the United States. Nor is it clear that in countries ruled by the principle of parliamentary sovereignty, government behaves more unjustly because parliament responds to majorities. At least, it is not clear that the injustices are more ominous than the ones found in the United States, where, as just mentioned, the Supreme Court has been the agent of injustice in many respects.

References

Abramovitz, Alan, and Steven Webster. "All Politics Is National: The Rise of Negative Partisanship and the Nationalization of U.S. House and Senate Elections in the 21st Century." Prepared for presentation at the Annual Meeting of the Midwest Political Science Association, Chicago, Illinois, April 16–19, 2015.

Achen, Christopher, and Larry Bartels. *Democracy for Realists: Why Elections Do Not Produce Responsive Government*. Princeton, NJ: Princeton University Press, 2016.

Aldrich, John. "Rational Choice and Turnout." *American Political Science Review*, 37 (1993): 439–450.

Arendt, Hannah. *The Human Condition*. Chicago: University of Chicago Press, 1978.

Arendt, Hannah. "On Violence." In *Crises of the Republic: Lying in Politics; Civil Disobedience; Thoughts on Politics and Revolution*. New York: Harcourt Brace Jovanovich, 1972.

Aristotle. *The Politics*. Translated by Carnes Lord. Chicago: University of Chicago Press, 2013.

Avery, James. "Does Who Votes Matter? Income Bias in Voter Turnout and Economic Inequality in American States from 1980 to 2010." *Political Behavior* 37 (2015): 955–976.

Barber, Benjamin. *Strong Democracy*. Berkeley: University of California Press, 2004.

Barry, Brian. "Comment." In *Political Participation*, edited by Stanley Benn. Canberra: Australian University Press, 1978.

Barry, Brian. *Justice as Impartiality*. Oxford: Oxford University Press, 1995.

Barry, Brian. *Sociologists, Economists and Democracy*. Chicago: University of Chicago Press, 1978.

Bartels, Larry. "Uninformed Votes. Information Effects in Presidential Elections." *American Journal of Political Science*, 40 (1996): 194–230.

Baum, Lawrence. *Ideology in the Supreme Court*. Princeton, NJ: Princeton University Press, 2017.

Beerbohm, Eric. *In Our Name*. Princeton, NJ: Princeton University Press, 2012.

Belman, Dale, and Paul J. Wolfson. "The New Minimum Wage Research," W.E. Upjohn Institute for Employment Research, *Employment Research*, 21 (2014): 4–5.

Bennet, Stephen, and Jeffrey Friedman. "The Irrelevance of Economic Theory to Understanding Economic Ignorance." *Critical Review*, 20 (2008): 195–258.

Bentham, Jeremy. *An Introduction to the Principles of Morals and Legislation.* Middletown, DE: First Rate Publishers.

Bentham, Jeremy. "Plan of Parliamentary Reform." In *Works*, edited by John Bowring. Edinburgh: William Tait, 1843.

Bentley, Arthur. *The Process of Government: A Study of Social Pressures.* Chicago: University of Chicago Press, 1908.

Benz, Mathias, and Alois Stutzer. "Are Voters Better Informed When They Have a Larger Say in Politics?" *Public Choice*, 119 (2004): 31–59.

Billingham, Paul. "Convergence Justifications within Political Liberalism: A Defence." *Res Publica* 22 (2016): 135–143.

Blais, Andrais. *To Vote or Not to Vote: The Merits and Limits of Rational Choice Theory.* Pittsburgh: University of Pittsburgh Press, 2000.

Bratman, Michael. *Shared Agency: A Planning Theory of Acting Together.* Oxford: Oxford University Press, 2014.

Brennan, Geoffrey, and Loren Lomasky. *Democracy and Decision: The Pure Theory of Electoral Preference.* New York: Cambridge University Press, 1993.

Brennan, Geoffrey, and Loren Lomasky. "Is There a Duty to Vote?" *Social Philosophy and Policy*, 17 (2001): 62–86.

Brennan, Jason. *Against Democracy.* Princeton, NJ: Princeton University Press, 2016.

Brennan, Jason. *The Ethics of Voting.* Princeton, NJ: Princeton University Press, 2012.

Brennan, Jason. "Polluting the Polls. When Citizens Should Not Vote." *Australasian Journal of Philosophy*, 87 (2009): 535–549.

Brittan, Samuel. "It Is Time to Jettison the Forecasts." *Financial Times*, December 9 (2007).

Buchanan, Alan. "Justice and Charity." *Ethics*, 97 (1987): 558–575.

Cabbane, Yves. "Participatory Budgeting: A Significant Contribution to Participatory Democracy." *Environment and Urbanization*, 16 (2004): 27–46.

Campbell, David. *Why We Vote: How Schools and Communities Shape Our Civic Life.* Princeton, NJ: Princeton University Press, 2008.

Caplan, Bryan. *The Myth of the Rational Voter: Why Democracies Choose Bad Policies.* Princeton, NJ: Princeton University Press, 2007.

Card, David, and Alan Krueger. *Myth and Measurement: The New Economics of the Minimum Wage.* Princeton, NJ: Princeton University Press, 2015.

Carpini, Michael, and Scott Keeter. *What Americans Know about Politics and Why It Matters.* New Haven: Yale University Press, 1996.

Chebub, Jose Antonio, and Adam Przeworksi. "Democracy, Elections and Accountability for Economic Outcomes." In *Democracy, Accountability and Representation*, edited by Susan Stokes et al. Cambridge: Cambridge University Press, 1999.

Chong, Alberto, and Mauricio Olivera. "Does Compulsory Voting Help Equalize Incomes?" *Economics and Politics*, 20 (2008): 391–415.

Chong, Dennis, Jack Citrin, and Patricia Conley. "When Self-Interest Matters." *Political Psychology*, 22 (2001): 541–570.

Christiano, Thomas. *The Constitution of Equality*. Oxford: Oxford University Press, 2008.

Christiano, Thomas. "Rational Deliberation among Experts and Citizens." In *Deliberative Systems: Deliberative Democracy at the Large Scale*, edited by John Parkinson. Cambridge: Cambridge University Press, 2012.

Christiano, Thomas. *The Rule of the Many: Fundamental Issues in Democratic Theory*. New York: Westview Press, 1996.

Ciccone, Anthony. "The Constitutional Right to Vote Is Not a Duty." 23 Hamline Journal of Public Law & Policy, 2002: 325–359.

Cicero. *On Duties*. Edited by M. T. Griffin and E. M. Atkins. Cambridge: Cambridge University Press, 1991.

Clark, Nicholas. "Explaining Political Knowledge: The Role of Procedural Quality in an Informed Citizenry." *Political Studies*, 3 (2016): 61–80.

Clarke, Rudolph. *Omissions: Agency, Metaphysics and Responsibility*. Oxford: Oxford University Press, 2015.

Constant, Benjamin. *On the Liberty of the Ancients Compared to That of the Moderns*. Available at https://oll.libertyfund.org/titles/constant-the-liberty-of-ancients-compared-with-that-of-moderns-1819.

Converse, Phillip. "The Nature of Belief Systems in Mass Publics." *Critical Review*, 18 (1964): 1–74.

D'Agostino, Fred. "The Idea and the Ideal of Public Justification." *Social Theory and Practice*, 18 (1992): 143–164.

Dahl, Robert. *Democracy and Its Critics*. New Haven: Yale University Press, 1989.

Dahl, Robert. *Who Governs?* New Haven: Yale University Press, 1961.

Dewey, John. *Intelligence in the Modern World: John Dewey's Philosophy*. Edited by Joseph Ratner. New York: Modern Library, 1939.

Dewey, John. *The Public and Its Problems*. New York: H. Holt, 1927.

Downs, Anthony. *An Economic Theory of Democracy*. New York: Harper, 1957.

Dworkin, Ronald. *A Matter of Principle*. London: Clarendon Press, 1985.

Drop, Jeffrey, and Wendy Hansen. "Purchasing Protection? The Effect of Political Spending on U.S Trade Policy." *Political Research Quarterly*, 57 (2004): 27–37.

Druckman, James, and Lawrence Jacobs. *Who Governs? Presidents, Public Opinion and Manipulation*. Chicago. University of Chicago Press, 2015.

Druckman, James, Erik Peterson, and Rune Slothuus, "How Elite Partisan Polarization Affects Public Opinion Formation." *American Political Science Review*, 107 (2013): 57–79.

Eberle, Christopher. *Religious Conviction in Liberal Politics*. Cambridge: Cambridge University Press, 2002.

Elmendorf, Christopher, and David Schleicher. "Informing Consent: Voter Ignorance, Political Parties and Election Law." *University of Illinois Law Review, 213* (2013): 363–432.

Epstein, Lee, Christopher Parker, and Jeffrey Segal. "Do Justices Defend the Speech They Hate? An Analysis of In-Group Bias in the Supreme Court." *Journal of Law and Courts*, 6 (2018): 237–262.

Esmer, Yilmaz, and Thorleif Pattersson. "The Effects of Religion and Religiosity on Voting Behavior." In *The Oxford Handbook of Political Behavior*, edited by Russell Dalton and Hans-Dieter Kinglemann. Oxford: Oxford University Press, 2007.

Feinberg, Joel. *Freedom and Fulfillment*. Princeton, NJ: Princeton University Press, 1992.

Feinberg, Joel. *Harm to Others: The Moral Limits of the Criminal Law*. Oxford: Oxford, University Press, 1984.

Feinberg, Joel. "The Moral and Legal Responsibility of the Bad Samaritan." *Criminal Justice Ethics*, 3 (1984): 56–69.

Ferejohn, John, and Morris Fiorina. "The Paradox of Not Voting: A Decision Theoretic Analysis." *American Political Science Review*, 68 (1974): 525–536.

Finkel, Steven. "Personal Influence, Collective Rationality and Mass Political Action." *American Political Science Review*, 83 (1989): 885–903.

Fishkin, James. *The Limits of Obligation*. New Haven: Yale University Press, 1982.

Fowler, James. "Altruism and Turnot." *Journal of Politics*, 68 (2006): 674–683.

Funk, Carolyn. "The Dual Interest of Self-Interest and Societal Interest in Public Opinion." *Political Research Quarterly* 53 (2000): 37–62.

Galbraith, James, and Travis Hale. "State Income Inequality and Presidential Election Turnout and Outcomes." *Social Science Quarterly*, 89 (2008): 887–901.

Galston, William. "Civic Education and Political Participation." *Political Science and Politics*, 37 (2004): 263–266.

Galston, William. "Political Knowledge, Political Engagement, and Civic Education." *Annual Review of Political Science*, 4 (2001): 217–234.

Gaus, Gerald. "Does Democracy Reveal the Voice of the People? Four Takes on Rousseau." *Australasian Journal of Philosophy*, 75 (1997): 141–162.

Gaus, Gerald. "Is the Public Competent? Compared to Whom? About What?" *Critical Review*, 20 (2008): 291–311.

Gaus, Gerald. *Justificatory Liberalism: An Essay on Epistemology and Political Theory*. Oxford: Oxford University Press, 1996.

Gaus, Gerald. *The Order of Public Reason.* Cambridge: Cambridge University Press, 2010.

Gaus, Gerald, and Kevin Vallier. "The Roles of Religious Conviction in a Publicly Justified Polity: The Implications of Convergence, Asymmetry and Political Institutions." *Philosophy and Social Criticism*, 35 (2009): 51–76.

Gelman, Andrew, Aaron Edlin, and Noah Kaplan. "Voting as a Rational Choice: Why and How People Vote to Improve the Wellbeing of Others." *Rationality and Society*, 19 (2007): 293–314.

George, Tracey, and Lee Epstein. "On the Nature of Supreme Court Decision Making." *American Political Science Review* 86 (1992): 323–337.

Gilens, Martin. "Inequality and Democratic Responsiveness." *Public Opinion Quarterly*, 69 (2005): 778–796.

Gilens, Martin, and Benjamin Page. "Testing Theories of American Democracy: Interest Groups, Elites and Average Citizens." *Perspectives on Politics*, 12 (2014): 564–582.

Goldman, Alvin. "Why Citizens Should Vote: A Causal Responsibility Approach." *Social Philosophy and Policy*, 16 (1999): 201–217.

Goodin, Robert. "Institutionalizing the Public Interest: The Defense of Deadlock and Beyond." *American Political Science Review*, 90 (1996): 331–343.

Goodin, Robert. *Reflective Democracy.* Oxford: Oxford University Press, 2003.

Goren, Paul. "Core Principles and Policy Reasonings in Mass Publics." *British Journal of Political Science*, 31 (2001): 159–177.

Graetz, Michael, and Ian Shapiro. *Death by a Thousand Cuts: The Fights over Taxing Inherited Wealth.* Princeton, NJ: Princeton University Press, 2005.

Griffin, John, and Brian Newman. "Are Voters Better Represented?" *Journal of Politics*, 67 (2005): 1206–1227.

Gronlund, Kimmo, and Henry Milner. "The Determinants of Political Knowledge in Comparative Perspective." *Scandinavian Political Studies*, 29 (2006): 386–406.

Guerrero, Alex. "Against Elections: The Lottocratic Alternative." *Philosophy and Public Affairs*, 42 (2014): 135–178.

Hayek, Friedrich. "The Use of Knowledge in Society." *American Economic Review*, 35 (1945): 519–530.

Held, Virginia. "Can a Random Collection of Individuals Be Morally Responsible?" *Journal of Philosophy*, 67 (1970): 471–481.

Hill, Lisa, and Jason Brennan. *Compulsory Voting: For and Against.* Cambridge: Cambridge University Press, 2014.

Hoppe, Hans-Herman. *Democracy: The God That Failed.* New Brunswick, NJ: Transactions Publishers, 2001.

Howe, Paul. "Political Knowledge and Electoral Participation in the Netherlands: Comparisons with the Canadian Case." *International Political Science Review*, 27 (2006): 137–166.

Hume, David. "Of the Original Contract." In *Political Essays*, edited by Knud Haakonssen. Cambridge: Cambridge University Press, 2006.

Isaacs, Tracy. *Moral Responsibility in Collective Contexts.* Oxford: Oxford University Press, 2011.

Jankowski, Richard. "Altruism and the Decision to Vote: Explaining and Testing High Voter Turnout." *Rationality and Society* 19 (2007): 5–34.

Jones, Morris. "In Defense of Apathy: Some Doubts on the Duty to Vote." *Political Studies*, 2 (1954): 25–37.

Kant, Immanuel. *Foundations of the Metaphysics of Morals.* Translated by Lewis W. Beck. Indianapolis: Bobbs-Merrill, 1959.

Kiewiet, Roderick, and Andrea Matozzi. "Voter Rationality and Democratic Government." *Critical Review*, 20 (2008): 313–326.

Kinder, Ronald, and Roderick Kiewiet. "Sociotropic Politics: The American Case." *British Journal of Political Science* 11 (1988): 129–161.

King, Martin Luther, Jr. "Civil Right No 1: The Right to Vote." *New York Times Magazine*, March 14 (1965): 26–27. Reprinted in *A Testament of Hope: The Essential Writings of Martin Luther King, Jr*, edited by James Washington. New York: Harper Collins, 1991.

Kleining, John. "Good Samaritanism." *Philosophy and Public Affairs*, 5 (1976): 382–407.

Kutz, Christopher. *Complicity.* Cambridge: Cambridge University Press, 2000.

Landermore, Helene. *Democratic Reason.* Princeton, NJ: Princeton University Press, 2011.

Lau, Richard, and David Redlawsk. "Advantages and Disadvantages of Cognitive Heuristics in Political Decision Making." In *Controversies in Voting Behavior*, edited by Richard Niemi. Washington, DC: CQ Press, 2011.

Lau, Richard, and David Redlawsk. "Voting Correctly." *American Political Science Review*, 91 (1997): 585–598.

Leighley, Jan, and Jonathan Nagler. *Who Votes Now?* Princeton, NJ: Princeton University Press, 2014.

Lichtenberg, Judith. "Negative Duties, Positive Duties and the New Harms." Ethics, 120 (2010): 557–578.

Lijphart, Arend. "Unequal Participation: Democracy's Unresolved Dilemma." *American Political Science Review*, 91 (1993): 1–14.

Locke, John. *Essays on the Law of Nature.* Oxford: Oxford University Press, 2002 [1663].

Lopez-Guerra, Claudio. *Democracy and Disenfranchisement: The Morality of Electoral Exclusions.* Oxford: Oxford University Press, 2014.

Lovett, Francis. "Machiavelli, Civic Virtue, and the Problem of Stability." Paper presented to the Annual Meeting of the American Political Science Association, 2013.

Lupia, Arthur. "How Elitism Undermines the Study of Voter Competence." *Critical Review*, 18 (2006): 217–232.

Lupia, Arthur, and Matthew McCubbins. *The Democratic Dilemma: Can Citizens Learn What They Need to Know?* Cambridge: Cambridge University Press, 1998.

Mackie, Gerald. "Rational Ignorance and Beyond." Unpublished manuscript available at http://pages.ucsd.edu/~gmackie/documents/RationalIgnoranceAndBeyond.pdf.

Mackie, Gerald. "Why It's Rational to Vote." In *Rationality, Democracy, and Justice: The Legacy of Jon Elster*, edited by Claudio Lopez-Guerra and Julia Maskivker. Cambridge: Cambridge University Press, 2015.

Manin, Bernard. *The Principles of Representative Government*. Cambridge: Cambridge University Press, 1997.

Mansbridge, Jane. *Beyond Adversary Democracy*. Chicago: University of Chicago Press, 1983.

Maravall, Jose Maria. "Accountability and Manipulation." In *Democracy, Accountability and Representation*, edited by Adam Przeworski et al. Cambridge: Cambridge University Press, 1999.

Martin, Paul. "Voting's Rewards: Voter Turnout, Attentive Publics, and Congressional Allocation of Federal Money." *American Journal of Political Science*, 47 (2003): 110–127.

Maskivker, Julia. "Being a Good Samaritan Requires You to Vote." *Political Studies*, 66 (2018): 409–424.

Maskivker, Julia. "An Epistemic Justification for the Obligation to Vote." *Critical Review*, 28 (2016): 224–247.

Mayo, H. B. "A Note on the Alleged Duty to Vote." *Journal of Politics*, 2 (1959): 319–323.

McChesney, Fred. *Money for Nothing: Politicians, Rent Extraction, and Political Extorsion*. Cambridge: Cambridge University Press, 1997.

McCright, Aaron, and Riley E. Dunlap. "Anti-reflexivity: The American Conservative Movement's Success in Undermining Climate Science and Policy." *Theory, Culture & Society*, 27 (2010): 100–133.

Mele, Alfred. "Ultimate Responsibility and Dumb Luck." *Social Philosophy and Policy*, 16 (1999): 274–293.

Mill, John Stuart. "*Considerations on Representative Government.*" In *On Liberty and Other Essays*, edited by John Gray. Oxford: Oxford University Press, 2008.

Mill, John Stuart. *Later Letters 1848–1873*. Edited by Francis Mineka and Dwight Lindley. Toronto: University of Toronto Press, 1972.

Mitchell, Karlyn, and Douglas Pearce. "Professional Forecasts of Interest Rates and Exchange Rates: Evidence from the Wall Street Journal's Panel of Economists." *Journal of Macroeconomics*, 29 (2007): 840–854.

Monroe, Alan. "Public Opinion and Public Policy: 1980–1993." *Public Opinion Quarterly*, 62 (1998): 6–28.

Mounk, Yascha. *The People versus Democracy*. Cambridge, MA: Harvard University Press, 2018.

Mueller, Dennis, and Thomas Strattman. "*The Economic Effects of Democratic Participation*." *Journal of Public Economics*, 87 (2003): 2129–2155.

Murphy, Liam. "The Demands of Beneficence." *Philosophy and Public Affairs*, 22 (1993): 267–292.

Nagel, Thomas. *Mortal Questions*. New York: Cambridge University Press, 1979.

Nagel, Thomas. *The View from Nowhere*. Oxford: Oxford University Press, 1986.

Nozick, Robert. *Anarchy State and Utopia*. New York: Basic Books, 1974.

Olivella, Santiago, and Joseph Uscinski. "The Mediating Impact of Conspiracy Thinking on Climate Change Attitudes." Prepared for the "Suspect Science: Climate Change, Epidemics, and Questions of Conspiracy" conference, September 17–19, 2015, at the Centre for Research in the Arts, Social Sciences and Humanities, University of Cambridge, Cambridge.

Page, Benjamin. "That Same Old Song: Somin on Political Ignorance." *Critical Review*, 27 (2015): 1–5.

Page, Benjamin, and Martin Gilens. *Democracy in America? What Has Gone Wrong and What We Can Do about It*. Chicago: University of Chicago Press, 2017.

Page, Benjamin, and Robert Y. Shapiro. *The Rational Public: Fifty Years of Trends in Americans' Policy Preferences*. Chicago: University of Chicago Press, 1992.

Parfit, Derek. *Reasons and Persons*. Oxford: Oxford University Press, 1984.

Parker, Glenn. *Congress and the Rent-Seeking Society*. Ann Arbor: University of Michigan Press, 1996.

Pateman, Carole. *Participation and Democratic Theory*. Cambridge: Cambridge University Press, 1970.

Pettit, Phillip. *On the People's Terms: A Republican Theory and Model of Democracy*. Cambridge: Cambridge University Press, 2013.

Pettit, Phillip. *Republicanism: A Theory of Freedom and Government*. Oxford: Oxford University Press, 2012.

Pettit, Phillip, and Michael Slote. "Satisficing Consequentialism." *Proceedings of the Aristotelian Society*, 58 (1984): 139–176.

Phillips, Anne. *The Politics of Presence*. Oxford: Oxford University Press, 1995.

Pitkin, Hanna. *The Concept of Representation*. Berkeley: University of California Press, 1969.

Pontusson, Jonas, and David Rueda. "The Politics of Inequality: Party Mobilization and Left Parties in Advanced Industrial States." *Comparative Political Studies*, 43 (2010): 675–705.

Popkin, Samuel. "The Factual Basis of Belief Systems: A Reassessment." *Critical Review*, 1 (2006): 233–254.

Popkin, Samuel. *The Reasoning Voter: Communication and Persuasion in Presidential Campaigns*. Chicago: University of Chicago Press, 1994.

Quaile Hill, Kim, and Jan E. Leighley. "The Policy Consequences of Class Bias in State Electorates." *American Journal of Political Science*, 36 (1992): 351–365.

Quong, Jonathan. *Liberalism without Perfection*. Oxford: Oxford University Press, 2010.

Rawls, John. "Justice as Fairness: Political Not Metaphysical." *Philosophy and Public Affairs* 14 (1985): 223–251.

Rawls, John. *Political Liberalism*. New York: Columbia University Press, 2000.

Rawls, John. *A Theory of Justice*. Cambridge, MA: Harvard University Press, 1971.

Reich, Michael, Ken Jacobs, and Annette Bernhardt: "Local Minimum Wage Laws: Impacts on Workers, Families and Businesses," Institute for Research on Labor and Employment, IRLE Working Paper No. 104-14, March 2014.

Reidy, David. "Rawls' Wide View of Public Reason: Not Wide Enough." *Res Publica*, 6 (2000): 49–72.

Richardson, Jeremy. "Government, Interest Groups, and Policy Change." *Political Studies*, 48 (2000): 1006–1025.

Riker, William, and Peter Ordeshook. "A Theory of the Calculus of Voting." *American Political Science Review*, 62 (1968): 25–42.

Ringquist, Evan, Kim Quaile Hill, Jan Leighley, and Angela Hinton-Andersson. "Lower-Class Mobilization and Policy Linkage in the U.S. States." *American Journal of Political Science*, 39 (1995): 75–86.

Ripstein, Arthur. "Three Duties to Rescue: Moral, Civil, and Criminal." *Law and Philosophy*, 19 (2000): 751–779.

Rousseau, Jean-Jacques. *On the Social Contract*. Translated by Donald Cress. Cambridge: Hackett, 1987.

Runciman, David. "Why Not Eat an Éclair?" Review of Tuck's *Free Riding* in *Boston Review of Books*, 30 (2008).

Sanchez Cuenca, Ignacio. "The Political Basis of Support for European Integration." *European Union Politics*, 1 (2000): 147–171.

Sandel, Michael. "Reply to Critics." In *Debating Democracy's Discontent: Essays on American Politics, Law, and Public Philosophy*. Edited by Anita L. Allen et al. Oxford: Oxford University Press Online.

Scanlon, Thomas. "Contractualism and Utilitarianism." In *Ethical Theory: An Anthology*, edited by Russ Shafer-Landau. London: Wiley Blackwell, 2013.

Scanlon, Thomas. "Preference and Urgency." *Journal of Philosophy*, 72 (1975): 655–669.

Scanlon, Thomas. *What We Owe to Each Other*. Cambridge, MA: Harvard University Press, 2000.

Schafer, Armin. "Republican Liberty and Compulsory Voting." Working Paper No. 11/17, Max Planck Institute for the Study of Societies, Cologne, 2011.

Schwartzman, Micah. "The Completeness of Public Reason." *Politics, Philosophy, and Economics*, 3 (2004): 191–220.

Schwartzman, Micah. "The Sincerity of Public Reason." *Journal of Political Philosophy*, 19 (2011): 375–398.

Sears, David, and Carolyn Funk. "The Limited Effect of Self-Interest on the Political Attitudes of the Mass Public." *Journal of Behavioral Economics*, 19 (1990): 247–271.

Sen, Amartya. *The Idea of Justice*. Cambridge, MA: Harvard University Press, 2011.

Sen, Amartya. "Rational Fools: A Critique of the Behavioral Foundations of Economic Theory." *Philosophy and Public Affairs*, 6 (1977): 317–344.

Shaffer, Stephen. "Policy Differences between Voters and Non-voters in American Elections." *Western Political Quarterly*, 35 (1982): 496–510.

Shapiro, Ian. *The State of Democratic Theory*. Princeton, NJ: Princeton University Press, 2003.

Shapiro, Robert, and Yaeli Bloch-Elkon. "Political Polarization and the Rational Public." Paper prepared for presentation at the Annual Meeting of the American Political Science Association, 2006. Available at http://themonkeycage.org/Shapiro%2520and%2520Bloch.pdf.

Sharman, Amelia. "Mapping the Climate Sceptical Blogosphere." *Global Environmental Change*, 26 (2014): 159–170.

Singer, Peter. "Famine, Affluence and Morality." *Philosophy and Public Affairs*, 1 (1972): 229–243.

Somin, Ilya. *Democracy and Political Ignorance*. Palo Alto, CA: Stanford University Press, 2013).

Stacey, Gordon, and Gary Segura. "Cross-National Variation in the Political Sophistication of Individuals: Capability or Choice?" *Journal of Politics*, 59 (1997): 126–147.

Stilz, Anna. *Liberal Loyalty*. Princeton, NJ: Princeton University Press, 2009.

Stokes, Susan, Adam Przeworski, and Bernard Manin, eds. *Democracy, Accountability and Representation*. Cambridge: Cambridge University Press, 1999.

Taleb, Nassim. *The Black Swan: The Impact of the Highly Improbable*. New York: Random House, 2007.

Talisse, Robert. "Does Public Ignorance Defeat Deliberative Democracy?" *Critical Review*, 16 (2004): 455–463.

Tetlock, Phillip. *Expert Political Judgment: How Good Is It? How Can We Know?* Princeton, NJ: Princeton University Press, 2005.

Thompson, Judith. "In Defense of Abortion." *Philosophy and Public Affairs*, 1 (1971): 47–66.

Tingsten, Herbert. *Political Behavior: Studies in Election Statistics.* London: Arno Press, 1975.

Tuck, Richard. *Free Riding.* Cambridge, MA: Harvard University Press, 2008.

Valentini, Laura. "Social Samaritan Justice: When and Why Needy Fellow Citizens Have a Right to Assistance." *American Political Science Review,* 109 (2015): 735–749.

Vallier, Kevin. "Convergence and Consensus in Public Reason." *Public Affairs Quarterly,* 25 (2011): 261–280.

Vallier, Kevin. *Liberal Politics and Public Faith: Beyond Separation.* Oxford: Routledge, 2014.

Waldron, Jeremy. "The Principle of Proximity " NYU School of Law, Public Law Research Paper No. 11-08, 2011.

Waldron, Jeremy. "A Right to Do Wrong." *Ethics,* 92 (1981): 21–39.

Waldron, Jeremy. "Votes as Powers." In *Rights and Reason: Essays in Honor of Carl Wellman.* New York: Kluwer Academic Publishers, 2000.

Wall, Steven. "Freedom, Interference, and Domination." *Political Studies,* 49 (2001): 216–230.

Wartenberg, Thomas. *The Forms of Power: From Domination to Transformation.* Philadelphia: Temple University Press, 1990.

Williams, Bernard. *Moral Luck.* Cambridge: Cambridge University Press, 1981.

Williams, Bernard, and J. J. C. Smart, eds. *Utilitarianism: For and Against.* Cambridge: Cambridge University Press, 1973.

Williamson, Vanessa. *Read My Lips: Why Americans Are Proud to Pay Taxes.* Princeton, NJ: Princeton University Press, 2016.

Zaller, John. *The Nature and Origins of Mass Opinion.* Cambridge: Cambridge University Press, 1992.

Zaller, John, and Stanley Feldman. "A Simple Theory of the Survey Response: Answering Questions versus Revealing Preferences." *American Journal of Political Science,* 36 (1992): 579–616.

Index

For the benefit of digital users, indexed terms that span two pages (e.g., 52–53) may, on occasion, appear on only one of those pages.